Praise for *After the Mask*
Students an

"After the Mask" is a critical post pandemic read for educators, school administrators, and even parents. Dr. Jenson and his team take the reader on a journey through the science behind the many possible effects of the pandemic on our students. Stress is placed on the critical impact on student mental health rather than academic setbacks. The book is full of realistic strategies, resources, and powerful information written in reader-friendly and conversational language. There will indeed be "battles to fight" as we try to return to some sense of normality. This book will make everyone better able to mount an attack!"

- Sally Roberts, Ph.D., Associate Professor and Associate Dean Emeritus, School of Education & Human Sciences, University of Kansas.

"In *After the Mask*, Dr. Chris Jenson takes on our youth mental health crisis with an inspiring call to action for teachers and their school communities that is both audacious in its reach yet refreshingly practical in its researched plan that believes in—and respects—the power of teachers."

- Joe Robertson, Kansas City Star education reporter (retired)

"Students and staff are both experiencing rapid and erosive changes with mental health. *After the Mask* offers a practical and thoughtful way to address these concerns in school districts across the United States."

- Ms. Kristi Dixon, Kansas Outstanding School Counselor of the Year 2016-2017, Kansas School Counselor Association (KSCA)

ISBN Paperback: 978-1-64184-705-6

AFTER THE MASK:

A GUIDE TO CARING FOR STUDENTS AND SCHOOLS

An evidence-based approach for navigating the prolonged erosion of student mental health in the midst of deep-seated teacher burnout and a devastating pandemic.

CHRISTOPHER JENSON, M.D.
With Jessica Sorcher, M.S. and Rachael Sorcher, B.A.

To my beautiful wife and daughters, who teach me how to love a little more each day.
- Chris Jenson

To Mom, Dad, and Caroline for empowering us to dream big, and to our family and friends for being our biggest cheerleaders- we love you!
- Jessica and Rachael Sorcher

Acknowledgments

Dr. Sally Roberts
- Thank you for being a lifelong champion of education and always willing to take a frantic phone call from a rookie teacher. Your contribution to our book is deeply appreciated.

Blue Valley Southwest High School, Mental Health Support Team
- Thank you for engaging in the peer-review process of the SEAL Ambassador Program Evaluations. Your insight allowed us to craft tailored tools that will help school staff measure the program's impact and make meaningful adjustments for the future.

Taylor McKillop
- Thank you for making *After the Mask* come to life with a beautiful book cover. Your eye for design is unmatched!

T and L Jenson
- Thank you for your extremely wise words - "When things get really hard, and you are thinking about quitting, just remember why you started in the first place." You are awfully wise for being under ten years of age!

Table of Contents

Introduction: Three things to know before you begin

The introduction i) provides brief insight into the authors and their qualifications, ii) highlights the consistent approach to data throughout the book, and iii) establishes rules and promises for the reader.

Part One: State of the student union...What students face today

Examine school-aged children's vulnerabilities and mental health trends over the past two decades and explore what schools were doing to address the escalating issues.

Chapters:

Part Two: Cough, cold, and collapse...The impact of COVID-19

The impact of SARS-CoV-2 is not limited to the millions of people it infected. It has also changed the outlook and operations of the BILLIONS of people it isolated.

Chapters:

Part Three: Immunity through community...Strategies for students and staff

Evidence-based strategies that improve student mental health without exceeding staff training or creating additional work burden outside of class.

Chapters:

Appendix Information

Appendix A, B, and C offer all the supplemental material referred to in Part Three. This includes sample lesson plans, classroom strategies for teaching self-esteem and self-efficacy, identification of transferable skills for most occupations, and various assessments of the SEAL Ambassador Program.

INTRODUCTION: Three things to know before you begin

Ferris Bueller was right—life moves pretty fast; if you don't look around once in a while, you could miss it. I realize this whimsical observation could apply to any year of life, but it seems to carry more weight amidst the rapidly evolving chaos of the COVID-19 pandemic. I often think of Ferris' nostalgic line (at least nostalgic for 1980s fans) during the rare quiet moments of the day and wonder quite simply...*did we miss it? Are we still missing it?* Hear me out. While much of the world, myself included, applied their full focus and attention to a nasty sequence of RNA and proteins known as SARS-CoV-2, every other aspect of life continued to barrel ahead at full speed. I suppose that shouldn't be a surprise. There is no pause button for the game of life. But have we all been so blinded by COVID's sphere of influence that important issues in our communities and personal lives have been put on hold or even forgotten? If so, will that come back to haunt us?

Let's not sugarcoat it. A lot has changed, and even more pushed aside. We may currently live in an adaptive state, but it doesn't change the fact that our daily existence remains a fast-paced sprint through life. Arguably, COVID is at the front of that race. This microscopic assailant, smaller than the width of human hair, has zipped across cities, farms, playgrounds, and millions of lives in a matter of months. That's pretty fast, friends. As quickly as the virus entered our homes and workspaces, its departure will be a much slower event. The effects of prolonged isolation, persistent fear, sudden anger, newfound anxiety, chronic depression, and various forms of social tension have changed people. And when you change enough people, you begin to change populations. Our schools are not exempt from this. Students, staff, and parents endured the most captivating and wide-reaching psychological stress test of the last hundred years. And mind you, the prior claim doesn't even include the added impact for those that experienced moderate to severe illness from SARS-CoV-2. It's daunting to think about. But sadly, there is no appreciable time to pause. Life forges ahead.

The discussions in this book are designed to address the challenges of this pandemic and the years following. With that in mind, *After the Mask* arms you with meaningful evidence, expert insight, and realistic strategies— all of which you can implement in your school and classroom. Why? Because educators, perhaps more than ever, need definitive guidance to address the social, emotional, and academic complications associated with the pandemic. School districts demonstrated that they needed assistance minimizing the impact of COVID-19 during 2020. They appropriately reached out to local health departments and helpful clinicians to hastily create operational guidelines. The goal was to put students and staff back in the classroom while minimizing the impact of the virus. And although this was far from a flawless process, there were some bright spots along the way. Educators, clinicians, and public health leaders all rose to the occasion and did the best they could during an imperfect situation.

Given this, it's reasonable and expected for school officials to continue requesting guidance, at least for the next few years, as they navigate the fallout from COVID. As a former physician, public school educator, and current chief health advisor, I would be honored to play a small role in that. So here I am, firing away at a laptop with no less than 16 academic journal articles spread across my dining room table. I feel a call to help. It's one cathartic way to heal from 2020. But before we jump into this book at a pace that rivals Ferris Bueller's Ferrari adventure, I think you deserve to know the following three things. They serve as the backbone to this introduction and the book at large. Please consider:

1. Who comprises our author team? What value do we bring?

2. What is our approach to data and demographics?

3. What rules and promises do we maintain for the reader?

Who comprises the team? What value do we bring?

Let's start with me, your lead author and 2018 grape spitting champion for 3rd hour Anatomy. I have been blessed with a serendipitous ride through life. My background starts with a career in emergency medicine followed by a CDC fellowship that focused on public health initiatives in education. Now, sprinkle in four years of experience serving as a medical consultant for school districts across the United States, ten years of teaching high school science, and my current position of chief health advisor for a school district of 25,000 students and staff. It's a wild career path, but one that I would not trade for anything. My prior experiences have led me down a path to a niche that I love—advising school leadership on how to best address health concerns within schools in an evidence-based fashion.

I would not be where I am today without classroom experience. I enjoy the concept of teaching so much that I became captivated by the shiny side of education, believing that teaching offered me an opportunity to invest in the next generation and right many of the wrongs we see in the world today. Sounds good, right? I still believe it is. Of course, education also provided me the opportunity to develop some amazing life skills. Please review a few of my favorites below:

- Presenting in front of large audiences with unexpected, untimely, and critical technology fails

- Learning about small machine maintenance (known as photocopier usage)

- Treating second degree burns to the skin from toner cartridges (also known as photocopier usage)

- Learning how to talk to three people at once while returning an email

- Eating lunch with your left hand while using your gloved right hand to pass out sheep brains

My point is that I taught long enough to understand the ins and outs of a classroom. And I also taught long enough to laugh and cry about my job. I need you to know upfront that classroom experience helped frame the strategies we present in Part 3 of this book. They are evidence-based and scientifically supported...but equally important, these recommendations represent something a **teacher** believes is practical and would **want** to implement.

So, what about the rest of this team? Well, good news, I brought in some young, enthusiastic, and brilliant talent. Jessica and Rachael Sorcher are the co-authors and counterbalances to my infectious sarcasm. Both of them attended Miami University (Ohio), graduated with numerous accolades, and have a strong interest in public health and mental health concerns among youth. Jessica chased down a Master of Science, focused on health promotion, and will begin a PhD in community health program in the fall of 2021. Rachael is currently a Master of Public Health student at Boston University School of Public Health, has a special interest in health equity at the local and global level, and was selected as a 2021 Pulitzer Center Reporting Fellow. I am convinced Jessica and Rachael represent some of the most brilliant young minds in America. But if you want insight into their personality, here you go. Before the age of 20, they supervised a charity event with a meager budget of $560, yet raised over $63,000 for families struggling to afford their child's cancer treatment. This snapshot defines their talent and character. But from your perspective as a reader, Jessica and Rachael increase the value you'll get out of this book through their diligent searches for reliable evidence, cross-checking sources, and adamantly ensuring that our team holds to the book's mission. Their public health backgrounds and perspective helped us to explore the connection between mental health, education, and well-being.

What is our approach to data and demographics?

The sad reality is that you, as an educator, have another huge and nebulous year ahead of you. Public perception (right or wrong) is that schools will repair the devastation of this pandemic and be ready to operate in a "normal" fashion well before they turn on the lights for Friday night football. That doesn't seem fair nor realistic, huh? Nevertheless, that's where a lot of communities are right now with their thought process. And those perceived expectations add much pressure to the educational system. Teachers already have an infinite number of things to do and an infinitely small amount of time to do them. As a fellow educator, I am aware of that. That's why we worked tirelessly to make sure this book is worth your time. It was one of the focal points of our writing.

So, what does the book offer? Here are some questions you should ponder:

1. Will *After the Mask* solve every problem in your classroom?

2. Is it likely this book will change state standards and national mandates?

3. Will our efforts help you self-actualize all your complex feelings regarding education and come to terms with the budget limitations of your school district?

Answer key (1,2,3) = Nope.

Fair and honest coming right at you there. But, that's also the beauty of it. This book is **NOT** about the distractors, red tape, and bureaucracy found in education. I am not here to blow sunshine up your backside and pretend we can change the constraints that are well outside of our control. That would be a waste of your time and mine. Instead, this book takes you back to the very fundamental reasons why you wanted to give so much of yourself to this job—a chance to better a child in a way that is far more important than any content you have taught or will teach. That is a promise coming from a former ER doc, secondary school teacher, and most of all, a loving dad. Yep, above all else, I am a father who desperately wants to see thoughtful changes implemented for his two young girls, who are both flying down the pathway of public school.

So, what is our approach to the analysis and recommendations we provide? Simple. Diligently research meaningful data from multiple sources that guide us to practical suggestions and strategies. It's the best way to provide evidence for change. So, get ready. I am about to rain down upon you a tsunami of high-level science from the American Academy of Pediatrics, Centers for Disease Control, American School Counselors Association, leading universities, and accomplished researchers around the world of public health and education. At times, it will be like drinking from a fire hose of data. Don't worry about that. Our team takes this information and translates it into **something you WANT to implement in your classroom**. That, we believe, makes this book absolutely worth your time. And if you're curious how we did that, the plan is right below. Full transparency.

- Examine quantitative evidence that substantiates likely vulnerabilities in current school-aged children, all of which influence their mental health and resilience BEFORE the pandemic hit.

- Assess and determine if COVID-19 improved, worsened, or made no appreciable impact on the pre-pandemic vulnerabilities of current students (Gen Z).

- Diligently gather data for underserved and underrepresented populations, ensuring these cohorts are part of the discussion and included in proposed plans for improvement.

- Explore specific evidence-based strategies that an educator can implement in their school or classroom, addressing student uncertainty, depression, resilience, and anxiety **without** asking them to be a health care provider or social worker…because chances are, you're not.

As forecasted above, this book occasionally takes a deep dive into the mental health situation of school-aged children. It's important to understand that mental health and its related conditions are largely shaped by social, physical, and economic environments.[1] These environments place health, and more specifically, mental health, at the intersection of five critical factors. The U.S. Department of Health and Human Services suggests the five key social determinants of health include the following (with examples), as seen in Figure 1[2]:

1. Economic Stability—housing, employment, food insecurity, etc.

2. Education Access and Quality—early childhood development, literacy level, high school graduation, etc.

3. Social and Community Context—racism, discrimination, incarceration, etc.

4. Health Care Access and Quality—health literacy, access to health care, access to primary care, etc.

5. Neighborhood and Built Environment—exposure to crime and violence, exposure to toxic chemicals and substances, housing quality, etc.

Figure 1

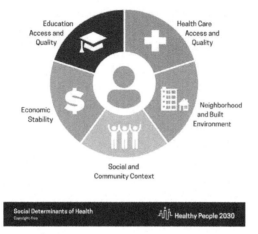

Social Determinants of Health

Our team is acutely aware that the social determinants of health underlie and contribute to health inequities.[4] As such, we do our best to consider these inequities and incorporate them into our discussion. We are also mindful that all school and student populations vary. With that in mind, I want to stress that this book is not a guide for one type of school. It isn't here to solely benefit well-funded suburban schools or unique magnet opportunities. That's not our goal. Furthermore, the proposed approaches in this book are most definitely not for one race, ethnicity, gender, or sexual orientation. Everything we discuss in this book is meant to benefit *all* schools, educators, and students. I suppose you could say that is the guiding mission of our book—make it as widely applicable as possible to help as many students and educators as possible.

What rules and promises do we maintain for the reader?

Our team created a series of rules to guide the framework of this book and how we wanted to interact with you, the reader. I share them with you now so we can be in sync from the very beginning.

RULE #1 — We believe in the concept of evidence-based decision-making. When we chat, claims need to be supported by facts. As such, I do my best to introduce plenty of data and sources for you to refer to as we build a logical thought process. No one wants this book to be a lengthy rant regarding what Chris Jenson would like schools to do for students. Instead, this book represents what scientific evidence **demands** we all do for our children.

RULE #2 — I love to be with people and talk. Just talk. As such, the tone of this book is very conversational and brings all the public health and medical info to the same level that I find myself using with my close teacher friends in the hallways. This is good and bad. Good in that this entire book is a no-nonsense conversation. Bad in the sense that English and literature instructors around the nation are well within their rights to tear apart my writing. That's fine, I can take it. In the end, I chose this style so that you and I might feel like we are sipping our coffee in between classes, chatting like friends, and crying a little on the inside as we watch a student rip their locker door off the hinges to free a stuck backpack.

RULE #3 — I do not have every answer. My wife can promise you that. But, I know where to find good answers for developing mental health and resilience in kids. Also, I will not make the preposterous claim that a hundred or so pages of writing, even when backed up with high-powered scientific data, will make you something you are not. Although you listen to children discuss their feelings, you are not a therapist. Despite your best intentions to fix the pain in a student's life, you are not a physician. And when the world is crashing down around your students, you are not their parents. By definition, your calling is to educate children and prepare them for life. That's true whether you are a veteran teacher, a newbie, a librarian, a paraeducator, a principal, or the sweet cafeteria staff member at White Oaks Elementary that repeatedly snuck me extra chocolate milk in 1982. Regardless of your role, I am sure of this: at the end of this book, you **WILL** see that you have the right skills to make the changes our young adults and students desperately need. I promise that. And keep in mind, I don't promise much in today's rapidly evolving world.

This book has value. I feel strongly that our efforts will change how you use your classroom in a way that you control. That's what I would want as an educator. And if that's not enough, I am 176% confident that this book is better than any professional development day. Why? You can set down the book right now and grab an adult beverage. Go ahead. I'll wait for you. Catch you at Chapter 1.

Introduction References

1. World Health Organization & Calouste Gulbenkian Foundation. (2014). *Social determinants of mental health*. https://apps.who.int/ iris/bitstream/handle/10665/112828/9789241506809_eng.pdf;jsessionid=C61101288B945CF23F261611AD1D4611?sequence=1

2. U.S. Department of Health and Human Services, Office of Disease Prevention and Health Promotion, & Healthy People 3030. (2021). *Social determinants of health*. https://health.gov/healthypeople/ objectives-and-data/social-determinants-health

3. Healthy People 2030, U.S. Department of Health and Human Services, & Office of Disease Prevention and Health Promotion. *Social determinants of health*. Retrieved February 22, 2021 from https://health. gov/healthypeople/objectives-and-data/social-determinants-health

4. Centers for Disease Control and Prevention. (2019, December 19). *NCHHSTP social determinants of health*. https://www.cdc.gov/nchhstp/socialdeterminants/faq.html

PART ONE

State of the student union...What students face today

Examine the vulnerabilities and mental health trends of school-aged children over the past two decades and explore what schools were doing to address the escalating issues.

1

Who's staring back at you?...
Classroom identity

The first day of class is always a rush. It doesn't matter how long you've been teaching or how hard you pretend it's just another day. Kids come together with hopeful expectations and a buzz of conversation regarding summer trips, funny experiences, and the latest trends, all of which quickly circulate through your classroom. I've always thought day one was a magical moment. Everyone starts with a clean slate, and how many times in life can you do that? The sacred first day of school is full of hope and promise. No one can ruin that.

And then, the classroom door shuts. Reality hits. You scan the room to find three students keenly investigating the propane gas valve for a lab station, four students frantically logging into a website for concert tickets, one laughing because their friend was struck in the eye by a pen's spring, and many other random acts of life that involve a smart-phone. All in all, there are 33 sets of youthful eyes staring at you but don't worry, your room accommodates 28. It's in that exact moment that you begin to wonder: *who are these people before me?*

On paper, at least, your job is to deliver the state standards for this grade in such exemplary fashion that each of these little cherubs moves onward to become world leaders and refer to you as their primary inspiration. Your thoughtful lesson planning combined with the perfect execution of differentiated instruction, blended learning, and experiential investigation over the next few months will lead all these kiddos to become content ninjas by May. You are their Jedi master, and they are the perfect little Padawan (for all the Millennial teachers, you may now Google Padawan...oh wait, you already asked Siri).

Alright, let's take back some of that sarcasm and discuss what you do, what I do, and for that matter, what we all strive to do as caring educators in the classroom. To start, we work hard to teach kids content and knowledge. We aspire to make lessons exciting and provide students with creative opportunities. We do our best to add flexibility to our classrooms because children learn at different speeds, and we want all of our kiddos to feel like they are on a path to success. All of this occurs in classrooms across America. Every one of these tasks is important to learning. However, there is one critical element that I have yet to mention, and I would argue that it's the most important thing educators do: we invest time and effort to get to *know* our kids.

Educators form relationships with students in such a way that we know their strengths and weaknesses. We have insight into our student's fears, dreams, and motivations. We spend enough time with our classroom family to gain a fair amount of information regarding new friendships, failed friendships, waxing and waning relationships, and what goes on at home. In short, the eight hours we spend with our students daily leads us to know parts of their lives that their parents may not be aware exist. That is pretty powerful when you step back and consider the depth of that relationship. It illustrates how vital an educator is to the life of a student. However, I suspect you already know that, including the responsibility that comes with it.

Post-pandemic, educators will see a good percentage of their students more than their parents, psychologists, therapists, and doctors. Gulp. That hits home for me on many levels. While I agree that it's not an educator's job and/or responsibility to solve health problems in children, there **IS** an opportunity to provide meaningful help within the scope of our training. I like that. In fact, I love it. I love the opportunity to intervene with a student a lot more than supervising a practice ACT, which a substantial number of the kids in the room don't care about anyway. Like you, I joined the teaching ranks to help children navigate life and feel good about themselves. I am not looking to produce Rhodes Scholars, but rather kids that are passionate about something in life and have the skills to better their lives. So, if you feel the same and are excited about the chance to reprioritize student well-being above grading, this is definitely the time to do it. Kids desperately need you.

The stark reality check is that there is extensive and profound public health data, which I share in later chapters, that demonstrates concerning mental health trends in school-aged children before the pandemic hit and how COVID-19 has accelerated these trends. So, please keep reading, friends. It will quickly become clear that teachers *have* to be part of the solution when dealing with the fallout of COVID-19, at least if we want a meaningful solution.

All this said, the unprecedented force of COVID-19 is going to impact your classroom, which is largely comprised of Generation Z, on a scale we may not have seen before. We need to prepare for that. We have to plan for something far more important than the state standards and test prep work. We need a comprehensive plan for school culture and life. Please hear me out. To do that, we have to understand this particular generation's strengths and vulnerabilities on a macro-scale. This broad understanding gives us some insight into how we address problems plaguing our students on a micro-scale.

This ideology should apply to **all** the kids in your classroom, and not just the ones with IEPs or enthusiastic hand-raising. It needs to be useful for the quiet girl in the back corner who struggled to make eye contact with you today because she just got destroyed on social media. It should be relevant for the boy who always has his earbuds in, perhaps in an attempt to look busy, hiding the fact that he doesn't have friends in your class. And, it even applies to the popular boy that is extra kind and seems to have it all together, but as an adolescent, you know cannot possibly have the perfect life he portrays... making you wonder, *why does he not want to admit that?*

In a few chapters, data in this book will quickly demonstrate that it's never been more imperative to connect and know **ALL** the students that pass through your halls. Why? Because they all just experienced a mental stress test that no university would ever get ethical approval for: worldwide isolation with exposure to death, job loss, divorce, and all the usual problems of life, but without the ability to talk to someone unmasked or ask for a hug. So, let's take the next few pages to garner a closer look at the students staring back at you in the classroom and get to know, arguably, the world's most vulnerable generation.

Generalities about generalizations

Typically, I despise stereotypes and generalizations. They often lead to incorrect assumptions when applied to specific people and individual situations. And, I suppose in many ways, broad sweeping generalizations do nothing more than expose one's ignorance. However, there are times when understanding probable risks and benefits for a specific population can come in very handy. A great example is in medicine. Allow me to highlight:

- Diabetes - is every diabetic patient the same? Absolutely not. Are diabetics defined as a person by their blood sugar disorder? Of course not. But, it's critical to know that almost all diabetics become confused and sweaty when their blood sugar is too low. Why do they do this? Because that's how diabetes operates. Recognizing predictable outcomes (sweaty with behavior change) from predictable stressors (low blood sugar) can be life-saving.

- Depression - does every individual with depression consider suicide? Of course not. And if someone with depression contemplated suicide, would they chat about it? Tough to say. But, it is likely that an individual contemplating suicide would experience other changes in their sleep, appetite, long-term plans, and manifestations of hope. Why? Because this is how major depressive disorders work. And once again, recognizing predictable outcomes (change in daily acts of living) from predictable stressors (severe depression) can be life-saving.

So, is there value in exploring Generation Z in the same manner that health care providers explore abnormalities within the human body? Most definitely, yes. We need to know how Gen Z is built to understand how they process information, communicate, and tend to operate. By doing so, we can establish a likely norm of predictable outcomes and how these individuals would most likely respond in the face of a significant stressor. As mentioned before, this recognition allows us to gain insight into the strengths and vulnerabilities of the 69 million Gen Z students in the same manner that physicians understand millions of diabetics macroscopically in the United States.[1]

Who is Gen Z?

How is Gen Z characterized? What is their reputation? It turns out that they are not just an extension of Millennials. Instead, the world's second youngest generation has been busy carving out their own unique perspectives, interests, and expectations (just reference the media reports on skinny jeans and side parts). Most of the 69 million members of this generation were born between 1997 and 2012, placing the younger participants in our classrooms and the older cohort taking their first shots at the job market. Thus, Generation Z currently occupies an exciting and formative time of human life.

Over the following few pages, I intend to highlight several critical points of interest that help us understand and connect with Gen Zers in a more meaningful fashion. What do I consider meaningful? Well, the type of conversations that allow you to go beyond last night's sports scores, the latest TikTok sensation, and whether AP Calculus was designed by the prince of darkness. It's time to be something more than a friendly educator. It's time to get back to helping kids the way educators wanted to in the first place—by being an instrumental force in their lives. Please don't forget that positively impacting kids is the original reason you endured an educational law class, a chaotic student teaching environment, and still deal with a suboptimal salary. But hey, working with kids is what we love. It's why we all began this adventure. So, please give yourself permission to go back to those feelings and that mission because educators need to connect with this generation in a much deeper way than we ever have.

The social and emotional stress of a pandemic has exposed numerous concerns and accelerated deficits that were previously found among these kiddos. This generation will need us. They will value a trusted and caring adult far more than a content expert in multiplication. Although, TRUST x LOVE = CONTENT. And by content, I refer to both connotations: knowledge and happiness.

With all that in mind, what is the deal with Gen Zers? How do they operate? To answer these questions well, let's briefly compare them to Millennials and Gen X, establishing a rough appreciation for how Gen Z fits in. This idea also allows us to see how Gen Z relates to the rest of their school community, seeing as the average age of a teacher in the United States today is 42.6 years old.[2] By the way, thoughtful and irrefutable science demonstrates that 40 is the new 30. You're welcome, my fellow Motrin users. At any rate, let's take a brief jog through history to help see where Gen Z fits in schools and society.

We'll start by rolling back the clock to Millennials. Born between 1981 and 1996, Millennials are old enough to remember 9/11 in terms of the details and the significance of this event, unlike Gen Z.[3] These individuals grew up through the Iraq and Afghanistan wars, as well as the Great Recession, and subsequently experienced the impacts of these political and economic crises. Beyond the timing of their birth, Millennials have also been positively influenced by meaningful diversity; until Gen Z, Millennials were the most diverse generation the United States had seen.[3]

As you might imagine, there are some similarities between Gen Z and their predecessors. Like Gen Z, Millennials grew up during a technology explosion. However, a hallmark difference between these neighboring generations is that Millennials *adapted* to new technology as it hit the market

(Walkman → mp3 player → iPod → smartphones), while Gen Z was *born* into it—it's second nature.[4] In large part, Gen Z has difficulty remembering a time when they did not have a small computer at their fingertips connecting them to the **entire** world. That is something to always remember: technology is just a natural part of life to Gen Z, not an upgrade.

Now, let's set our time circuits for bubble gum pop music, neon leggings, and a whole lot of Ronald Reagan. Gen Xers, born between 1965 and 1980, are largely the parents of Gen Z. This is a critical point of interest, because, like it or not, parents influence their children. That becomes more obvious the further we travel through life. And trust me, we will dive into the depths of Gen X's impact on your classroom shortly. However, for now, just know that Gen Xers are often referred to as the "neglected middle child" due to their position between two large, well-known generations: Millennials and Baby Boomers.[5] Gen X attitudes on social and political issues are more conservative than Millennials, yet more liberal than their Baby Boomer predecessors. Several of U.S. history's most critical events, such as the Vietnam War, the Gulf War, JFK and MLK's assassinations, as well as the moon landing, shaped their upbringing.[6] In stark contrast to Millennials and Gen Z, this generation bore witness to the innovations in technology that have changed modern society. In short, they have lived more years of their life without iPhones than with, braved a time without texting, and remember when the only way to see a movie was at the theater. Gasp!

As we look at the generational differences along a continuum, we can quickly identify some key influences or events that explain why one cohort has shifted away from its predecessors' tendencies. Experience and emotion shape us. And if the influence is profound enough, it doesn't just shape you; it helps mold your entire generational cohort. Researchers are fascinated by this phenomenon. There are plenty of scholarly articles on the topic, and a wonderful author named Anna Liotta even wrote an entire book on it entitled *Unlocking Generational Codes*.[7] So, with that in mind, what are the biggest influencers of Gen Z? Is there anything that we can say has definitively shaped a common thought pattern amongst the kiddos that sit in your classroom today? We could argue about a lot of possibilities. Most of them would be good and worth consideration. However, I also feel confident that if we keep our list extremely short, we will inherently select the most impactful influences upon Gen Z—ones that we would all agree upon.

To do just that, I began to read a large volume of articles about Gen Z. These reviews covered a wide bandwidth of material ranging from recent research from the American Psychological Association, corporate opinions from Deloitte, academic opinions from various universities, to even some YouTube videos created by Gen Zers (which I must confess, came to my attention from my Gen Z daughter). At the end of this investigation, two points of interest were continuously referenced as critical determinants when it came to shaping the common trends, tendencies, and thought patterns of many Gen Zers. Any guesses? I am going to skip the awkward ten-second teacher pause for understanding. The answers are: i) parental influence and, ii) technology. Yep; parents and a smartphone. That's what most experts believe makes the Gen Z world go round.[8,9] Let's take some time to deep dive into these two areas.

Parental persuasion - Impact of Gen X upon Gen Z

Parents are extremely important to a child's life, even the imperfect ones like me. Although, I was smart enough to marry my wife, giving our daughters a favorable chance in the end. You're welcome, girls. Self-deprecating humor aside, I want to point out that all kids need and long for a parental figure in their lives. And Gen Z is no different. But the reality is that not every home contains the 1950s image of a nuclear family with mom and dad, two kids, a dog, and a picket fence. Most of the world does not operate that way. The key is that there needs to be a positive adult influence in a kiddo's life who offers love and guidance.

That said, many circumstances in life can make an impact upon a child. Family life, history, opportunities, and the conditions surrounding us all contribute to the people we become. I have seen some of the happiest friends and students reside with a single guardian, who might struggle to pay bills and can't shower them in toys, but provides a constant downpour of love and support. In contrast, I have also seen wealthy students from affluent suburbs miserable, as their parents pressure them to maintain a perfect family image, while mom abuses prescription drugs and dad has an affair with his secretary. And finally, I will never forget a wonderful friend who went on to become an architect after being the sole survivor of a car accident, losing his parents and spending the rest of his childhood with his grandmother. There may not be a "normal" family out there. Nevertheless, they are undeniably family.

I mention all this because I take to heart that no family is the same. Additionally, there's no formula for what works the best, or I suppose, what works the worst. I acknowledge that. Individual considerations for a child's family situation are critical for the health of that student. However, I do think it's worth our time to examine how many guardians of Gen Z, regardless of their gender, race, role, etc., might operate. This creates a macro-level trend that can help guide our thinking regarding how many students within Gen Z operate when influenced by their guardians—in the same manner that health care providers consider how many diabetics on a macro-level operate when influenced by their low blood sugar.

Recall that individuals from Gen X are the most common guardians for Gen Z students. Gen Xers are best known for being the "latchkey" survivalists that took care of themselves after school until their parents arrived and braved a time period of high divorce rates and economic hardships.[4] This is important. Why? Keep in mind that most caring parents, regardless of race, religion, or economics, follow one predictable creed: give your children all the things you did *not* receive in childhood. Sound familiar? You probably first heard this from your grandparents, and Gen X moms and dads are certainly no different. Now, I'm not trying to suggest the 1970s and 1980s were devoid of fun activities and adventures (most even legal), but I am going to point out that many Gen Xers felt "alone" after school and somewhat forgotten.[10] These conflicting feelings and loneliness have inspired some Gen X parents and guardians to make sure they are always present in their child's life. This goal is not a bad thing in moderation. However, as teen eye rolls will confirm, it may also be a parental overcorrection for what they lacked in childhood, and they are going back to the unwritten creed to make sure their kiddo has a better shake at life.

As such, we see Gen X parents compensate, and sometimes overcompensate, for all the wrongs they want to right in their version of parenting. This may lead to "lawnmower" parenting, where parents seek to always be present and mow down any obstacle in their child's way. This intention seems innocent enough, in that some Gen X guardians felt that they had to figure out too much on their own and don't want their child to experience that stress. However, this line of logic has its problems. Dr. Penny Rue, Vice President for Campus Life at Wake Forest University, explains this well. Dr. Rue points out that Gen X "[will] try to give their children the safe and secure childhood they didn't have at all, so we will likely see some fragility in Gen Z that we see in late Millennials."[4]

To Dr. Rue's point, educators have already noticed this trend in parenting style, and it's capturing the attention of the behavioral science experts. There is plenty of research that examines how behavioral practices, including ones implemented by Gen X parents, impact childhood growth and development.[11] There are also plenty of observational studies that connect parenting styles to a child's self-esteem, allowing Gen X moms and dads to see where they might fit in.[12] And then there are some articles that really offer some direct and vivid feedback about Gen X parenting, as we see from Mr. Neil Howe, who has an article on The American Association of School Administrators website:

"When these Gen-X "security moms" and "committed dads" are fully roused, they can be even more attached, protective, and interventionist than Boomers ever were. Web junkies, they will monitor Edline and Blackboard sites nightly, send e-mails to school board members, trade advice on blogs, and look up teacher credentials. Flex workers, they will juggle schedules to monitor their kids' activities in person. Speedy multitaskers, they will quickly switch their kids into—or take them out of—any situation according to their assessment of their youngsters' interests."[13]

Wow. That detailed depiction from Mr. Howe forces any parent to pause and reflect on their level of intervention in their child's life. But all that said, I don't believe our educational leaders, nor certainly myself, are trying to suggest that the Gen Z kiddos in your classroom are products of the greatest parenting fail in the last millennium. Far from it. Like any generation of parents, Gen X guardians have their strengths and weaknesses. They will impact their children but not define their children. And, that's how parenting has really operated for the last thousand years or so. But the point is this: in situations where overparenting does occur, there can be significant setbacks, and Gen Z is at risk for that. I intend to explore those risks in just a moment. However, before we do, I want to clarify something important. Please keep in mind that I am part of the Gen X parenting cohort. I read opinions and research regarding Gen X parenting, and I try to take them to heart. In the end, I believe that my wife and I, as well as the friends we admire, are at least halfway decent parents. But I also realize that I am not a parenting expert. I average at least three to four parenting failures a day.

All sarcasm aside, I feel compelled to point out that there are also many benefits when Gen X parents are (extremely) involved in their child's life. I can refer you to mountains of clinical research that demonstrates that time with children strengthens a family. *The Journal of Marriage and Family* has an article that does a wonderful job highlighting this and proving that quality of time trumped quantity of time.[14] However, when parent involvement in a child's life crosses over into persistent intercession on a child's behalf, this may create an unintentional setback. Why? Because despite the parent's best intentions, this repetitive behavior creates a situation where a child becomes too dependent upon their guardian(s) to consistently make plans for them and solve all of their problems. Why does that matter? Over time, this parenting practice can diminish resilience and increase ambiguity in a child's life, as these students are unintentionally conditioned to look for someone else to eliminate their challenges. That's not beneficial for a child.

Now, go one step further. What happens when these kiddos need their parents to intervene and fix some pretty significant challenges that have arisen from a pandemic? Even if your dad is Dr. Anthony Fauci, it's unlikely he can single-handedly address the loneliness, uncertainty, financial worries, sick family members, and loss of support that millions of school-aged children just experienced. So, what happens when a mom can't intervene on her kid's behalf and solve all problems related to the pandemic? You guessed it. It teaches a child that the plan they've put all their faith and confidence into does not work—at least not always.

The stressors that came with this pandemic have been big problems, not small ones kids can shrug off. I can promise you, albeit unscientifically, that the 152 students I taught science to in 2020 did not hold back on voicing concerns during Zoom classes; they wanted the problems of isolation, anxiety, fear, and so forth to be solved immediately. And that was in April of 2020. We had barely begun. However, I suppose their concerns were not a surprise. But, what threw me for a loop was their persistent line of questioning to determine who at the school district was responsible for various hardships that had nothing to do with school? It seemed as though they were grasping for solutions from other people they relied upon since the last few weeks had shown that their parents couldn't simply mow down this barrier caused by COVID-19.

I suspect that this realization—knowing parents can't fix everything—likely imploded the very operational framework for problem-solving that some Gen Zers relied upon. I am not alone in my thoughts here. Dr. Jenny Grant Rankin, an educator and author for *Psychology Today*, points out in an NBC article that "Kids who receive the best of everything and don't have opportunities to practice defeat will later struggle when coping with life's messy nature."[15] Dr. Rankin explains this principle of cause and effect extremely well. I wonder, on a scale of messiness, where COVID-19 falls? I can't answer that. However, later in this book, we will examine impactful data that highlights concerning trends in mental health before and during the pandemic. And I will admit upfront, the outcome data has further convinced me to believe this pandemic was REALLY messy.

At any rate, a fair number of children in your classroom may have succumbed to this realization when dad, aunt, grandma, or whomever cares for them couldn't fix SARS-CoV-2 and all the crappy things that came along with it. So, what's the impact? At the very least, it's a mini epiphany and stressor for their developing mind. But like all coming of age moments, good or bad, expect behavior change. There will likely be a notable number of students in your classroom who re-enter school a little shaken. Maybe not on the surface, but I assure you it will be there. Here is why. Any time your reliance and faith in something is tested, it results in a small amount of doubt and ambiguity, at least until the challenge can be resolved.

COVID-19 will fade, so in that regard, some issues will improve at a superficial level. But depending upon the age and insight of your students, many will realize that their problem-solving method failed. When it mattered a great deal, the people that these children placed the greatest faith in could no longer create instantaneous solutions for them. This was likely unsettling for many Gen Zers because up to this point, caretakers may have eliminated most difficulties for them—until they couldn't. That's a hefty line of logic to process as an adult, let alone a Gen Zer in school. I wonder if those kids are looking for someone to reinspire confidence and perhaps show alternate paths to problem-solving and resilience...someone like a teacher.

Air, water, technology - Essentials for life

So, if you're impressed by the impact of Gen X parenting upon a good chunk of your students, then I can't wait to bring you up to speed on the influence of technology. Let me use simple math to set the tone for our discussion. The average parent spends somewhere between 1-2 hours of quality face time with their child each day. If that seems low, don't feel too bad. The value has doubled since the 1960s.[16] Now, enter technology. The average child with a cell phone spends four to seven hours with that device daily. Seven hours? Choose a swear word to mutter quietly. Before we investigate how and why this infatuation with technology is critically important in terms of measurable outcomes, allow me some latitude for a quick story, which also sets the framework for what lies ahead.

While waiting for a flight in an airport one afternoon, I watched a young teenage boy lose his mind over the loss of airport Wi-Fi. This led to a sudden reliance upon LTE service. His dad didn't understand the reason for his son's lamentations, so he asked him, "What's the big difference between Wi-Fi and LTE if I'm the one paying for your data anyway?" His son replied with a well-constructed response regarding internet upload and download speeds on LTE compared to the superior performance of fiber-based Wi-Fi. I couldn't help but listen. Now, for the record, I greatly admired the patience of this father and how he chatted with his very intelligent son. But after about three minutes of back-and-forth discussion, the grievances joined together into one final lamentation from the teenager: "it shouldn't take 10 seconds to load this web page! It should be now!" The dad smiled. Then he calmly reminded his son that the phone was connecting with a satellite *IN OUTER SPACE*, and perhaps he could just appreciate that things like that even happen. The point is this: most of Gen Z coexists with technology. Taking it away from them, even in the slightest manifestation, is probably comparable to me telling you not to use your dominant hand for a few hours.

A byproduct of that coexistence with technology is familiarity and confidence. There is no doubt that Gen Z is tech-savvy beyond anything we have seen in other generations. *The Guardian*, a newspaper in the United Kingdom, appropriately coined the term "digitally innate" when referring to the students in today's classroom.[17] What does that mean? It simply highlights that this generation has been raised side by side with technology. The first attempt at a smartphone? 1992. First iPhone? 2007. And then a seemingly infinite amount of phone apps that followed right after. Social media has also been a routine part of life for this crew, and touch screen technology is not new for them either...rather, it is the norm. This became even more readily apparent for me when I chatted with a kindergarten teacher that mentioned how MAP testing can be a nightmare with five-year-olds. Why? Because the students have never seen a computer mouse, and when told to use the mouse, they press it against the computer screen where their fingers would normally make contact.

Laughs aside, Gen Zers are superb with technology. Most comb the internet at insanely rapid speeds and are adept at searching for any kind of information. They also stay on top of new tech updates, platform upgrades, and are likely to be early adopters of new technology. As such, they expect the internet to be readily available and digital applications to improve rapidly. These are normal expectations of life for many Gen Zers. The older half of this generational cohort want internet access to be so readily available that college football stadiums are now installing Wi-Fi to keep up with the times. Wait, aren't people there to watch the game?

Although internet skills offer a lot of benefits—knowledge and the ability to communicate—being online constantly has its downsides. The Washington Post reported on a 2019 review that found eight-to-twelve-year-olds spend an average of 4 hours and 44 minutes a day online, while teens put this to shame with an average of 7 hours and 22 minutes. This does not include time spent on homework. Let your mind fully wrap around those numbers, as teens are spending an entire corporate workday online and somehow going to school too.[18] But not all kids have smartphones. So, maybe this isn't as bad as we think, right? Well, on second thought... in 2018, the Pew Research Center confirmed that 95% of teens have access to smartphones, and 45% believe they are online "constantly."[19] Ugh.

Now, if you're a classroom teacher, I suspect you're not surprised by those screen time numbers. Students seem to habitually, almost obsessively, find reasons to pull their phone out and quickly check notifications. Some will even habitually check their appearance with the camera app. This is common behavior, and to some extent, old news, as cell phone restriction in schools has been a hot topic for quite some time now. However, our interest in cell phones and technology is not based on school policy. Rather, we strive to examine how technology influences Gen Zers' lives inside and outside of the classroom. Let's go ahead and do that.

Filtering

Gen Z is phenomenal at filtering information at a rapid rate. Whether it is app upgrades, Snapchats, Instagram notifications, or simple text messages, Gen Z persistently filters info during their day. Why? The amount of incoming information can be extraordinary. A 2015 study reported that the average person receives 64 push notifications in a day.[20] Adolescents were likely well above that average, and phone use has only increased since those results were collected. All that adds up to a student who examines the information on their phone with the following perspective: *Does this information apply to me? Do I care right now? Should I respond immediately?*[21] Given that Gen Z practices this mental exercise for around four to seven hours a day, can you see how it becomes a pervasive pattern of thought for life in general?

I mention this filtered viewpoint, used by some Gen Zers because if a teacher's attempt to form a meaningful connection with a student did not pan out on a particular day, it might not reflect incompatible personalities but rather, too many things were happening at that moment. The educator's good intentions ended up on the wrong side of the student's filter. As such, it's not enough as an educator to mention something interesting in general. Gen Zers need it to be interesting for *them*. Like it or not, this is a byproduct of persistent filtration. All the more reason to take time as an educator to learn what a student pursues in life and use that knowledge to connect. Students need to internalize that when a teacher talks, their words "apply to me, and I should care." This can be burdensome to teachers. However, for some Gen Zers, this may be how meaningful relationships begin.

Opportunity cost - Screen time vs. anything else

When you Google "cell phone impact on behavior," you receive 135,000,000 results. That's all? Come on, Google, try a little harder. The influence of technology upon behavior and thought process is an enormous area of interest for researchers, educators, and parents alike. Many of these investigations look into how specific applications, such as YouTube or TikTok, impact focus and attention.[21] Other studies look at the quantitative time spent on devices. But regardless of how a phone or tablet is used, any time away from human interaction can take a toll on the developmental life of a child.[22] Why? Because humans still have yet to figure out how to be in two places at once. Time and attention with devices eliminate valuable moments spent doing alternative activities with other people, such as talking, laughing, and engaging with emotional cues. As such, there is an opportunity cost that comes with technology, and it needs to be considered.

For all the non-business people like myself out there, here's a quick tutorial on opportunity cost and the implications it brings forth. The corporate world defines opportunity cost as the loss of potential gain from alternative choices when one specific alternative is chosen over others. Make sense? If not, let me rephrase. Another possibility is to think of opportunity cost as the benefit that *could have* been enjoyed had a specific choice not been made to eliminate it as an option. If you're still stuck, don't feel bad. Here's how my eight-year-old just explained it to me a few weeks ago, "So if I choose ice cream for dessert, the side effect [opportunity cost] is that I can't enjoy a chocolate bar, since I can only pick one thing... because you and Mommy make my life hard." Hopefully, one of those definitions connects with you.

Why does opportunity cost matter? If a student spends four to seven hours on their phone outside of school, they choose to interact with their phone instead of with family or friends. This means, unless they are Facetiming (or some variant thereof), they are NOT having in-person connections most or all of that time. Some lost opportunities that occur within those seven hours each day could be: i) socializing with friends, as texting and talking are very different in terms of brain involvement and emotional response ii) reassurance from loved ones that can be validated with nonverbal cues, and iii) perception of reality, as most social media accounts reflect highlights instead of everyday events. Thus, there is fallout from choosing direct messages and texts as a primary form of communication. As amazing as mobile devices and technology are, there is no like or share button that can replace the value of a confirmatory smile or a much-needed hug. And that, my friends, is an enormous opportunity cost.

Side effects of artificial intelligence

Sometimes technology does some wonderful things, and Gen Zers are acutely aware of this. The students in your classroom have grown up in an interconnected world where just about anything is possible with the click of a mouse or touch screen. Think about the following:

- Need some special wet brush markers for an art class? You can order them through your Amazon app in about 60 seconds. It's faster if you don't want to read about the subtle differences between the first four types that pop up on the initial search. My eight-year-old daughter only needed 48 seconds, to be exact. Still not fast enough? Just ask Alexa to do it for you.

- Need to know how to restart your gas fireplace after the pilot light goes out? YouTube has over 20 experts showing you how...and that's just for our particular model.

- Want to watch the latest Disney movie? You could buy tickets through Fandango. Or why do that? There is still COVID. Just start it on Disney + before you finish microwaving the popcorn.

Keep in mind that none of these scenarios are upgrades for Gen Z. They are just a part of life—a life they have known since they could utter the phrases "Momma," "Dadda," and "iPhone."

Now, I'm not saying any of this is a bad thing. Technology offers convenient and easier ways to navigate life. That's one reason why we pay premium dollars for these devices and continue to follow the latest upgrades. I have no problem admitting that I appreciate the time-saving opportunities technology affords me and the family time it creates for my little crew. For example, just last night, I ordered from my favorite restaurant via the UberEats app, providing delivery to our door so that I could avoid cooking and use that time to play a board game with my daughters. In my book, that's a good thing.

However, experts point out that as we increase convenience, we may be decreasing opportunities to problem solve. What do they mean by that, and why would they question my Uber Eats decision? Well, every problem you and I solve requires four distinct steps: i) identify the problem, ii) determine the cause(s) of the problem, iii) design a solution that addresses or mitigates the causes, and iv) implement the solution.[23] This process holds true whether you are solving the dilemma of dinner or something far more serious. However, let's keep things simple for now and go back to the culinary conundrum I had last evening. I'll walk you through the process.

- Identify the problem—I don't have time to play with my daughters right now because I need to prepare dinner.

- Cause(s)—There is limited time between my arrival home from work and the preferred time for our family to eat. Also, my girls do not enjoy food prep, so this is not an option for us to spend time together.

- Solution—I will have someone else make dinner. This frees up time for me to hang out with my lovely daughters and lose to them in Princess Monopoly.

- Implementation—I order food through the UberEats app.

Make sense? Wonderful. Except that it's not completely wonderful. Here's the catch. The outlined example above represents a pared-down problem-solving process. It's so simple that most of us can do all four steps intuitively and nearly simultaneously in our brain. However, there is an issue that you may not have caught that becomes important with big problems far beyond the scope of dinner. Technology, whether it be YouTube or Wikipedia, takes steps two and three of the problem-solving process away from us. Yep, a piece of software, automated and thoughtfully programmed, can make assumptions about the likely cause of the problem you input and has an algorithm to select solutions. You get those results from your device and then simply implement them. This is what we love about it... tech support takes away our need to think. All we have to do is define the problem for the tech support, and it should implement a well-designed solution. This is exactly what the UberEats app did for me. It assumed I had a time constraint and pointed out restaurants in my area, categorized by the estimated time of delivery and taste preferences, and then facilitated the payment and logistics of the food arriving at my home. All I had to do was touch my phone screen, and therefore, implement the solution I wanted. Twenty-five minutes later, there was yummy food at my front door.

What I described is the basis of artificial intelligence (AI). We may find it helpful and convenient, such as when it comes to a quick dinner solution, but if you're a Millennial or older, you've learned how to problem solve without AI. For Gen Z, who has grown up with persistent use of AI, there may be a steep downfall. Researchers have begun to investigate it.

- University of California, Los Angeles (UCLA) professor Dr. Patricia Greenfield and colleagues analyzed more than 50 studies on how technology impacts learning. The outcome from this meta-analysis was that critical thinking and analysis skills quantitatively decline the more people use technology, while visual skills improve.[24]

- A recent article in Forbes points out, "As automation systems, deep learning algorithms, and AI get more skilled at certain tasks, humans have to do them less, which could over time make us *less* skilled."[25]

- An article in the *Journal of the Association for Consumer Research* presented a study that investigated how the simple presence of a cell phone, beyond the countless notifications and noises, can alter thought process and cognition.[26]

- New York Times best-selling author Dan Brown wrote a spectacular book, entitled *Origin*, which casts a supercomputer with advanced AI that helps the protagonist navigate thrilling challenges and solve complex problems.[27] It's a fantastic and entertaining story. It also concludes with a carefully constructed suggestion that humans are devolving over time, as much of our creative abilities and problem-solving is being replaced by technology.

So, what's the harm with all this? Students that consistently rely upon technology to augment problem-solving struggle when there is no AI capability available. This may seem like a minor setback for trivial issues. However, for large and meaningful problems in a student's life, this setback could develop into a collapse. Students may feel a sense of ambiguity, restlessness, and concern when they don't know how to approach an ill-defined issue without tech support. Think about it. There is no app to order a solution for a child's emotions surrounding their parents' divorce. There isn't a whole lot on YouTube for guidance on how to select a college after a parent loses their job, and their younger sibling, who also aspires to go to college, is two years behind them in high school. And finally, I have yet to see great tech help regarding navigating the polarized opinions pertaining to this recent pandemic, especially for a child who lost their grandmother to COVID-19.

I am not saying that Gen Z does not know how to problem-solve. Rather, for many Gen Zers, their pathway to solutions involves a piece of technology. This makes them more prone to problem-solving deficits and subsequent frustration when compared to other population cohorts. As such, they will need to see the relevance of practicing problem-solving in school in order to build skills for the complex issues of life that can't be solved by a cell phone.

How does information about Gen Z improve my classroom or school?

With the critical help of expert insight, this chapter has constructed a working model for how many Gen Zers operate. Or, more accurately, how they are influenced to operate. Either way, this is important. Think back to the example with diabetes at the beginning of this chapter. Recall that an operational model of diabetes allows health care providers to look for aggressiveness, sweating, and confusion in diabetics. Why? Because this is how diabetes tends to operate when sugars are low. Please also keep in mind that an operational model will **not** apply to all the students in your class. No generalization ever does. However, this insight does allow us to be knowledgeable regarding trends, tendencies, and thought patterns. See if you can identify a few:

- A student states that a friend has become cryptic in their messages posted on Snapchat, especially regarding their future plans. This act of vague booking may be the only clue offered regarding thoughts of suicide.[28]

- A student mentions that their dad isn't around as much anymore because of business trips. Part of the student's ambiguity and fear may be due to the fact that dad is their "go-to" for problem-solving, especially for tough issues.

- A student mentions that their phone was taken from them as a consequence. Maybe that's an inconvenience to you as an adult. However, a cell phone to a Gen Zer is a part of normal daily life. Anticipate increased manifestations of anxiety, distractibility, and potentially poor classwork as the Gen Zer deals with "fear of missing out" as a chunk of their normalcy has been yanked from them.

The ability to recognize predictable responses to known stressors can be helpful and, sometimes even life-saving. Although we recognize this as educators and parents, we need to practice it. Gen Z may be statistically brilliant, tech-savvy, and worldly in their views, but they also seem to have a distinct set of vulnerabilities. Every generation does. But not every generation has endured a pandemic in their youth that has preyed upon their vulnerabilities. Understanding some of the concerns, setbacks, and obstacles that many of the students in your classroom internalize should allow you to deepen connections with them. Educators have the opportunity to help this cohort of students bounce back and see their own intrinsic value. Doing that without a text message or a "like" may be challenging, but that's what needs to be done.

Chapter 1 References

1. NPD Group. (2020). *Guide to Gen Z: Debunking the myths of our youngest generation.* https://www.npd.com/wps/portal/npd/us/news/tips-trends-takeaways/guide-to-gen-z-debunking-the-myths-of-our-youngest-generation/

2. Taie, S., & Goldring, R. (2020). *Characteristics of public and private elementary and secondary school teachers in the United States: Results from the 2017–18 National Teacher and Principal Survey First Look* (NCES 2020- 142). U.S. Department of Education. Washington, DC: National Center for Education Statistics. Retrieved February 22, 2021 from https://nces.ed.gov/pubsearch/pubsinfo.asp?pubid=2020142

3. Dimock, M. (2019, January 17). *Defining generations: Where Millennials end and Generation Z begins.* Pew Research Center. https://www.pewresearch.org/fact-tank/2019/01/17/where-millennials-end-and-generation-z-begins/

4. Rue, P. (2018). Make way, Millennials, here comes Gen Z. *About Campus, 23*(3), 5–12. https://doi.org/10.1177/1086482218804251

5. Taylor, P., & Gao, G. (2014, June 5). *Generation X: America's neglected "middle child."* Pew Research Center. https://www.pewresearch.org/fact-tank/2014/06/05/generation-x-americas-neglected-middle-child/

6. Pew Research Center: U.S. Politics & Policy. (2016, December 15). *Americans name the top historic events of their lifetimes.* https://www.pewresearch.org/politics/2016/12/15/americans-name-the-top-historic-events-of-their-lifetimes/

7. Liotta, A. (2011). *Unlocking generational codes.* Aviva Publishing.

8. Gomez, K., Mawhinney, T., & Betts, K. (n.d.). *Welcome to Generation Z.* Deloitte & Network of Executive Women. https://www2.deloitte.com/us/en/pages/consumer-business/articles/understanding-generation-z-in-the-workplace.html

9. The Wharton School of the University of Pennsylvania. (2019, January 22). *Make way for Generation Z in the workplace.* https://knowledge. wharton.upenn.edu/article/make-room-generation-z-workplace/

10. Arnett, D. (2019, March 27). *As Baby Boomers and Millennials grab headlines, the lost Generation X asks, "what about us?"* The Boston Globe. https://www.bostonglobe.com/ metro/2019/03/27/baby-boomers-and-millenniels-grab-headline s-lost-generation-asks-what-about/dFBmDXxpRo2I1mIKR0gnfI/ story.html

11. Hosokawa, R., & Katsura, T. (2018). Role of parenting style in children's behavioral problems through the transition from preschool to elementary school according to gender in Japan. *International Journal of Environmental Research and Public Health, 16*(1), 21. https://doi. org/10.3390/ijerph16010021

12. American Psychological Association. (2017, June). *Parenting Styles.* https://www.apa.org/act/resources/fact-sheets/parenting-styles

13. Howe, N. (2010). *Meet Mr. and Mrs. Gen X: A new parent generation.* The School Superintendents Association. https://www.aasa. org/SchoolAdministratorArticle.aspx?id=11122#:~:text=As%20 parents%2C%20they%20will%20be,to%20monitor

14. Milkie, M. A., Nomaguchi, K. M., & Denny, K. E. (2015). Does the amount of time mothers spend with children or adolescents matter? *Journal of Marriage and Family, 77*(2), 355–372. https://doi.org/ doi:10.1111/jomf.12170

15. Spector, N. (2019, March 27). *Why "lawnmower parenting" is like robbing your kids-And how to actually help them.* NBC News. https://www.nbcnews. com/better/lifestyle/why-lawnmower-parenting-robbing-your-kid s-how-actually-help-them-ncna987526

16. Renner, B. (2020, January 25). *Modern family: Average parent spends just 5 hours face-to-face with their kids per week.* Study Finds.

17. Povah, C., & Vaukins, S. (2017, July 10). *Generation Z is starting university – but is higher education ready?* The Guardian. https:// www.theguardian.com/higher-education-network/2017/jul/10/ generation-z-starting-university-higher-education-ready

18. Siegel, R. (2019, October 29). *Tweens, teens, and screens: The average time kids spend watching online videos has doubled in 4 years.* The Washington Post. https://www.washingtonpost.com/

technology/2019/10/29/survey-average-time-young-people-spend-watching-videos-mostly-youtube-has-doubled-since/

19. Anderson, M., & Jiang, J. (2018, May 31). *Teens, social media, & technology 2018*. Pew Research Center. https://www.pewresearch.org/internet/2018/05/31/teens-social-media-technology-2018/

20. Pielot, M., & Rello, L. (2017). Productive, anxious, lonely: 24 hours without push notifications. *Proceedings of the 19th International Conference on Human-Computer Interaction with Mobile Devices and Services*, Association for Computing Machinery. 1–11.https://doi.org/10.1145/3098279.3098526

21. McCarthy, C. (2018, July 21). *Can cell phone use cause ADHD?* Harvard Health Publishing: Harvard Medical School. https://www.health.harvard.edu/blog/can-cell-phone-use-cause-adhd-2018073114375

22. Lowry, L. (2016). *Facebook vs face-to-face: How technology threatens parent-child interaction*. The Hanen Centre. http://www.hanen.org/Helpful-Info/Our-Views-on-the-News/Facebook-vs-Face-to-Face--How-Technology-Threatens.aspx

23. Centers for Disease Control and Prevention (CDC). (2014). *Introduction to Public Health*. In: Public Health 101 Series. Atlanta, GA: U.S. Department of Health and Human Services. https://www.cdc.gov/training/publichealth101/public-health.html.

24. Wolpert, S. (2009, January 27). *Is technology producing a decline in critical thinking and analysis?* UCLA Newsroom. https://newsroom.ucla.edu/releases/is-technology-producing-a-decline-79127

25. Bernard, M. (2016, October 13). *Is stupidity a dangerous side effect of big data driven AI?* Forbes. https://www.forbes.com/sites/bernardmarr/2016/10/13/is-ai-making-us-stupid/?sh=628de9a04df3

26. Ward, A. F., Duke, K., Gneezy, A., & Bos, M. W. (2017). Brain drain: The mere presence of one's own smartphone reduces available cognitive capacity. *Journal of the Association for Consumer Research*, *2*(2), 140–154. https://doi.org/10.1086/691462

27. Brown, D. (2017). *Origin*. Knopf Doubleday Publishing Group.

28. Berryman, C., Ferguson, C. J., & Negy, C. (2018). Social media use and mental health among young adults. *The Psychiatric Quarterly*, *89*(2), 307–314. https://doi.org/10.1007/s11126-017-9535-6

2

Helmets, pads, and other protection... Protective vs. risk factors

Educators love to connect dots. It's one of the things that principals and teachers do exceptionally well and find delight in. There is an undeniable rush a teacher feels when they help a child make a connection, or conversely, identify the missing link a child needs to grasp before understanding a topic. In these moments, educators can get creative and provide the perfect drawing, insightful video, helpful mnemonic, or crazy story to help students connect the dots. Some staff might suggest that it's one of the best moments that comes with teaching.

So, with that in mind, let's connect some dots upfront. However, this time it will be for our benefit, not our students... at least, not yet. You are now aware of some operational trends found within much of Gen Z. That's a good start, but it's not enough to make changes in your classroom. Let's build upon that knowledge and connect it to other valuable dots, which also contain critical pieces of information. Here's a brief outline of the connections that need to be made.

- First Dot (Chapter 1): Identify important points of influence for school-aged children, and how those influences help predict the operational patterns, stress points, and responses for many Gen Zers.

- Second Dot (Chapter 2): Discuss how a wide array of protective factors and risk factors impact both perspective and resilience in the face of life's challenges. Some of these factors are unlikely to be modified by educators. However, factors that fall within the skill sets of educators should serve as our focus for potential intervention.

- Third Dot (Chapter 3): Based upon the forecasted vulnerabilities within Gen Z, examine meaningful outcome data to see if these predicted areas of concern translate into actual mental health challenges.

- Fourth Dot (Chapter 4): Are we using our time in school effectively when it comes to mitigating the mental health concerns and specific challenges for much of Gen Z?

These are the dots that we need to connect before finishing Part 1 of this book. If I do my job well, we should all have a common foundation regarding many of the challenges and concerns that the students in your classroom deal with on a regular basis. And perhaps more importantly, we gain some insight into what kind of support scaffold many students will need in order to navigate their post-COVID school years in a healthy manner.

Oh, the stressors you will encounter!

Before I dive into protective and risk factors, getting all "science-y" on you, it's important to understand what they mean. Most of us are familiar with the idea that it takes grit, resilience, and determination to power through life's challenges. The problem is that these are ill-defined words attached to complex concepts, and it's essential to understand what protective and risk factors represent and the impacts they have on our lives. Keep in mind that the most prominent force that protective and risk factors interact with is stress. Therefore, allow me to lay down some foundational concepts regarding stress and how it impacts school-aged children. All people are affected by stress at one time or another. However, adolescents seem to take the brunt of it. Let's segue into the awkward years.

Every generation struggles with the tween and early teen years. My co-authors and friends refer to this period as the "bangs and fangs" phase, when their middle school appearance included a bowl cut, vampire dental aesthetic, and high fashion ponchos with gym shoes (which will be cool again soon, right?). But regardless of fashion trends, adolescence brings physical, social, and emotional changes that can make it a bumpy ride. We all remember it. It includes tough moments, like shifting friendships, first relationship woes, combating peer pressure, or for some, looking after their younger siblings so their parents can work a second job. These examples demonstrate a small possibility of the many common stressors in an adolescent's life. Now, add to it the realization that school is more than a fun place to do art and hang with friends; it has implications that impact your opportunities after high school. For many kids, these challenges are a high-stress cross to bear.

None of this is my personal opinion. It's well documented. A global study examining around 11,000 students, ages 11-19, found that the most significant stressors in study participants' lives included i) school, ii) parents, iii) peers, and iv) romantic relationships.[1] This is a common trend in adolescence that spans many generations. You might even consider it a baseline for the normal growth and development of tweens and teens. But recently, life added a whole new layer of unexpected stress that came from the SARS-CoV-2 pandemic.

To no surprise, the challenges of this pandemic have made their mark in many areas. The American Psychological Association examined stress in America and found in 2020 that two out of five Gen Zers aged 13-17 reported that their stress level increased over the past year. In particular, 81% of those Gen Z students were negatively impacted by the pandemic due to changes from school closures.[2] These kids' lives (and school as we knew it) were turned upside down in a matter of days. And they weren't alone. Teachers, principals, bus companies, lunch service staff...we all had to adjust on the fly. However, adults have had years of experience and have a greater sense of resilience and self that should help. What about the students?

The answers we provide may or may not shock you. First, remind yourself of what they had to deal with. Try to look at this through the eyes of a sixth-grader, a brand-new kindergartner, or a graduating senior that watched all the special moments they dreamed of erased in one press conference. Our students were thrown into atypical and unexpected learning environments (ex. online, hybrid, and adjusted in-person formats) within a matter of days. This was a shift the overwhelming majority of them had never experienced before. What was the impact?

In 2020, 52% of Gen Z students reported decreased motivation to complete schoolwork, 47% felt they did not learn as much as in previous years, and 45% had difficulty concentrating on schoolwork.[2] Obviously, this isn't good. Prolonged stress in adolescence can set up lasting conditions that lead to mental health problems like anxiety and depression.[3] However, stress itself is just one piece of the puzzle that impacts mental health. There are other pieces—time to examine the competing forces in the battle of resilience: protective factors and risk factors.

Protective factors and risk factors - Mental health wellness and resilience

At a bare minimum, risk factors are the "characteristics at the biological, psychological, family, community, or cultural level that precede and are associated with a higher likelihood of negative outcomes."[4] Opposite to risk factors, protective factors are the "characteristics associated with a lower likelihood of negative outcomes or that reduce a risk factor's impact."[4] Together, the presence, absence, or blend of risk and protective factors significantly impact student mental health.[5]

Now, these risk and protective factors exist in various interconnected domains, such as at the individual, peer, family, school, and community levels. Let's walk through an example to illustrate the presence of these factors in your students' lives. See if you can pick out a few things that benefit this hypothetical individual and some characteristics or exposures that make them more likely to struggle.

- Sara is a 17-year-old girl with a complicated home life, yet you would never know, as she displays a happy-go-lucky demeanor at school. Her parents constantly fight, and as an only child, she is often caught in the middle of arguments. Sara is what you would describe as a social butterfly and relies upon her relationships at school and basketball to distract her from the stress at home. In March of 2020, Sara's school switched to an all-online format, and in-person activities were canceled for the foreseeable future. Her parents' usual arguments increased in frequency and size as both of her parents started working from home, and her family began experiencing financial trouble. Sara could no longer see her friends at school or activities, and she was largely confined to her bedroom to escape from the arguments. Sara wanted nothing more than to talk to her friends, but she never Facetimed them because she was afraid her friends would hear her parents arguing in the background. The once social butterfly now desperately awaits the day she can escape the pressures of her home life and return to her safe haven amongst her friends at school and on the basketball court. However, for now, Sara is lonely and more down than she has ever been in her life.

As teachers, we often know quite a bit about the daily happenings at school, ranging from who rants about their parents, who backstabs their friends, and even who changes in the bathroom from mom-approved outfits into more trendy attire. As educators, we notice many things. However, we don't notice everything. Our impressions are confined to the eight hours of school. And unless a student confides in a staff member, how could we know anything beyond our students' worlds at school?

Before COVID-19, I would have never known "Sara's" home life was rough and just how important her school relationships and involvement in activities were, at least not in the capacity that she relied on them to protect her mental health state. Now, once Sara is back at school, I may be able to pick up on her slight change in mood. However, the scariest part is that I may not. Sara, who is intelligent and capable, might still maintain a false impression of her happy-go-lucky demeanor. Why? Because this is what people expect out of her, at least that is what Sara believes. So, in the face of heightened risk factors like family conflict, isolation, and financial stress, Sara is "off-balance." What do I mean by this? Think of a playground see-saw. Sarah's risk factors may currently outweigh her protective factors, tilting the see-saw toward a poor mental health state. This imbalance is not what we want. Now, Sara's fictitious example is a narrow depiction of several factors that influence a student's life, but nonetheless, it illustrates some of the hidden stressors school-aged children deal with. Let's take a look at a wider distribution of risk and protective factors. The table below is not close to an exhaustive list but highlights some of the most prominent risk and protectve factors in Gen Zer's lives today.

	Individual	Peer	Family	School	Community
Risk Factors	1. Low self-esteem 2. Social isolation	1. Bullying 2. Associated with students who use drugs	1. Family conflict 2. Parental unemployment	1. School violence 2. Poor academic achievement	1. Community-level stressful/traumatic events 2. Community violence
Protective Factor	1.Emotional self-regulation 2. Good coping skills	1. Prosocial friendships 2. Close relationship with non-deviant peers	1. Connected to a positive adult in the family who serves as a mentor 2. Clear expectations for behavior	1. Support in developing skills/interests 2. Engagement in school activities	1. Safe community 2. Positive norms

Table adapted from Youth.gov and CDC

I could write an entire book (people have) discussing risk and protective factors that impact our students today, and it might still barely scrape the surface of possibilities. Fortunately, that effort is not needed for our purposes. Instead, what's important to know is that the presence of one risk factor increases the chances of a student experiencing more risk factors and decreases the likelihood of experiencing protective factors. And, the more risk factors students experience, the more likely they are to develop a condition that impacts their mental health.[4] This is a cumulative problem that adds intensity, so to speak, with each additional risk factor. It's almost like an exponential curve for all the math wizards out there.

But for those that don't love math, allow me to provide an analogy through imagery. Let's say you are rowing a boat upstream and have access to a set of wooden oars and a rudder to help you navigate. The oars and rudder serve as your protective factors and allow you to select your path, giving you a sense of control. At first, the river current, which is a risk factor, is minimal, and you are making great headway to your destination upstream. However, within minutes, the current increases (multiplying risk factor) in strength, and you are now struggling to maintain your momentum.

It's not long before the current becomes overpowering, and your once dependable oars are no longer strong enough to help you overcome the obstacle of the ever-increasing current, AND you can no longer select the path you want to take. You start slowly drifting downstream because you have lost control and will continue to do so. Fortunately, somebody comes along and offers you help, towing you to your destination. It took outside help to navigate this problem and get your boat to safety. As educators, I think you can understand how drifting downstream in this scenario is similar to when students, overwhelmed with risk factors, lose their way. This is when they need outside help, which in our analogy came in the form of a towboat.

As teachers, we cannot control the current—as much as we so desperately want to. We impact our students in many ways, but our reach is largely limited to inside the school walls. For example, we cannot snap our fingers and change a student's negative family dynamic, a parent's unemployment status, or the rate of violence within our student's community. However, we have a remarkable ability as educators to specifically impact critical influences on a student's life: self-efficacy and self-esteem. Now, I'm confident that you have seen presentations regarding self-efficacy and self-esteem one too many times, but I want you to understand why these often overused terms are essential to strategies discussed in Part 3 of this book. So, you'll need to understand self-esteem and self-efficacy in a more informed and meaningful way. Allow me to elaborate.

Like you, I've sat through hours of professional development and memorized most of the buzzwords related to positive classroom environments. This is different. I'm not looking for you to smile a lot and comment on the latest TikTok trend to make your students laugh. Rather, I am asking you to change a person. Change them in a way that when they are alone and challenged, they have what it takes not to fall apart.

Appreciate this opportunity. It's a big one! You, as an educator, have the ability to impact what are arguably two of the largest risk AND protective factors present in our kiddos' lives. If you can swing your students from feeling bad about themselves or not believing in their abilities to feeling confident and sure they can survive whatever is in front of them... then you are exactly what students need right now, more than ever after a terrible and isolating pandemic. This may be the most critical lesson you ever teach.

The impact of self-esteem and self-efficacy is so important that you and I will take a deep dive into the behavioral and cognitive science understanding of these factors. As I said, we need to understand these influences far beyond the professional development presentations that tossed them around as educational buzzwords (no offense to PD). The buy-in is this: it is imperative to understand the science behind self-esteem and self-efficacy to see the value of the approaches proposed later in this book. With that, game on.

Self-efficacy

Self-efficacy refers to an individual's belief in their ability to succeed in a certain situation or accomplish a given task. Self-efficacy influences the way people feel, think, and act.[6] But it's more than that. Self-efficacy serves as a major determinant in Social Cognitive Theory (SCT), which was developed by a prominent researcher and psychologist at Stanford University, Albert Bandura. The SCT asserts that people are self-reflecting, self-regulating, and are both influencers of and influenced by their social environment.[7] There are two main types of self-efficacy: generalized self-efficacy and domain-specific self-efficacy.

- Generalized self-efficacy refers to people's belief in their general ability to cope with universal challenges across the span of life, including their ability to deal with accompanying stress. A generalized self-efficacy example might include an individual's personal impression of how they would likely handle job promotions, aging, or becoming a parent. These are wide-scale considerations and/or events.

- Domain-specific self-efficacy refers to people's confidence in their ability to handle tasks and use skills in *specific* situations.[8,9] A domain-specific example could include a student who has low self-efficacy in math class because they do not have confidence in their ability to solve algebraic equations. However, this could drastically change the next semester when they are acing their geometry class.

So, how is this helpful? I admit there is still no definitive consensus regarding the relationship between domain-specific and general self-efficacy, including how they influence each other and to what extent. However, we DO know they are intertwined. The world of social science and behavioral health has demonstrated that whether you are dealing with domain-specific or general, there is a benefit to boosting self-efficacy. As such, self-efficacy, in any capacity, yields positive results.

Let's get more specific and examine data regarding student self-efficacy from an educator's perspective and in the context of your classroom or school. It has been found that self-efficacy is related to important motivational concepts like optimism, engaging in goal creation, asking for help at school, and personal value.[10] Students with high self-efficacy are likely to exhibit actions such as the following: problem-solve effectively, manage their time wisely, show more persistence, procrastinate less, and have less state anxiety (about an event) as well as trait anxiety (a personal characteristic).[10]

Take a moment to consider all of the elements we discussed regarding self-efficacy. I'm hopeful you now see this determinant as either a protective factor or risk multiplier and no longer an educational buzzword for professional development. The stark reality is that students need you to grasp its importance. Development of positive self-efficacy **must** be part of the solution, and that is a non-negotiable **must**. Self-efficacy is a requirement if we truly want to improve the situation for many Gen Zers and every cohort thereafter because it represents a dominant and successful coping resource when an individual is under a mountain of stress. And may I gently remind you, this is where we find Gen Z today—digging out from under that mountain.

Please also be aware that positive self-efficacy has been linked to improved overall health and well-being. The perception and belief that you can "do hard things" adds resilience and strength that decreases depression, minimizes anxiety, and improves quality of life.[11] We have known this for decades as we study the immune and endocrine systems. High levels of stress can increase chemicals known as cortisol and adrenaline. The Mayo Clinic reminds us that these substances are not meant to be elevated for long periods of time and can easily "wear down" your body. Alternatively, low levels of cortisol and adrenaline, during times where there is no physiologic need, contribute to a better immune system, calm demeanor, and focused thought pattern.[12] One last thought before we sign off on self-efficacy. What happens if you have a well-adjusted child that hits a slump and experiences a few consecutive school years with diminished self-efficacy? Is that hard to bounce back from? I mention this because it seems that every child experiences ups and downs at some point. Here's our answer. A study by Moksnes and colleagues found that adolescent girls, who had significantly higher stress in all domains (including peer pressure, school performance, home life, romantic relationships, etc.), simultaneously demonstrated lower self-efficacy and lower life satisfaction in all metrics as compared to boys.[11] So yes, the chronic impairment of self-efficacy puts these adolescent girls at theoretical risk for an increased chance of a future mental health challenge. But as you will see in Chapter 3, this risk is more than theoretical. It translates to real-life impairment. That kills me a little as a dad with two daughters at home.

Self-esteem

Onward to self-esteem. It is a concept that I internalize quite well. Not to brag, but very few people understand the self-worth that correlates with a 4% on a college organic chemistry exam in a pre-medicine track. In an attempt to collect my dignity, I had a meeting with my professor, but it ran short when he couldn't stop laughing about my low score. Yep, I am the right expert to discuss variations in self-esteem.

Essentially, the operational perspective of self-esteem encompasses an individual's sense of self-worth and reflects how they, and how they believe others, perceive their physical image, abilities, successes, etc.[13] The more positive views someone holds regarding these qualities and characteristics, the higher their self-esteem tends to be. The opposite is also true. Now, please keep in mind that self-esteem is not static. It changes drastically throughout the human lifespan. One global study examining the self-esteem of nearly 330,000 people, ages 9-90, found that self-esteem levels are highest in childhood, decline precipitously during adolescence, increase gradually during adulthood, and then decline again in old age.[14] This means that many school-aged children are persistently at risk for self-esteem issues based upon the chronology of life. Furthermore, long-term suppression of self-esteem can lead to a chronic change in perspective toward one's value. So, shouldn't we *always* be addressing this?

Like many aspects of childhood development, we know that self-esteem does not measure equally in all children. Research has found the following risk factors for increasing the likelihood of low self-esteem: i) females were almost twice as likely for impaired self-esteem as males, ii) those who were sensation seekers or rebellious were 50% more likely to have impaired self-esteem, and iii) obese teens were twice as likely to have impaired self-esteem than those who were considered normal weight.[15] Those examples are just the tip of the iceberg when it comes to determinants and influencers of self-esteem. Differences regarding self-esteem can also exist among various races; a study examining self-esteem among a large cohort of high school students found African-American students scored the highest, followed by Whites, then Hispanics, and Asian Americans.[16] Additionally, a meta-analysis from Dr. Bernadette Gray-Little and colleagues demonstrates that low-income Blacks have a higher perception of self-esteem than low-income Whites.[17]

Now, I happily admit that when I read through all the journals and reports I garnered on self-esteem, my goal was to find a pattern, both for this book and for my stunningly average parenting. More specifically, I wanted to know what elevates self-esteem to consistently healthy levels. Some useful answers come from the characteristics of students who have been shown to have higher self-esteem. There are many, but some prominent ones include: students with parents who are responsive, students with parents who set clear expectations, students with good grades, and students who participated in a team, club, or sport.[15] Boosting someone's self-esteem requires surpassing the superficial level of gifting compliments on an outfit choice, taste of music, or new glasses. Don't get me wrong, everybody loves a good compliment, and we should continue to hand these out like candy. However, if we want to change how someone fundamentally views themselves, it takes some deeper thought into your students' worlds—especially their online worlds, as this is where Gen Z lives for a part of their day.

We've already determined the omnipresence of technology and social media in Gen Zer's lives today, but it's important to talk about the *implications* of social media on our students' self-esteem. The Center for Generational Kinetics studied exactly this and found that Gen Z, more so than any other generation, believes social media greatly impacts how they view themselves, how others view them, their popularity, happiness, and well-being.[18] This makes a great deal of sense; as further explained by J Ryan Fuller, "participants [in a study] experienced lower state self-esteem and poorer self-evaluations after exposure to a person with a high activity social network."[19]

As a student scrolls through a news feed, they don't see the average depictions of life or the often shared experiences of dealing with the many stressors present in adolescents' lives. Rather, they see the best of life and the best of friends. Social gatherings, birthdays, silly nights out, prom dates... it's all there and almost inescapable. In less than 10 minutes, anyone can see hundreds of dreamy photos plastered all over Instagram (or Finstagram), Snapchat, TikTok, and three other platforms I probably don't even know exist. An article from the Child Mind Institute highlights the sentiment most school-age children feel when they scroll through their social media feeds, "See: pretty coffee, pretty girl, cute cat, beach trip. It's all like that. Everyone looks like they're having the best day ever, all the time."[20] As such, kids are almost forced to compare their worst moments to others' best when, really, only the great moments are documented.

Truthfully, we have known about this impact of social media for some time. So, what's new? Well, when many of those Gen Zers were at home on varying degrees of lockdown, what do you think they did during those boring days? Yep. More time online. A Forbes article from 2020 points out that at least 57% of surveyed users admitted that their daily screen time average increased during the pandemic by one hour or more, adding up to seven or more extra hours a week.[21] As such, the kiddos coming back to you in the fall may feel especially deflated if they couldn't even go to the grocery store, but several friends have beachside photos in Florida. This makes for a very lonely scroll during an already profoundly isolating time.

But don't trust my opinion; look at the data. Dr. Jean Twenge, a professor at San Diego State University, shares with us a "[recent] study found that adolescents who spent the most time on social media and the least time in face-to-face social interactions reported the most loneliness."[22] Now, given that loneliness is a risk factor for numerous mental health problems, we should be concerned that screen times dramatically increased during the isolating times of a world lockdown. However, what makes matters worse, is that this persistent interaction with social media, which in turn can enhance loneliness, actually mirrors the physiologic trends of a positive feedback cycle. And positive feedback loops will amplify a response until the cycle breaks. Take a moment to study a simplified example below.

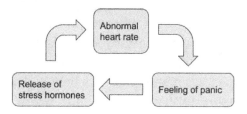

All this said, educators know that developing positive self-esteem at all grade levels is a wise investment. However, it often gets lost in the shuffle with meetings, grading, administrative expectations, and so forth. I am guilty of this too. Let's be better than that. Go back and take a look at the vulnerabilities of Gen Zer's and examine, once again, their ferocious consumption of screen time. Creating a classroom experience that elevates the self-esteem of all students quickly becomes a top priority again.

Educators have the opportunity to emphasize and model positive metrics of self-worth and demonstrate their value while their students' phones are off. When done correctly, this improves the self-esteem AND the self-efficacy of their students. This is, without question, a critical task if schools seek to model good mental health practice and how to approach challenges in life. I urge you to take this to heart. If you do, suddenly your math class becomes extremely important to ALL kids, and not just the ones that like math (if they exist).

It is your opportunity, not responsibility, to leverage your lesson plans to promote self-esteem and self-efficacy. But, keep in mind it's a great opportunity. And good news. There are a million ways to do this. You get to be creative as an educator. But in the end, I think any activity that convinces your Gen Z students that their concept of worth doesn't have to come from likes, shares, and numbers of followers is a fantastic start.

So, what do I do with all of this information?

I fully admit that I tossed a heavy amount of social science and introductory psychology at you in this chapter. However, it was critical to understand the importance of self-esteem and self-efficacy at a new level. But to help, and in true teacher fashion, allow me to share a study guide. Below are the take-away concepts that are critical for later chapters in this book:

- All of us, regardless of our race, economics, gender, or religion, navigate our lives amid protective factors and risk factors, which in turn, impact our feelings of self-worth and resilience.

- Protective factors are the attributes or influences that help an individual positively respond to stressors and/or diminish the negative emotions and risks in their life.

- Risk factors represent a modifier that is more likely to contribute to negative thoughts, negative outcomes, negative feelings of self-worth, and a non-healthy state.

- From a mathematical and behavioral perspective, the more protective factors someone has, the better off they are when it comes to handling challenges, stressors, and negative aspects of life. The more risk factors someone has in their life, the greater their propensity toward negative outcomes and an unhealthy state.

- There are many protective factors and risk factors. Our opportunity as educators is to maximize the positive protective factors and diminish negative factors that we can realistically influence in our schools. For most students across the nation, this will involve working on self-esteem and self-efficacy, as they can be either protective or risk factors, making them a high yield area to influence.

Now, if you are wondering how to put all these thoughts into practice, don't worry. Part 3 of this book will quickly become your friend. It shares specific evidence-based strategies you can use in your classroom, and I am happy to create this scaffold for you. Because let's be honest. After this long and hellacious pandemic school year, you are tired. *Really tired.*

In fact, judging by conversations I've had with a good number of fellow educators, some of you are even broken. Please know you're not the only one. Teaching during a pandemic has been a soul-sucking attempt to connect with students through laptops, intermittent Wi-Fi, muted zooms, ever-changing goals, frustrated parents, anxious students, suboptimal expectations, and to finish it off...an uncountable number of worries. Wow. That, my friends, is truly a dumpster fire.

But each day, you got out of bed, perhaps reluctantly, and you taught to the best of your abilities. As a dad, I thank you for that. But as a fellow educator, health advisor, and former physician, let me do more than thank you. Allow me to help you. You most definitely deserve it. Part 3 of this book hands you a road map for maximizing protective factors and mitigating risk factors, along with other realistic solutions you can utilize as an educator to do the one thing you always wanted to do since student teaching—better the lives of others.

Chapter 2 References

1. Persike, M., & Seiffge-Krenke, I. (2011). Competence in coping with stress in adolescents from three regions of the world. *Journal of Youth and Adolescence, 41*(7), 863–879. https://doi.org/10.1007/s10964-011-9719-6

2. American Psychological Association. (2020). *Stress in America™ 2020: A national mental health crisis.* https://www.apa.org/news/press/releases/stress/2020/sia-mental-health-crisis.pdf

3. American Psychological Association. (2019, October 24). *How to help children and teens manage their stress.* https://www.apa.org/topics/child-development/stress#:~:text=Prolonged%20stress%20can%20cause%20high,becoming%20more%20common%20in%20youth.

4. Substance Abuse and Mental Health Services Administration. (2019, July 18). *Risk and protective factors.* https://www.samhsa.gov/sites/default/files/20190718-samhsa-risk-protective-factors.pdf

5. Youth.gov. (n.d.). *Risk and protective factors.* https://youth.gov/youth-topics/youth-mental-health/risk-and-protective-factors-youth

6. Bandura, A. (1977). Self-efficacy: Toward a unifying theory of behavioral change. *Psychological Review, 84*(2), 191–215. https://doi.org/10.1037/0033-295X.84.2.191

7. Bandura, A. (1991). Social cognitive theory of self-regulation. *Organizational Behavior and Human Decision Processes, 50*(2), 248–287. https://doi.org/10.1016/0749-5978(91)90022-L

8. Schwarzer R., & Jerusalem M. (1995). Generalized self-efficacy scale. In J. Weinman, S. Wright, & M. Johnston (Eds.), Measures in health psychology: A user's portfolio. Causal and control beliefs (pp. 35- 37). Windsor, England: NFER-NELSON

9. Pajares F. & Schunk D.H. (2001). Self-beliefs and school success: Self-efficacy, self-concept, and school achievement. In R.Riding & S.Rayner (Eds.), Self-perception (pp.239-266). London: Ablex Publishing.

10. Usher, E. L., & Pajares, F. (2008). Sources of self-efficacy in school: Critical review of the literature and future directions. *Review of Educational Research*, *78*(4), 751–796. https://doi. org/10.3102/0034654308321456

11. Moksnes, U. K., Eilertsen, M.-E. B., Ringdal, R., Bjørnsen, H. N., & Rannestad, T. (2019). Life satisfaction in association with self-efficacy and stressor experience in adolescents – self-efficacy as a potential moderator. *Scandinavian Journal of Caring Sciences*, *33*(1), 222–230. https://doi.org/10.1111/scs.12624

12. Mayo Clinic. (2019, March 19). *Chronic stress puts your health at risk*. https://www.mayoclinic.org/healthy-lifestyle/stress-management/ in-depth/stress/art-20046037

13. American Psychological Association. (2021). Self-esteem. https:// dictionary.apa.org/self-esteem

14. Robins, R. W., Trzesniewski, K. H., Tracy, J. L., Gosling, S. D., & Potter, J. (2002). Global self-esteem across the life span. *Psychology and Aging*, *17*(3), 423–434. https://doi.org/10.1037/0882-7974.17.3.423

15. McClure, A. C., Tanski, S. E., Kingsbury, J., Gerrard, M., & Sargent, J. D. (2010). Characteristics associated with low self-esteem among U.S. adolescents. *Academic Pediatrics*, *10*(4), 238-44.e2. https://doi. org/10.1016/j.acap.2010.03.007

16. Bachman, J. G., O'Malley, P. M., Freedman-Doan, P., Trzesniewski, K. H., & Donnellan, M. B. (2011). Adolescent self-esteem: Differences by race/ethnicity, gender, and age. *Self and Identity*, *10*(4), 445–473. https://doi.org/10.1080/15298861003794538

17. Gray-Little B, Hafdahl AR. Factors influencing racial comparisons of self-esteem: A quantitative review. *Psychological Bulletin*. 2000;126(1):26-54. 10.1037/0033-2909.126.1.26

18. The Center for Generational Kinetics, & Dorsey, J. (2016). *iGen tech disruption: 2016 national study on technology and the generation and Millennials*. https://genhq.com/wp-content/ uploads/2016/01/iGen-Gen-Z-Tech-Disruption-Researc h-White-Paper-c-2016-Center-for-Generational-Kinetics.pdf

19. Fuller, J. (2015, March 27). *Social media use and self-esteem*. New York Behavioral Health. https://newyorkbehavioralhealth.com/ social-media-use-and-self-esteem/

20. Jacobson, R. (2021). *Social media and self-doubt.* Child Mind Institute. https://childmind.org/article/social-media-and-self-doubt/

21. Suciu, P. (2020, May 21). *Screen time and social media use among teens continues to rise.* Forbes. https://www.forbes.com/sites/petersuciu/2020/05/21/screen-time-and-social-media-use-among-teens-continues-to-rise/

22. Twenge, J. M., Spitzberg, B. H., & Campbell, W. K. (2019). Less in-person social interaction with peers among U.S. adolescents in the 21st century and links to loneliness. *Journal of Social and Personal Relationships*, *36*(6), 1892–1913. https://doi.org/10.1177/0265407519836170

3

An apple a day doesn't always keep the doctor away...Mental health trends

When I was a junior in high school, I spontaneously decided to join the speech team. My parents were surprised by this choice. I was already knee-deep in varsity track, band, and holding down a part-time job. Nevertheless, I saw some value in learning how to present in front of an audience, and I loved to debate issues. It seemed like a great career prep activity. But what's most important to know is that the out-of-town field trips with my girlfriend had nothing to do with it. Let's move forward.

I actually have a reason for mentioning my serendipitous involvement with the speech team. It affords me the opportunity to share some wisdom from my outstanding coach, Robert Seitz. Mr. Seitz bore some resemblance to Santa Claus, with rosy cheeks, a white beard, and a genuine sparkle in his eye. Additionally, Mr. Seitz would not hand you a present unless you truly earned it. All good things. But, there were also some differences. He was not afraid to tell you when something needed to improve or yell when you failed to listen. Perhaps all of this made him a corporate version of Santa? Anyway, in the middle of my extemporaneous practice sessions, I would often see him cross his arms, fake yawn, and belt out, "Will I hear some evidence before I fall asleep, as your personal opinion does not concern me." Harsh words, but also effective. Because amid his sarcasm, we all knew that his goal wasn't to scorn us but rather instill in our minds that data drives arguments.

With that in mind, I think Mr. Seitz would agree that you need and deserve some high-powered evidence. It's time to determine if the predictions around many Gen Zers are well-founded or just headlines with juicy claims. To do this, we will be dissecting (good science word) some outcome data from the Centers for Disease Control and Prevention, National Institutes of Health, and a few other institutions that employ people far more intelligent than me, but definitely not as stunningly average looking. My wife promises. Stop laughing. It's my self-esteem we are talking about.

Anyway, if you're not a science person by nature, let me illustrate the enormous difference between scientific predictions and measurable outcomes. Ready? Tornadoes. Hear me out. I can use physics, math, and my limited understanding of meteorology to explain how a tornado works by addressing centripetal motion, wind velocity, and force. These concepts are important and should paint a conceptual understanding of what tornadoes might do, serving as reasonable predictors.

However, if you really want to know what tornadoes are capable of, then examine their immense power with outcome measurements. What do I mean? How about determining the mass of the flipped car you see before you? Or calculate the force needed to peel boards off of a deck. Finally, take a moment and solve for the pressure difference needed across a large glass window to make it shatter. All of these are measured outcomes. They are the result of a tornado, and you can assess their severity and impact. Let's be honest, outcome data always feels more relevant when it demonstrates what a predicted problem can potentially do.

So far, we have considered evidence-based predictions of many Gen Zers vulnerabilities. Using the tornado analogy, these vulnerabilities predict what Gen Z can do, or more specifically, are at risk of doing. To refresh your memory, I listed some prominent vulnerabilities from Chapter 1 in the table below.

Influencing Agent	Vulnerability	Predicted (Potential) Outcome
Parent/ guardian	Excessive reliance upon guardian mitigating and/or eliminating difficult challenges or barriers	1. Diminished resilience 2. Inhibited ability to self-advocate 3. Ambiguity and anxiety when a guardian is unavailable or unsuccessful at mitigation

Technology	Excessive social media use	1. Increased screen time correlates with increased mental health challenges 2. Elevated risk of diminished self-worth partly due to constant "comparison" 3. Increased anxiety related to notifications and fear of missing out 4. Depending upon total screen time (ex: 7 hours per day), the opportunity cost for face-to-face relationships
Technology	Artificial intelligence	1. Although apps and AI can be convenient, they remove various steps in problem-solving, taking away this skill from the user
Technology	Rapid results from inquiries	1. Need to filter information at exceedingly fast rates and potential risk for focusing only upon data that applies to the user

As an educator, the vulnerabilities in the table sadden me. We all care about our second family—the kids in our classroom. But from the perspective of a former physician, these challenges do much more. They stir up concerns in the clinical part of my brain. The predicted outcomes of these vulnerabilities forecast a situation where a good chunk of children in Gen Z are potentially lonely, anxious, and fragile. All of those factors increase students' chances of anxiety, depression, and suicidal ideations. Yikes. Will we see that in our outcome data? How many students in Gen Z fall into this predicted trap? These lovable students are tech geniuses and kind-hearted—most of them seem fine in school. Are all of these mental health concerns really lurking below the surface? Those are the questions we need to answer.

The value of outcome data regarding mental health trends involving Gen Z

Full disclosure: before I jump headlong into activities that require both lobes of my brain, I need coffee. It's the way I work. And for more than 20 years, coffee has helped me pull off many feats of strength, ranging from all-nighters in college, treating critical patients in the ER, to most amazingly, putting together Playskool kitchen sets at 1:00 a.m. on Christmas morning. I mention this because if coffee is your superpower, too, then please grab a cup. I'm serious. Because in just a second, as promised, I'm about to drop a tidal wave of science upon you, and I think we will both need to be on our "A" game.

Alright, take a long sip, and let's start. The predictions regarding the vulnerabilities of Gen Z are well researched and seem reasonable thus far. However, they are not evidential proof that the students in your classroom, let alone a sizable portion of Gen Z, are struggling with specific issues. Only meaningful outcome data can confirm or deny that. So, it's important that we grab accurate information to measure all of the relevant predictions from expert clinicians, psychologists, and behavioral specialists. Is that hard to do? Well, yes and no.

We are fortunate that the Centers for Disease Control and Prevention, National Institute of Mental Health, and American Academy of Pediatrics have been tracking mental health trends in children for a long time. Additionally, there is an abundance of recent independent studies that further shed light on Gen Z's mental health. All in all, the bulk of work has been done for us. We just need to understand the numbers, their relevance, and if they align with the predicted outcomes.

How does that work? Well, that's my problem to solve. All you need to do is read and pay attention. So, please keep drinking your coffee. Now, the first thing to do is to ask the right set of questions. This, in turn, should guide us to meaningful data, putting us closer to the answers. With that in mind, here are some initial thoughts to consider:

- If a substantial number of Gen Zers are at risk for anxiety, then we should discover a spike in mental health visits and an escalating amount of generalized anxiety diagnoses over the past decade. Is there data to support this?

- Are current students lonely and at risk for self-deprecating thoughts? These are notable risk factors. If so, major depressive disorders may be on the rise proportional to the population.

- What about resilience? Do a large number of Gen Zers falter in the face of complex problems? Are things so problematic that they see their situation as unsolvable and consider a terrible and heartbreaking way out? If so, attempted suicide and suicidal ideations might be following an unfavorable trajectory.

Those are a few examples of the approximately 80 questions I considered while launching into this book. In the end, the investigation into those questions tends to show overlap and points of emphasis. And with that understanding, it appears that our best scientific data will be found in five main areas of focus over time: i) the number of mental health-related visits to qualified practitioners, ii) trend in anxiety disorders diagnosed, iii) evidence for the prevalence of major depression diagnoses, iv) rate of substance abuse within age groups, and v) trend in youth suicide and suicidal ideations. These areas of focus offer quantitative outcomes, which is ideal for comparing one year to another. And, there is another advantage with numeric data in this case. Mental health, especially in children, is a very sensitive topic. People can all easily be swayed by emotion and opinions. However, numbers aren't ruled by emotion and, to the best of my knowledge, allow science to be measured.

Focus #1 - Trends in mental health visits

According to the World Health Organization, mental health is "a state of well-being in which every individual realizes his or her own potential, can cope with the normal stresses of life, can work productively and fruitfully, and is able to make a contribution to his or her community."[1] However, we all know that the concept of mental health is obviously much more than this definition. There is emotion tied to these words. For some, mental health is a taboo term, as there has always been a stigma surrounding the topic. It's sad to think about and even worse to see in action. To be honest, this surprises me. Despite all the advancements we have made with accommodating exceptionalities at schools and offices, supportive attitudes for those with mental health challenges is lagging. This is particularly concerning as one-in-six adults in the U.S. live with a mental illness.[2]

To really internalize this issue around mental health, you need and deserve to know more. An influential study from *World Psychiatry* exposes this phenomenon all too clearly when they take a deep dive into the concept of stigma and how it applies to social and emotional issues. Mental health patients are persistently "challenged by the stereotypes and prejudice that result from misconceptions about mental illness."[3] Because of these stereotypes and prejudice, those with a mental illness are sometimes deprived of well-paying jobs, suitable housing, adequate health care, and a variety of social relationships—all things that help make up a quality life.[3] But here is where things get more damaging, the stigma around mental health is an obstruction to much-needed treatment. The American Psychiatric Association (APA) reports that over half of individuals with mental health concerns do not seek out help for various reasons, including being fearful of people treating them differently and/or losing their employment.[4] The APA asserts this barrier to care is due to prejudice and discrimination against people with mental illness. This creates a dangerous feedback cycle in the sense that many individuals with mental health problems feel the need to hide them, allowing the problems to grow over time and increase the pressure to mask them.

Eventually, these individuals reach a point where compensatory mechanisms fail, and hiding their challenges is no longer possible. On that fateful day, the individual might unleash an emotional roller coaster in front of their peers or share thought disturbances that are concerning. Everyone is surprised, and the individual experiencing the mental health crisis often lands in the emergency department, getting screened for acute psychiatric illness. As a former ER doc who cared for these patients, I can promise you that the most common words I heard from co-workers, friends, and even family to describe the events leading up to their ER visit were: "weird," "crazy," "embarrassing," and "scary." Not very empathetic terms, if you ask me. Are you surprised by all this? You shouldn't be. Here is a simple exercise for you and your colleagues to consider. Just follow the steps below and engage in self-reflection.

STEP 1: Have you ever refrained from hanging out with someone or collaborating on a project with them because their blood sugar is occasionally too high? What if a coworker intermittently wheezes when breathing around pollen? What if your teaching partner sometimes develops blemishes on their skin when they are embarrassed; is that a deal-breaker in terms of collaborating with them? STEP 2: Have you ever excluded someone from a gathering because they're "kind of a downer" or just not much fun? What about if a coworker flies off the handle now and then with random thoughts while talking fast and persistently interrupting you? Does that bother you more than the person in Step 1 who occasionally wheezes? Do you find them hard to be around? Just one more question, and please be honest. Would you ever trust a teenager with significant autism with anything more than a simple job? You know, the same kiddo that everyone in the IEP meeting said should dream big?

STEP 3: Does the term "bad" mental health refer to individuals that have the presence of a diagnosis? On the other side of the coin, does "good" mental health imply the absence of a mental health diagnosis? Can a person with clinical depression that is being treated have better overall mental health than an overworked and angry colleague with no history of mental health diagnosis?

STEP 4: Take a moment to reflect on all three steps. The only person that needs to know your answers is you. But I'm curious. Does implicit bias, which is not at the forefront of your consciousness, impact your thoughts on mental health? What coworkers or situations are you more tolerant of? Any ideas why? You might consider taking another sip of that coffee because this reflection is very important.

With all of the stigma around mental health treatment, you would think that Gen Zers might be distrustful of reaching out to qualified providers, which in turn means they avoid care? Asking for medical assistance is a process that requires considerable courage and trust. This can be especially tough to do when an individual is under emotional duress or experiencing thought disturbances. Now, pile on another layer. Do the projected vulnerabilities of many Gen Zers make them even more resistant to asking for help? Diminished self-advocacy and impaired problem-solving might add to their hesitancy, right? Apparently, not. At least outcome data would suggest otherwise. As you are about to learn, mental health visits are definitely rising as of late, and Gen Z is leading the pack. Let's take a look at a powerful piece of data published in *Pediatrics*, an academic journal for the American Academy of Pediatrics. Not too long ago, Dr. Luther Kalb and his team examined the results of the National Hospital Ambulatory Medical Care Survey.[5] This survey spanned from 2011 to 2015 and provides insight into what types of concerns and ailments result in emergency room visits increase, decrease, or remain static over four years. Additionally, we can fractionate this data to look at specific subgroups, such as Gen Z, and scale for the population.

Kalb and colleagues quickly noticed that between 2011-2015, there was a 28% overall increase in mental health visits to the emergency department per 1,000 youth across the country. More importantly, the most significant jump in a given subpopulation was the 54% upward spike in adolescent visits. Gen Zers demonstrated more need for mental health assessment and support than other age groups and past cohorts of adolescents. But that's only the tip of the iceberg. When we fractionate the adolescent data further, the numbers reveal that specific subgroups are accessing care more often. This likely correlates to an increased need for mental health care. Kalb's hard work demonstrated that the largest growth in adolescent visits to the emergency department for mental health concerns was found in Hispanic patients, who experienced a 91% jump, followed by African Americans, who moved upward 53%.[5] That's significant growth in just four years. Furthermore, these measurements confirm that a sizable portion of Gen Z is struggling, with specific cohorts feeling the impact more so than others.

Increased visits among Hispanic and African American populations leads to additional questions. There are obviously several variables in play and multiple possibilities to consider. For example, are the numbers rising in these subpopulations because health care providers are finally doing a better job of screening for mental health challenges and concerns in African American and Hispanic children? Or, are families within these subgroups currently more willing to share mental health concerns, where they may have been leery of doing so in the past? One more possibility, are African American and Hispanic children under increased pressure, dealing with additional vulnerabilities when compared to non-Hispanic whites and other groups? All of those questions are extremely important and need to be further investigated so that communities, including schools, can support our students and their specific needs. It's clear that we don't have all the answers yet. It will take more focused research. However, this inquiry is undoubtedly needed, and I recommend that you continue to follow the topic.

As you might suspect, Kalb and his team are not the only researchers worried about this topic. Another study in *Pediatrics* by Dr. Charmaine Lo and colleagues tapped into the National Pediatric Readiness Project to investigate if the percentage of mental health cases were increasing in terms of total emergency department visits.[6] The guiding hypothesis was straightforward: if youth visits for mental health needs are increasing, then the amount of time and resources committed to mental health treatment for pediatric patients should represent a larger percentage of total ER visits.

So, what did Lo's study find? Overall, the number of pediatric visits to the emergency department was stable over 10 years (2007-2016), at least when it came to the total volume of patients. However, the fraction of cases associated with child mental health took a huge jump upward. Visits to the ER for deliberate self-harm and all mental health disorders increased by 329% and 60%, respectively.[6] Lo's publication suggests that this is a widespread phenomenon, with increased visits occurring in emergency departments of many different patient sizes and settings. Even low-pediatric-volume facilities (up 53%) and nonmetropolitan areas (up 41%) rose significantly. Thus, the rise in mental health services for school-aged children is not limited to academic referral centers or large cities. Rather, this is a trend that we see in medical centers everywhere, regardless of demographics. We should expect the same for schools.

Before we leave the topic of mental health visits entirely, it's important to address a question that I suspect many of you (highly-caffeinated) readers have. Why did these large-scale studies only look at emergency departments when it came to assessing pediatric mental health? As a former emergency medicine physician, I can promise you with a large degree of confidence that emergency departments serve as the national safety net for sudden exacerbations in mental health. Remember, this is a medical diagnosis veiled in stigma. Very few patients are comfortable admitting that they have a thought or mood disorder. As such, they are often not identified until they hit a breaking point. As mentioned earlier, that breaking point often involves the ER.

But to be thorough, let's go beyond the perspective of clinicians and consider another data source: the Centers for Disease Control and Prevention (CDC). That's right, America's largest and most respected public health agency is not just for dealing with viral pandemics. The CDC tracks all sorts of public health concerns, and the mental health of America's youth is an important one. Below are some pieces of worrisome data:

- National Hospital Ambulatory Medical Care Survey data from 2018 demonstrate that the number of visits to emergency departments with mental health, behavioral, and neurodevelopmental challenges as the primary diagnosis was approximately 4.9 million cases. This agrees with Kalb and Lo's studies, further demonstrating that mental health visits are sharply on the rise.[7,8] And that's one year, mind you.

- The CDC reports on their webpage for adolescent mental health that more than 1 in 3 high school students had experienced persistent feelings of sadness or hopelessness in 2019, a 40% increase since 2009.[9] Some groups are more affected than others. These feelings were especially common among lesbian, gay, or bisexual students as well as female students.[9]

Keep in mind that this is all pre-pandemic information, which means that well before COVID-19 stole all the news headlines, our hard-working friends down in Atlanta began to worry that a mental health epidemic was on the rise. This includes a wide bandwidth of ages, races, and socioeconomic situations. And as you are beginning to see, school-aged children are not spared from this phenomenon.

Studies such as those by Lo and Kalb, and many other notable articles in academic journals, demonstrate that Gen Zers need an increase in mental health support. This will, undoubtedly, be explored further, and I would not be shocked if the volume of pediatric visits continues to rise for some time. I encourage you to follow these developments. And for those that are curious about solutions, allow me to highlight an important piece of information: both the CDC and American Academy of Pediatrics publicize that connections with trusted adults is fundamental to good mental health in children.[10,11] Given that most students are at school 40 hours a week, I am pretty confident that leading health experts will argue that educators need to be part of the plan to address youth mental health concerns.

Focus #2 - Assessment of anxiety in youth

Anxiety. I am going to pick on myself here. Is it weird that I worry about anxiety in kids? Isn't that the most counterproductive thing you've heard of? Don't answer. The simple fact is that I'm not alone. As an educator, I hear my colleagues discuss the following daily: i) test accommodations for anxiety, ii) quiet rooms for anxiety, iii) alternate assignments for anxiety, and iv) attending formal IEPs for anxiety. It seems to be an everyday occurrence. To no surprise, a study examining data from the 2016 National Survey of Children's Health found that 7.1% of children aged 3-17 years (which is approximately 4.4 million) are currently diagnosed with an anxiety disorder of some form.[12] But, children, like adults, have always had to deal with the challenges of anxiety. This is nothing new. So, the question that really needs answered is, how is the rate of anxiety changing over time? Let's go back to our public health authorities yet again. Both the National Institutes of Health and CDC maintain a large amount of longitudinal data regarding the prevalence of anxiety through the years.

One helpful piece of information, which captured the attention of the CDC, comes from a study originally published in the *Journal of Developmental and Behavioral Pediatrics* from 2018.[13,14] It does a nice job showing the escalating presence of anxiety over much of the 2000s.

- Patients diagnosed with anxiety or depression, among children aged 6–17 years, increased from 5.4% in 2003 to 8% in 2007 and again to 8.4% in 2011–2012.[13] This demonstrates a consistent rise over approximately nine years.

- The data above was investigated further, isolating anxiety from depression. The results demonstrate that patients diagnosed with anxiety disorders alone increased from 5.5% in 2007 to 6.4% between 2011–2012.[13]

Those may seem like relatively low percentages to you but multiplied across a large country of 330 million, that's an enormous number of children in our schools. However, there is more. The CDC website also shares a study by Dr. Reem Ghandour and colleagues, which found that anxiety is often intertwined with other behavioral or mental health diagnoses. Data from this study published in 2019 demonstrates the following.[12,14]

- For children aged 3-17 years with anxiety, about 1 in 3 have concurrent depression (32.3%).[12]

- For children aged 3-17 years with behavior problems, more than 1 in 3 also have anxiety (36.6%), and about 1 in 5 also have depression (20.3%).[12]

- This relationship is also reciprocal. About 3 out of 4 children aged 3-17 years with depression demonstrate anxiety (73.8%). Additionally, almost 1 in 2 have behavior problems.[12]

I would humbly suggest that there are two takeaways from these data points. First, anxiety appears to be on the rise. We see this in a diverse spread of pediatric age groups. Educators at all grade levels need to be aware of this escalating problem, as anxiety will appear in all classrooms on a more frequent basis. Secondly, anxiety is often intertwined with other behavioral or mental health diagnoses. This is particularly relevant as anxiety may often go unnoticed and unaddressed.

What do I mean? Imagine a second-grade kiddo diagnosed with ADHD who is medicated. That child will likely do well in school and has a lot to look forward to each day.

However, there will be days when that child may struggle to focus, interrupt others more often, and have a hard time sitting still. All of those symptoms fit with ADHD, right? Agreed, but those are symptoms. They do not represent the driving force that leads to those hyperactivities. The question that's relevant for a teacher is: what's accelerating the ADHD symptoms that day? It could be treatment-related—perhaps they forgot to take a pill that morning or missed a few therapy sessions. This often happens. However, it could also be anxiety. Maybe that child had a seat change and is nervous around new students. Or, it could be more serious in nature. Such as wondering why Mom and Dad fight so much lately and why Mom doesn't go to work anymore? The point is that anxiety can often be a driving force of other behaviors and remain unrecognized and undiagnosed.

Now, just like we did with our exploration of mental health visits, let's cross-check our clinical data with some outside perspective. This time, let's dive into the world of health insurance. It seems like a weird viewpoint to assess anxiety, right? Well, as it turns out, not really. Insurance agencies have the opportunity to see all the billable diagnoses in patients and can track trends over time. They also use strict criteria, usually evidence-based, to validate a patient's diagnosis to ensure appropriate reimbursement. Thus, they have good insight into the prevalence of the disease across populations.

To demonstrate this, consider an insightful review from FAIR Health. This grandiose effort investigated 28 billion private health care claims between 2007-2017.[15] You may have come across this information before, as it was cited in an article by U.S. News and World Report.[16] At any rate, the study found the following regarding anxiety and youth:

- Generalized Anxiety Disorder (GAD) saw the greatest increase in insurance claim lines over this 10-year period. These claim lines increased by **217%**, accounting for

0.168% of all medical claim lines in 2007 to 0.523% in 2017.[15]

- Claim lines for GAD rose by greater percentages for college and high school individuals than any adult group.[15]

  o Claim lines for college-age individuals increased in share by **441%**, growing from 0.62% to 3.16% of all medical claim lines for young adults.

  o For high school-age individuals, GAD claim lines increased **389%**, rising from 0.4% to 1.77% of all medical claim lines for that age group.

I am not sure how to wrap my head around those percentages other than they are staggering. The jump in insurance claims for high school and college students, which Gen Z currently represents, provides further numeric evidence for a public health concern when it comes to anxiety in schools.

To no surprise, educators should anticipate this issue to spill over into our classrooms regularly. It's unfortunate, but it should not be unexpected. Anxiety has been insidiously creeping into the lives of school-aged children since the early 2000s. However, the math demonstrates a recent spike in anxiety-related issues. And in case you were unaware, our students can feel it. Pew Research Center reports that 70% of teens surveyed in 2019 stated anxiety was a major problem in their school community.[17] The adolescents surveyed prioritized anxiety as a bigger problem than alcohol misuse, drug addiction, and poverty. That's some telling data. Keep in mind that it's rare to get 70% of adolescents to agree upon anything. Anxiety appears to be leaving quite a mark on Gen Z.

Focus #3 - Depression trends in the pediatric population

Where does sadness end, and depression begin? It's tough to say, but psychiatrists have done an admirable job defining it for us in the Diagnostic and Statistical Manual of Mental Disorders (DSM-5). This hefty book serves as a clinical guide filled with detailed diagnostic criteria for just about every mental health challenge you could imagine, including all forms of depression. As educators, we obviously don't need to understand depressive disorders to the depth of an active clinician, so allow me to share the paraphrased version. To be diagnosed with depression, an individual must be experiencing five or more depressive symptoms in the DSM-5 for the span of at least two weeks, and one of the symptoms must be decreased mood and/or loss of interest and pleasure. Pretty complex criteria. However, it highlights the persistence and wide-reaching involvement of a major depressive disorder. True clinical depression is much more than a few bad days in a row. And, contrary to what some may think, depression is not a mental health challenge that you can get over in a weekend or by simply fixing your attitude.

As a former physician, I wince a little when I watch staff members or students tell someone with depression, "We just need to have a fun night out!" or ask, "Are you feeling better yet?" All of these comments are endearing with the right intentions, but they are naive in nature. Why? Depression involves a complex biochemical puzzle in the brain that is influenced by many variables. Like a real puzzle, when a piece is missing or transiently misshapen, the entire picture changes. As any good puzzle master will tell you, you can't force a piece into the wrong spot and pretend things are fine. Rather, you need to go back and examine how the pieces interact in the first place and realign the image. In real patients, that realignment could involve medications, such as Prozac or Paxil, or it might rely upon various forms of therapy. And, for many patients, it's a combination of both. But regardless of the exact treatment strategy, please understand that treating depression is a lengthy process that requires a lot of resilience on everyone's part.

Now, if we know so much about depression, can we predict who might develop it? Well, sort of. Psychologists and psychiatrists are aware of numerous risk factors for major depressive disorders, but these issues don't guarantee the development of the actual mood disorder. Nevertheless, below are some of the risk factors that the American Psychiatric Association and the National Institute of Mental Health look for [18,19]:

- Genetic—both family history of depression and presence of another pre-existing mental health disorder may elevate the risk of depression

- Biochemistry—transient imbalance of neurotransmitters and other chemicals in the brain due to other medical processes (ex: postpartum depression)

- Major life changes—situations that require significant lifestyle adjustments, such as the loss of a loved one (beyond normal grieving), job changes, and geographical moves

- Environmental factors—persistent exposure to powerful outside influences such as violence, neglect, abuse, or poverty

- Personality and outlook—those with impaired self-esteem, poor self-efficacy, or chronic stress have a greater propensity for major depressive episodes

This list is by no means exhaustive, but it does give us insight into many of the common risk factors related to depression. And what offsets those risk factors? Recall from Chapter 2 that our protective factors help build self-efficacy, self-esteem, and resilience, which help minimize or avoid tumultuous bouts of clinical depression.

So, where does Gen Z stand in the crosshairs of major depressive disorders? Given their predicted propensity toward anxiety, potentially impaired resilience, tendency to compare themselves to the best version of others (social media), and wavering metrics of self-esteem...we should be a little worried. But put the brakes on. Let's see what the data reports, starting with the Substance Abuse and Mental Health Services Administration (SAMHSA). SAMHSA has some powerful information from the 2017 National Survey on Drug Use and Health (NSDUH). Below is a sufficient window into their research[20]:

- An estimated 17.3 million adults in the United States had at least one major depressive episode. This number represented 7.1% of all U.S. adults.

- The prevalence of major depressive episodes was higher among adult females (8.7%) compared to males (roughly 5.3%).

- The prevalence of adults with a major depressive episode was highest among individuals aged 18-25 (approximately 13.1%). This encompasses a notable portion of Gen Z.

- The prevalence of major depressive episodes was highest among adults reporting two or more races (11.3%). This held true across several age groups, including portions of Gen Z.

The last two bullet points of that data dump captured my attention. First, SAMHSA clearly identifies that the most vulnerable age group for depression was the youngest one they studied. As pointed out, this happens to include some of the current members of Gen Z, but admittedly not all of the cohort. Second, the final bullet point mentions that individuals with a background of two or more races were impacted more profoundly. Given that Gen Z is the most diverse generation we've seen to date, this is a pivotal piece of data. It begs the question: does Gen Z contain larger subgroups of vulnerable kids, and that's why we see a larger impact when it comes to clinical depression?

This line of thought shouldn't be limited to racial diversity. It may also extend into other subpopulations of students. Take a look at the LGBTQIA+ cohort. While it's wonderful that students in Gen Z feel more comfortable (on average) disclosing their sexual orientation and gender identity than prior generations, it doesn't change the fact that the LGBTQIA+ community is under a high amount of pressure. The Youth Risk Behavior Survey trends from 2009-2019 illustrate that lesbian, gay, or bisexual youth are more than twice as likely to report experiencing feelings of sadness or hopelessness than their heterosexual peers.[9] Additionally, transgender and nonbinary youth are at an even higher risk for poor mental health outcomes, like depression or attempted suicide, than their cisgender and LGBQ peers.[21] As educators, we have to be aware of this outcome data to protect and support all children in our classrooms.

So far, most of the data that's been presented applies to the upper ages of Gen Z. What about the younger cohort that we see in schools? It would be nice to garner more information about them. As it turns out, in 2017, SAMHSA found that approximately 3.2 million adolescents aged 12-17 in the United States had at least one major depressive episode.[20] This is about 13.3% of the United States population aged 12-17 in case you are wondering. And, once again, mixed races show a higher propensity of risk, as seen below in Figure 1.[20]

Figure 1[22]

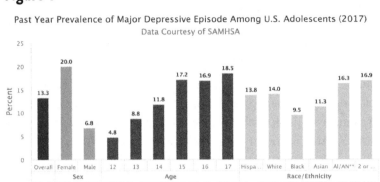

Past Year Prevalence of Major Depressive Episode Among U.S. Adolescents (2017)
Data Courtesy of SAMHSA

I wish I could say that depressive disorders have improved since 2017, but it doesn't appear that's the case. The 2019 National Survey on Drug Use and Health (NSDUH) shares additional cohort data that reaffirms the escalating trend. The number of adolescents aged 12-17 treated for a major depressive episode within the past year increased from 37.8% in 2005, which is around 800,000 patients, to 43.3% in 2019, which encompasses 1.6 million patients.[22] As such, the percentage of major depressive episodes for youth in 2019 was higher than the percentages in most years from 2005 to 2015, but admittedly, similar to the percentages from 2018. This increase in treatment should be expected. If more children are experiencing signs and symptoms of depression, then all things being equal, we should be treating more pediatric patients. Therefore, the NSDUH from 2019 is yet another way to cross-check diagnostic data and provide another credible resource when it comes to many Gen Zers struggling with depression. No one should turn a blind eye to this. Especially educators. Now is the time to recognize the risk and offer help.

Focus #4 - Substance misuse and abuse

After working in an emergency department located in downtown Chicago and experiencing ER care within a vibrant college town, I think it's fair to say that I'm familiar with substance abuse. It can be a horrendous journey for patients and one that typically starts in the most insidious of ways. Don't believe that substance abuse is sneaky? Let me ask you this. Would anyone take a single shot of tequila or snort a line of cocaine if they could see into the future, visualizing all the details associated with their first trip to the ER for an overdose? I promise you, the answer is no. And I think every nurse and physician I worked with would back me up.

That said, it's not lost on me that substance abuse does exist, and there must be a reason. There has to be a driving force for people to turn to a chemical for help instead of chatting with a friend, exercising outdoors, or watching *Love Actually* in your favorite joggers while eating a metric ton of nachos and ice cream (I am not saying that's been my solution twice in my life, but I'm also not denying it). All that aside, it's important to have insight regarding how people get lured down a destructive path, often against their wishes. If I can do that for you, then we are in a better position to speculate if Gen Zers are at risk.

Most roads to substance abuse start quite innocently. People turn to drugs and alcohol to fulfill a specific need. Typically, those with addictions will tell you that they only meant to use a particular substance as a temporary solution. You know, something to just take the edge off for a bit. The problem, of course, is that addiction is not temporary—it's a long-term burden. The National Institute on Drug Abuse does a great job of addressing the most common precipitating events that lead to substance abuse and are summarized below.[23]

- Behavioral and social pressures

  o Experience of feeling pleasure

  o Boost outcome performance (ex: mental sharpness or confidence)

  o Self-medication (ex: drink alcohol when stressed)

- Environmental and external influences

  o Lack of support systems (ex: feel unable to discuss an issue with family or friends)

  o Associated behavior (ex: Mom always has a drink when anxious, so maybe I should?)

  o Peer pressure (ex: desire to "fit in" while friends normalize drug use behavior)

- Escape strategy

  o A feeling produced by the drug or alcohol as a dissociative opportunity from problems

  o Self-medication for stress

Now, I think it's fair to say that drug and alcohol dependency is not a new phenomenon. I mean, I was born in the 1970s, and every time I asked my uncle what the age of disco was like, he would laugh and respond, "Not sure. It was hazy inside and out." It took me until high school to realize he probably wasn't joking. However, forget the 1970s and what my uncle may have done on the weekends. This book is only interested in how drug use over time might impact Gen Z.

So, let's start with the most commonly abused drug in school-aged children—alcohol. The CDC utilizes the Youth Risk Behavior Survey (YRBS) to track alcohol trends over time by age and other demographics. When it comes to current school-aged children, the data is positive. As of 2021, the most recent YRBS data demonstrates an overall decrease in underage alcohol consumption from 1991-2019. Below are a few important highlights[24]:

- The number of children that drank alcohol before age 13 years (other than a few sips) dropped from 32.7% in 1991 to 15% in 2019.

- High school students that had at least one alcoholic drink in the last 30 days also fell—50.8% in 1991 down to 29.2% in 2019. This was a steady decline over the entire duration of time.

Are we doing a better job convincing school-aged children (and Gen Z at large) to avoid drugs and alcohol? Or, have they switched from beer cans to bongs? I'm serious. Further data from YRBS demonstrates that marijuana use among high school students was variable between 1991-2019, demonstrating only a slight increase from 31.3% in 1991 to 36.8% in 2019, with a peak in 1999 (47.2% of teens).[25] This is also reassuring. It does not appear the reason alcohol use is down is because marijuana has replaced it. But, the former ER doc in me wondered, what about something stronger? Nope. Cocaine and hallucinogens also didn't budge much over those 10 years either—all good things to hear. I was just on my way to give a metaphorical high five to Gen Zers, and then I remembered vaping. You know, the extremely well-marketed stunt that proclaimed, "Love your lungs." Ugh.

E-cigarettes made an assault on social media that may represent one of the most successful influencers of teenage minds since the dawn of time. Sales of JUUL, the most commonly sold e-cigarette in the United States, boasted a sales increase of approximately 600% during 2016–2017. If you need the raw values, that's jumping from 2.2 million unit sales to 16.2 million unit sales in one year.[26] But there is more. The growth continued. The CDC reports that the number of adolescents using vaping devices rose another 78% during 2017–2018.[27] And, by 2019, an average of 27.5% of current high school students reported using e-cigarettes consistently.[28] Crap.

And, so there it was. E-cigarettes. In all their colors, sizes, and flavors, e-cigarettes prevailed as the champion. The evidence makes it clear that nicotine vapes had snuck in to become Gen Z's addiction of choice. But in fairness to school-aged children, this spike in e-cigarette usage was likely independent of the potential vulnerabilities of Gen Z. Rather, it was likely due to the stupendous marketing blitzkrieg, compounded with the help of social media. This made e-cigarettes more of a phenom for many kids, as opposed to an escape, a dissociative moment, or a coping mechanism. This makes the e-cigarette boom a little different from other storylines of substance abuse.

In the end, it's crucial to be fair and accurate. The data suggests that the consumption and abuse of alcohol, cocaine, marijuana, and hallucinogens have decreased in current school-aged children. As such, I would humbly argue that the pre-pandemic Gen Z has been a lot more mindful regarding substance abuse when compared to the glue-sniffing and mushroom eating bus riders I sat with during my freshman year of high school. Good job, Gen Zers. That's worth a "cheers" and another sip of your coffee.

Focus #5 - Suicidal ideations and self-harm

Above all else, do no harm. These well-known words remain one of the most influential guidelines in health care. Specifically, they remind clinicians that our intentions, ethics, and actions should never purposefully inflict harm to someone else. Patients are inherently vulnerable and need to be cared for in a kind and compassionate manner. Additionally, all patients need to be able to trust their health care provider, not in terms of being perfect with medical knowledge or skill, but rather in terms of honesty and genuine intentions. In many ways, much of the ethical and operational components of modern health care is built upon these words. Well, at least the part of health care that doesn't have to do with payment. It's a huge stressor when the ideology of "do no harm" is violated. Actions that fail to put the patient's needs, thoughts, and concerns first are potentially harmful and certainly abrasive for any caring health care worker to witness. In fact, I would argue that being part of an experience where a patient gets hurt is one of the worst outcomes a health care provider could endure during their career. At least most of us in health care imagined that to be the case...until you see a young, vibrant, and well-loved child purposely take their own life because they thought suicide was the *solution*. That's a soul-crushing moment. One that you certainly don't need to go to medical school to understand.

The unfortunate reality is that thoughts of suicide and attempts at self-harm appear to be on the rise. There is just no sugarcoating that. Dr. Holly Hedegaard and colleagues took time to examine the National Vital Statistics System (NVSS) from 1999 through 2018 and discovered the age-adjusted suicide rate in the United States increased 35%, from 10.5 to 14.2 per 100,000 population.[29] There is more bad news. This trend seems to be accelerating. The NVSS data shows the greatest increase in suicide rates over those 15 years occurred between 2013 up to present day.[30] Additionally, Gen Zers, particularly females, were one of the most impacted groups, putting school-aged children at high risk. And, it's important to note that this isn't just a high school problem, far from it. According to the CDC, in a report published in 2019, the greatest percent increase in suicide rates for a specific cohort was females aged 10-14.[31] That involves children in elementary and middle schools. As a dad with two young daughters, this scares the crap out of me.

Figure 2[29]

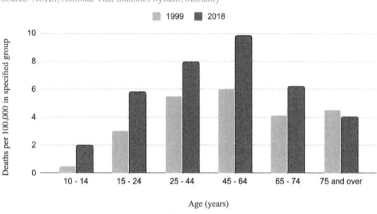

Suicide Rates for Females by Age Group, United States (1999-2018)
Source: NCHS, National Vital Statistics System, Mortality

Outside of the CDC, there are plenty of other institutions that have launched inquiries into suicide. It's just too important of a topic to ignore. Academic organizations across the United States are studying suicide intently, hoping to find the reason why these numbers are on the rise. And, the topic of suicide seems to persistently make the headlines. One example from PBS pulled together several pieces of research that were published by *The Journal of the American Medical Association* (JAMA).[32,33]

- In 2017, there were 47% more suicides among people aged 15-19 than in the year 2000. With more than 6,200 suicides among people aged 15-24, suicide ranked as the second-leading cause of death for people in that age group in 2017, trailing behind deaths from unintentional motor vehicle accidents, which claimed 6,697 lives.

- Among adolescents aged 15-19 years, the suicide rate in 2000 was 8 per 100,000. This frequency remained fairly stable for several years but saw a 3.1% increase from 2007-2014. An even larger jump to 10% was reported from 2014-2017.

- And what about recent graduates? Does leaving high school and acquiring maturity help things? Tough to say. For young adults aged 20-24 years old, the suicide rate was 17 per 100,000 in 2017, an increase from 12.5 per 100,000 in 2000.

Wow. It seems like any credible report demonstrates bleak results when it comes to suicide trends since 2000. I honestly don't know how to follow that data. Those numbers represent actual lives lost. Furthermore, they include students that our schools and communities cared about. That's tough to internalize. But in an effort to keep moving forward, there is some good news to consider. Each year, we learn more about youth suicide, allowing us to design more focused prevention strategies and screenings. This is something educators have the capacity to support, which is why this book will discuss several nonclinical strategies in Part 3 that educators have in their wheelhouse to implement. Because anyway you present the data, kids need us. That's the most important fact of all.

What should I take away from all of this?

Unless you're a biostatistician who enjoys cross-checking national data with statistical t-tests and p-values, I would hope that you are satisfied with the information presented. It's not just numbers. It reflects the stories of our students' lives. As such, it's my sincere hope that you see the "buy-in" for making changes. The numbers presented represent outcomes, which over time, show trends. As of now, these are concerning trends. You saw the data. Anxiety is on the rise, depression is far more prevalent, and the suicide risk for young girls is recently the highest it has ever been. And sadly, this information seems to correlate quite well with the predicted vulnerabilities of many students within Gen Z.

As we discussed before, numbers don't lie. But, they also don't create changes. Only relevant external influences can impact the variables associated with the cause. That's the cold but accurate, scientific description. However, there is another way to phrase that idea, which I prefer. Caring people that understand the cause of a problem usually want to help. And if caring adults lend a hand in an evidence-based way, their efforts can mitigate the cause(s) of a problem, which takes us one step closer to a solution. That will require intelligent, motivated, and empathetic people who spend considerable time with Gen Zers. And as I look at the day of a school-aged child, I'm pretty sure that would be parents and educators.

The challenges for at-risk students in Gen Z have been insidiously and quietly escalating for years, all hidden behind the veil of cell phones, headphones, and saying, "I'm fine." Scan your classroom. If it's anything like mine, you've got children in front of you right now that are navigating some of these obstacles. Which ones do you know about? More concerning, which ones do you **not** know about? And what is the next step to help all of them? That burden is on me to demonstrate. Just keep reading...and by all means, feel free to finish your coffee. Chapter 4 will be ready when you are.

Chapter 3 References

1. World Health Organization. (2018, March 30). *Mental health: Strengthen our response.* https://www.who.int/news-room/fact-sheets/detail/mental-health-strengthening-our-response

2. National Institute of Mental Health. (2021, January). *Mental health information: Mental illness.* https://www.nimh.nih.gov/health/statistics/mental-illness.shtml

3. Corrigan, P., & Watson, A. (2002). Understanding the impact of stigma on people with mental illness. *World Psychiatry, 1*(1), 16–20. https://www.ncbi.nlm.nih.gov/pmc/articles/PMC1489832/

4. American Psychiatric Association. (2020, August). *Stigma, prejudice, and discrimination against people with mental illness.* https://www.psychiatry.org/patients-families/stigma-and-discrimination

5. Kalb, L. G., Stapp, E. K., Ballard, E. D., Holingue, C., Keefer, A., & Riley, A. (2019). Trends in psychiatric emergency department visits among youth and young adults in the US. *Pediatrics, 143*(4). https://doi.org/10.1542/peds.2018-2192

6. Lo, C. B., Bridge, J. A., Shi, J., Ludwig, L., & Stanley, R. M. (2020). Children's mental health emergency department visits: 2007–2016. *Pediatrics, 145*(6). https://doi.org/10.1542/peds.2019-1536

7. Centers for Disease Control and Prevention. (2021, January 25). *National Center for Health Statistics: Mental health.* https://www.cdc.gov/nchs/fastats/mental-health.htm

8. Centers for Disease Control and Prevention. (2020, November 9). *Ambulatory health care data: Datasets and documentation.* https://www.cdc.gov/nchs/ahcd/datasets_documentation_related.htm

9. Centers for Disease Control and Prevention, Division of Adolescent and School Health, & National Center for HIV/AIDS, Viral Hepatitis, STD, and TB Prevention. (2020). *Youth risk behavior survey: Data summary & trends report 2009-2019.* https://www.cdc.gov/healthyyouth/data/yrbs/pdf/YRBSDataSummaryTrendsReport2019-508.pdf

10. Centers for Disease Control and Prevention. (2020, October 22). *Adolescent and school health: Connectedness can protect students from poor mental health outcomes.* https://www.cdc.gov/healthyyouth/mental-health/index.htm

11. American Academy of Pediatrics. (2019, October 21). *American Academy of Pediatrics provides guidance on helping children with mental health challenges.* HealthyChildren. org. https://www.healthychildren.org/English/news/Pages/Mental-Health-Competencies-for-Pediatric-Practice.aspx

12. Ghandour, R. M., Sherman, L. J., Vladutiu, C. J., Ali, M. M., Lynch, S. E., Bitsko, R. H., & Blumberg, S. J. (2019). Prevalence and treatment of depression, anxiety, and conduct problems in US children. *The Journal of Pediatrics, 206*, 256-267.e3. https://doi.org/10.1016/j.jpeds.2018.09.021

13. Bitsko, R. H., Holbrook, J. R., Ghandour, R. M., Blumberg, S. J., Visser, S. N., Perou, R., & Walkup, J. T. (2018). Epidemiology and impact of health care provider–Diagnosed anxiety and depression among US children: *Journal of Developmental & Behavioral Pediatrics, 39*(5), 395–403. https://doi.org/10.1097/DBP.0000000000000571

14. Centers for Disease Control and Prevention. (2020, June 15). *Children's mental health: Data and statistics on children's mental health.* https://www.cdc.gov/childrensmentalhealth/data.html

15. FAIR Health. (2019). *Spotlight on national behavioral health trends: A 10-year window into key mental health and substance abuse indicators* [White paper]. https://s3.amazonaws.com/media2.fairhealth.org/whitepaper/asset/Spotlight%20on%20National%20Behavioral%20Health%20Trends%20-%20A%20FAIR%20Health%20White%20Paper%20-%20May%202019.pdf

16. Gelburd, R. (2019, May 20). *Young people are increasingly represented in growing mental health insurance claims.* US News & World Report. https://www.usnews.com/news/healthiest-communities/articles/2019-05-20/young-people-increasingly-represented-in-growing-mental-health-insurance-claims

17. Pew Research Center. (2019, February). *Most U.S. teens see anxiety and depression as a major problem among their peers.* https://www.pewresearch.org/social-trends/2019/02/20/most-u-s-teens-see-anxiety-and-depression-as-a-major-problem-among-their-peers/

18. American Psychiatric Association. (2020, October). *What is depression?* https://www.psychiatry.org/patients-families/depression/what-is-depression

19. National Institute of Mental Health. (2018, February). *Mental health information: Depression.* https://www.nimh.nih.gov/health/topics/depression/index.shtml

20. Substance Abuse and Mental Health Services Administration. (2018). *Key substance use and mental health indicators in the United States: Results from the 2017 National Survey on Drug Use and Health* (HHS Publication No. SMA 18-5068, NSDUH Series H-53). Rockville, MD: Center for Behavioral Health Statistics and Quality, Substance Abuse and Mental Health Services Administration https://www.samhsa.gov/data/report/2017-nsduh-annual-national-report

21. Price-Feeney, M., Green, A. E., & Dorison, S. (2020). Understanding the mental health of transgender and nonbinary youth. *Journal of Adolescent Health, 66*(6), 684–690. https://doi.org/10.1016/j.jadohealth.2019.11.314

22. Substance Abuse and Mental Health Services Administration. (2020). *Key substance use and mental health indicators in the United States: Results from the 2019 National Survey on Drug Use and Health* (HHS Publication No. PEP20-07-01-001, NSDUH Series H-55). Rockville, MD: Center for Behavioral Health Statistics and Quality, Substance Abuse and Mental Health Services Administration. https://www.samhsa.gov/data/report/2019-nsduh-annual-national-report

23. National Institute on Drug Abuse. (2020, May 26). *The science of drug use: Discussion points.* https://www.drugabuse.gov/drug-topics/criminal-justice/science-drug-use-discussion-points

24. Centers for Disease Control and Prevention, Division of Adolescent and School Health, & National Center for HIV/AIDS, Viral Hepatitis, STD, and TB Prevention. (2020, August 20). *Trends in the prevalence of alcohol use national YRBS: 1991-2019.* https://www.cdc.gov/healthyyouth/data/yrbs/factsheets/2019_alcohol_trend_yrbs.htm

25. Centers for Disease Control and Prevention, Division of Adolescent and School Health, & National Center for HIV/AIDS, Viral Hepatitis, STD, and TB Prevention. (2020, August 20). *Trends in the Prevalence of Marijuana, Cocaine, and Other Illegal Drug Use*

National YRBS: 1991-2019. https://www.cdc.gov/healthyyouth/data/yrbs/factsheets/2019_us_drug_trend_yrbs.htm

26. King, B. A., Gammon, D. G., Marynak, K. L., & Rogers, T. (2018). Electronic cigarette sales in the United States, 2013-2017. *JAMA,* *320*(13), 1379-1380. https://doi.org/10.1001/jama.2018.10488

27. Gentzke, A., Creamer, M., Cullen, K., Ambrose, B., Willis, G., Jamal, A., & King, B. (2019). Vital signs: Tobacco product use among middle and high school students - United States, 2011-2018. *Morbidity and Mortality Weekly Report,* 68, 157-164. http://dx.doi.org/10.15585/mmwr.mm6806e1

28. Ali, F. R. M., Diaz, M. C., Vallone, D., et al. (2020). E-cigarette unit sales, by product and flavor type-United States, 2014–2020. *Morbidity and Mortality Weekly Report, 69,* 1313-1318. https://doi.org/10.15585/mmwr.mm6937e2

29. Hedegaard, H., Curtin, S., & Warner, M. (2020, April). *Increase in suicide mortality in the United States, 1999–2018.* National Center for Health Statistics: NCHS Data Brief, no 362.

30. Curtin, S., Warner, M., & Hedegaard, H. (2016, April). *Increase in suicide in the United States, 1999-2014.* National Center for Health Statistics: NCHS Data Brief, no. 241. https://www.cdc.gov/nchs/products/databriefs/db241.htm

31. Curtin, S. C., & Heron, M. (2019, October). *Death rates due to suicide and homicide among persons aged 10–24: United States, 2000–2017.* National Center for Health Statistics: NCHS Data Brief, no. 352. https://www.cdc.gov/nchs/data/databriefs/db352-h.pdf

32. Frazee, G., & Gorena Morales, P. (2019, June 18). *Suicide among teens and young adults reaches highest level since 2000.* PBS NewsHour. https://www.pbs.org/newshour/nation/suicide-among-teens-and-young-adults-reaches-highest-level-since-2000

33. Miron, O., Yu, K.-H., Wilf-Miron, R., & Kohane, I. S. (2019). Suicide rates among adolescents and young adults in the United States, 2000-2017. *JAMA, 321*(23), 2362–2364. https://doi.org/10.1001/jama.2019.5054

4

Do your homework...Are we using schools correctly?

Some of the most interesting conversations take place in the least glamorous settings. It's true. Think of the bizarre chatter you casually overhear in subways, grocery store checkout lines, and dive bars. I suppose hundreds of more locations could be added to the list, but I would ask that you draw your attention to a lesser-known gem. On its good days, this hot spot for gossip is certainly a front runner for the best news and most passionate rants. Are you guessing the White House Press Briefing Room? Nope. That's far too glamorous. I am referring to the one-star luxury you can only find within a school faculty lunch area. Typically situated amidst cinder block walls and bland paint colors, this space sits barren most of the day. It smells of old coffee and burnt skin, which is still adhered to the photocopier toner cartridge from a misguided color copy attempt. But I digress.

What's important to know is that this space bursts to life during a rushed lunch period, where educators exchange their energy, emotion, and disposable utensils, all while gulping down food fast enough to test the reliability of the human esophagus. I won't go into all the details of what I've heard (and overheard) during these lunch sessions. That would violate the "Las Vegas" rules agreement all educators implicitly understand— "what happens in the lunchroom, stays in the lunchroom." However, I am happy to share that these quick discussions have prompted me to: i) laugh, ii) cry, iii) silent laugh, iv) silent cry, v) choke while laughing and crying, and, finally vi), shoot Chobani yogurt out my left nostril after sneezing unexpectedly during a laugh. It really hurts, by the way. There may still be some coco loco flakes deep within my maxillary sinuses.

The point is, educators hear enough in the faculty lunch area to cover an enormous bandwidth of emotion and life. Many important issues are explored, argued, and solved in that architecturally modest room. And topics ebb and flow over time. But one of the most critical questions that seems to resurface every semester, as if it lingers within the walls of that room, is one you have probably asked yourself: are we using schools correctly?

That's an enormous question that carries intense emotion. I don't know how you answer that line of thinking without a long-winded and likely passionate response. Furthermore, asking if we are using schools correctly is, in many ways, a leading question. It's meant to inspire some sort of change, potentially shifting the pendulum of educational operations in one direction or the other. Sometimes that change can be good. Sometimes that change can be bad. And sometimes, that change can seem like a useless hoop to jump through just for the sake of making someone with little knowledge of how schools work happy. I need to ask for your grace and latitude as I pose that question again. And, in the interest of full transparency, let me forewarn you that I will put a twist on the question that allows me to generate an argument—one that will hopefully lead you to make subtle yet important changes in the classroom. But in the end, that's your decision, not mine. I am not your boss. However, I am reasonably well trained in science, fairly observant as a classroom teacher, and most of all, I feel morally compelled to do something with the data we learned about in Chapters 1-3. So, here is my spin on the question. I can remove excess educational red tape and send us down the right path by adding two words. Ready? Consider this: are we using schools correctly...**for kids?**

By now, you should be able to predict that my answer is "no." However, that's not an all-encompassing "no." I am not here to assassinate public education. Far from it. I enjoy and take pride in the fact that schools do many things exceptionally well. That means something to me. I would not have switched from a more profitable career in health care to designing cow heart replacement valves with students if I didn't believe in public education. Spoiler alert! I didn't switch jobs for the lucrative teacher salary either. I know, jaw-dropper. So, in fairness to the process, none of us (especially me) should comment on whether we are using school correctly for kids until we examine the following:

- What guides student learning in most school settings?

- How do we define success for students?

- Does our approach to education meet current student needs?

Now, I recognize that there are many more variables we could use to examine this topic—a lot more. However, based upon faculty lunch discussions and the U.S. Department of Education's website, the latter of which seems to be far more reliable, I think we are hitting three of the most critical points of interest. And, I promised myself that this book wouldn't rival the Warren Commission Report in terms of pages and confusing appendices. So, if you're still willing to lend me that grace and latitude I asked for, let's get started with the first assessment.

What guides student learning in most school settings?

If you know much about Dr. John Hattie, an educational guru from New Zealand that measured student influences, you might jump to answering this question with the following: "It's the teacher that guides student learning!" That would be my initial response as well. Hattie did a fantastic job investigating the scope and magnitude of 195 unique points of influence upon student achievement. His study spans several years, demonstrates statistical significance, and was updated in 2015 with new considerations.[1] Hattie's outcome data creates a visually pleasing comparison of where all these influences fall in relation to each other. And what's at the top of this list? The influence from a highly effective teacher.

Hattie's work substantiates that "collective teacher efficacy" makes a key difference in most students' academic journeys toward graduation and the world beyond. In many ways, I suppose Hattie has given every educator the data to take a brief time out, pat themselves on the back, and then argue for greater compensation based upon their value (which is another popular topic in the faculty lunch area). Anyway, Hattie's results make you feel proud to be an educator, right? One problem, though. Hattie's diligent efforts, which are impressive, do not answer the question I asked in the subtitle.

Recall that I suggested we investigate what guides student learning in schools. As important as educators are, they don't determine what is taught. Educators may have a lot of say in how a topic is taught but less influence when it comes to curricular selections. What seems to guide student learning in terms of content stems from standards and expectations, usually from the state level of governance. These directives outline exactly what is taught in school and sometimes how it is assessed. Does that sound a lot like a mandate? That's because it is. And if you're curious, the relative impact of a mandated curriculum was almost one standard deviation lower than the impact of an effective educator, according to Hattie's 195 points of influence.[1] Awesome.

All that said, I am certainly not looking to go rogue. I don't have any intentions of suggesting we toss out state standards, allowing us to teach whatever our hearts and souls find interesting that day. Not at all. As an educator myself, I see both the upside and downside of required teaching standards. They make sure that schools and staff are held accountable, which is intended to look out for the student experience. And, standards ensure an acceptable level of knowledge is transferred to every student in that state who takes that particular course. So, are state standards sometimes annoying and antiquated in their content? At times, yes. I think many educators feel that way. But, do they also serve a purpose that offers some positive student gain? Yes, again. We may not always want to admit it, but standards certainly do help students in some ways.

Irrespective of how you and I feel about standards, I'd like to suggest the most important thing to take away is this: I don't see them going away any time soon. These mandated points of instruction help define the borders of a metaphorical sandbox that we, as educators, and our students, as clients, are asked to play in each school day. I don't think any of us have the power to get rid of that sandbox entirely. Too many people in state and federal leadership positions want that sandbox there. Now, extending the metaphor a little further, we are allowed as educators to argue about the borders of the sandbox (content) or what toys (learning opportunities) are found within it, but that's about it. And if you're wondering why, I think the answer is a somewhat misguided conception—standards allow us to measure student "success."

The U.S. Department of Education spells this out for us, affirming that standards set goals for what students should know and be able to do while learning academic content. Our federal and state departments of education believe assessments actually serve as a mechanism to determine how much a student has learned and whether they have performed to a level of proficiency set by academic standards.[2] So, wait. If I have this right, the formula is something like this: i) learn specific content, ii) test specific content, and iii) compare test and proficiency scores regarding the specific content. If a student scores well, we pretend the specific content has made the child "successful." That is a convenient operational model. But, is it the best thing for the student?

Allow me to toss aside the sarcasm and go one layer deeper. I suspect there is more to this process in terms of what guides learning. Admittedly, some of this is strictly opinion. However, we do know with confidence that school districts and state departments of education need a way to measure how well the financial investment into schools is performing. To do this, they need a benchmark and some outcome data that determines if teachers, students, administrators, or whomever, achieved the benchmark. This also occurs at the federal level to some extent. Here's a perfect example: how does the Center for American Progress determine the efficacy of our current public education system in terms of success? Well, by comparing international test scores.[3]

Yep, they use test scores that correlate with academic points of interest to predict competitive performance in the world job market. Now, I can't speak for the Center for American Progress and agencies like them, but I would guess that they realize there are many confounding variables that surround a student's test scores, at least in terms of whether they will outperform a comparable student from Finland. Nevertheless, test scores are what leaders in education often reference when comparing successful students in the United States with those in other countries. And by the way, if you're interested in this topic, go read about the Programme for International Student Assessment (PISA). You'll get a healthy dose of what I am describing for you. Anyway, let's get back on track with this transparent observation: I am not an elected authority, and I clearly don't represent any state or federal department of education. I am guessing you are in a similar situation. However, I think it's a logical assertion that the obsession with local, state, and international test scores facilitates a quantitative performance, allowing governing bodies to make quick comparisons. Again, that is convenient for most parties involved, but definitely not the student.

So, when it comes down to it, what seems to play a very large hand in what guides student learning is not just the 195 points of influence that Hattie studied. Instead, the major player appears to be a somewhat controversial process that generates quantifiable data from specific exams, allowing school districts, states, and the federal government to comparatively assess their performance. Yep, it may very well be that benchmark data, finances, and convenience are key driving forces that guide student learning. Go ahead and let that sink in for a moment. I don't see much of that changing at the macro-level. But, don't fret. In Part 3 of this book, I will happily demonstrate that this organizational framework will not inhibit the strategies we can use in our classrooms to meet the needs of school-aged children.

How do we define success for students?

Allow me to go back to the U.S. Department of Education again and share a formula for student education.[4] It reads a little something like this.

- Step 1: Use standards to set clear and measurable goals in terms of what students should know and be able to do.

- Step 2: Utilize assessments to determine how much a student has learned and whether they have performed to a level of proficiency set by academic standards.

Now, somewhere in between the goals and the assessment is the curriculum. This curriculum is the basic operational guide of how you teach information that addresses the standards and sets students up to perform well on assessments that relate to those standards. Most curriculum decisions occur at the state and local levels. And, if you are a fortunate educator, you work in a district where there is some latitude in how the curriculum is implemented, which increases teacher autonomy.

However, the issue at hand is metrics of student success. And guess what? Similar to assessments of school district success, our local, state, and federal leaders like to use quantitative data, yet again, for evidence of student success. It makes sense. Numbers show relationships between students and can serve as a cut-off for scholarships and admissions to trade schools or universities. Furthermore, quantitative data that correlates with student "success" is an excellent way to track trends over time. Like the stock market, the percent gain or loss for a given period of time is an excellent way to substantiate improvements, failures, and trends. This makes standardized student testing a critical method to assess student performance...at least, at one point in time.

Interestingly, education's forced relationship between the concept of success and national standardized exams is so intertwined, even Google recognizes it. Look at the information I obtained after searching "best school districts and students in America" and the evaluation process each one utilized.

NATIONAL SCHOOL DISTRICT METRICS OF SUCCESS:

Award/ Recognition	Origin	Evaluation Material
National Blue Ribbon School	U.S. Department of Education[4]	• Whole school state assessment in top 15% of state • Subgroup performance in the top 40% of state for all subgroups • Graduation rate and career and college readiness scores
National High School Rankings	U.S. News & World Report[5]	• Proportion of 12th graders that passed one or more AP exams • Math and reading proficiency (based on state assessments) • Underserved student performance (state assessments) • College curriculum breadth (AP tests and scores)

Best School Districts in America	Niche.com[6] (influential website used by parents for high levels students and athletes to increase opportunities for college)	• States test scores • AP tests taken • AP tests passed • SAT scores • ACT scores • Public school district ranking

As you may have noticed, the three institutions that Google dropped in my lap(top) represent the impressions of the U.S. Department of Education, the national news media, and a search engine algorithm to locate the most successful schools in America. What do they all have in common? They all heavily rely on quantitative test scores to produce relative rankings. In short, they measure student success in terms of numbers. Yep, numbers again. Apparently, to be the best student in the best high school, you need to have the best numbers. This means that instead of looking at the ability of graduates to communicate effectively, problem-solve well, or demonstrate resilience at their first full-time job, institutions gather numbers from standardized assessments to see if a child will be on the right path for life following graduation. Again, this seems like an evaluation predicated upon convenience for the evaluators.

However, the information we just covered only describes school districts and larger cohorts in the educational landscape. How do we define success in terms of individual students? Maybe things are better here? Well, if you've taught for any amount of time, you already know the answer. Nevertheless, please review the criteria some prominent national awards use to assess applicants for eligibility. There seems to be a theme here that you may have seen before.

NATIONAL STUDENT METRICS OF SUCCESS

Award/Recognition	Origin	Evaluation Material
AP Scholars Program • AP Scholar • AP Scholar with Honors • AP Scholar with Distinction	AP College Board[7]	• Based upon scoring a minimum of a 3 or higher on three AP exams • With each level, more AP exams must be completed with an increasing scoring average
National Merit Scholarship Program	PSAT/ NMSQT[8]	Example for 11th graders: • Take the PSAT 10 in the spring of their sophomore year (or fall of junior year) and score in the top 10% by state • Earn a score of 3 or higher on two or more AP exams by their junior year (9th and 10th grade AP scores are considered) • Students must have a 3.5 GPA or higher in high school
U.S. Presidential Scholar	U.S. Department of Education[9]	• Score exceptionally well on the SAT or ACT • Additional metrics are applied after students meet the ACT/ SAT eligibility

Here we go again. It appears the evaluation of individual student success has fallen into the same trap as school districts. Quantitative data from national standardized tests appears to be the driving force behind determining student success or failure for certain prominent evaluators. But, wait. Maybe this is just because we reviewed a few national scholarships, and they need numeric cut-offs to limit the applicant pool? Let's look at other measurements of student success and see if there is a trend.

Take an online trip to the National Center for Educational Statistics (NCES) website. The NCES contains all types of powerful data on parameters that impact education. Seems promising. And then you run across everything you could possibly want to know about the SAT from 1967 forward, including how gender, race, and the state you are living in might impact your composite score. That's not terribly surprising since the NCES is a data-driven agency with "statistics" in its name, right? However, what made me chuckle is that I found the NCES website cited in several articles as a metric of (drum roll please)..."student success." It was all based on numbers, again.

If we are going to use convenient numbers over limited content and discrete points in time to assess students, then we need to find a way to add other aspects to their evaluation of success. Why? Numbers help us assess values, trends, and margins of error. As a science nerd, I love them. But, numbers probably aren't the best metric to evaluate the success of human beings, especially cohorts of them. There is so much more to humans. Consider the following:

- National Merit qualifiers and subsequent applications grew steadily to around 50,000 students per application cycle between 2017 to 2019. This means that the number of students with elite PSAT and AP scores is rising. That's great—more successful kids![8] This statistic makes you believe schools are improving over that two-year span!

- Around the same time (October 2016 and 2017), the National Center for Educational Statistics claims that approximately 523,000 15-to-24 year-olds left school without obtaining a high school credential. These dropouts accounted for 4.7% of the 11.1 million youth enrolled in grades 10-12 in 2017.[10] This is a much larger number than the small cohort of students that applied for the National Merit Scholarship Program. That's not great. This statistic paints a picture of schools struggling during those two years.

I wonder if a soft skill assessment would have split the middle and explained both of the above-bulleted trends. Were some subpopulations lacking basic professional traits needed to score well on a test independent of content knowledge? It makes you wonder.

My point is that it's not a wise idea to associate student success with quantitative assessments alone. These assessments can't possibly measure all of the skills and proficiencies a student learns and develops in school to take a test well or simply graduate. Furthermore, the published metrics of success typically focus upon the extremely high achieving student, representing a **small** percentage of all students. Take a look at those last two bullet points again. Are you really increasing overall student success in schools when the top 0.5% are improving, while at the same time half a million kids bailed on school over a 12-month period?

Before we wrap up this discussion, I want to acknowledge that I focused my efforts on large-scale agencies and popular assessments that most students and teachers are aware of. Clearly, I did not cover every option, or every opinion, associated with the topic of student success. I fully admit that. And if there is something particularly important to you that

I failed to cover, consider this my apology. But, the reality is this: there is not enough time, coffee, or Red Bull for me to do so.

We have talked about success from the perspective of districts and evaluatory bodies—all of which use numeric cut-offs for certain parts of their evaluation. Let's switch gears to a different perspective. How do educators inspire success? We focus on creative lessons at the classroom level to build soft skills and demonstrate student learning with exciting performance-based assessments. We encourage students to emphasize process over product and perhaps even give them the chance to reapply their efforts at a later date. And, on our good days, we take the time to point out to a student various career paths they might consider based upon their strengths and weaknesses. As educators, we do all of that. And you know what's cool? We often make headway and inspire a lot of those students to take steps forward in their lives. That's impactful.

And then, our building community does something to unintentionally undermine it all...like holding a special assembly for a student with a perfect 36 ACT score, or hosting an exclusive high-end breakfast with fancy food and real silverware, specifically for students that earned national or state recognition for their high exam performance. We have the best intentions, right? It seems harmless. Until the other students, which is only about 98% of your school, hear about the special event and wonder why they have never been recognized? Well, the answer I heard most from kids over the past decade of being a science teacher saddened me: "I'm not successful."

One final thought, it's important to recognize that most students in America will never receive high-level recognition for "success." Yet, these students will launch into the world and create a beautiful life that inspires others, and by many accounts, is wildly successful. They could be accountants, writers, engineers, or doctors. They could also be plumbers, electricians, carpenters, or Amazon delivery staff—remember, the people we all sang praises about in 2020?

I point this out for a reason. Recall that much of the quantitative data collected regarding student performance is often heavily skewed toward college-bound pathways. This is a trap we have been caught in for decades, and I struggle with why. It creates the impression that kids are not successful unless they pursue a college degree. This is erroneous and sad. Sad because all careers have value and offer opportunities for success. Sad again because how well you take a standardized academic test has never correlated with long-term happiness, at least not that I'm aware of. And finally, sad because quantitative assessments could be set up to examine student performance-based skills in kids, but the world of education is slow to do so. If you think I'm wrong, please take comfort in the fact that intense patient simulations and skilled actors are now part of medical training to assess **vital skills** in doctors, in addition to intellect. Why not evaluate like this at all levels of education? If the answer is because it's not convenient, then it needs to change.

I'm not alone in my thoughts here. A recent poll conducted by Gallup and the Northwest Evaluation Association (NWEA) reveals that 83% of teachers, 82% of parents and superintendents, and 83% of principals believe it is equally important to assess BOTH academic skills and nonacademic skills such as teamwork, critical thinking, and creativity **to measure success**.[11] But the issue runs deeper. Authorities outside of education are requesting that school districts prioritize developing life skills with greater emphasis than the current practice for many school districts. In 2018, The National School Boards Associations (NSBA) created a Commission to Close the Skills Gap to help advise school boards on how they can best prepare their students for their next steps in life.[12] Even the NSBA recognizes this gap we have described throughout this chapter.

Organizations from a variety of sectors were represented on the Commission and provided insight into what they think are the essential skills needed for success in the workplace. Some of these organizations represented in the Commission include the National Retail Federation, the American Hotel & Lodging Association, and the Manufacturing Institute. The Commission identified six "LifeReady" skills essential for students to master for success in school, employment, and life. These skills include 1) dependability and reliability, 2) adaptability and trainability, 3) critical thinking, 4) decision making, 5) customer focus, and 6) teamwork.[12]

This identified list of skills may not surprise you. We all know these are necessary to building and maintaining relationships, setting and achieving goals, and navigating life challenges. Just to hit this point home, when Gallup surveyed the general public and asked them the question, "how prepared do you believe most high school graduates are to be successful in college?" only 3% said very prepared, 22% said prepared, 56% said somewhat prepared, and 17% said not at all prepared.[13] Additionally, when Gallup asked the same population, "how prepared do you believe most of those with a high school degree only are to be successful in the workplace?" only 5% said very prepared, 17% said prepared, 58% said somewhat prepared, and 19% said not at all prepared.[13] What do you think you would say to the two questions above? Take a second to think about this. Regardless of their paths, I am worried our schools are not adequately preparing our students.

Does our approach to education meet current student needs?

In many ways, the amount of information tossed at you from Part 1 of this book may have resembled drinking from a firehose. But, if I did my job well, you are now in a position to understand the vulnerabilities, risks, protective and risk factors, and mental health trends of your students...at least, right up to the point of COVID-19. Nevertheless, I feel confident that you are qualified to answer the final question of Part 1. Here it is again: does our approach to education meet *student* needs? What are your thoughts? And please, don't feel like you need to rush to answer. Just start by thinking about how most schools operate.

- Does your ACT prep course practice the soft skills desperately sought by employers at all levels, providing a high likelihood of sustainability and promotion for your students?

- What about state assessments? Do your state assessments help identify and solve some otherwise hidden social and emotional needs for students in your class?

- Does your school football team address how to communicate with trusted adults regarding complex issues instead of leaving vague messages on social media and feeling sad when no one replies?

- And, what about music? Does your band program help trumpet players understand the link between the self-efficacy needed to practice a challenging piece of music and the resilience one of them will need three hours from now when a Snapchat story humiliates them?

- Does checking off the state standards for a unit help your kids with the crippling spike in anxiety among teenagers?

The answer, albeit sarcastically, appears to be "no," just like when we started this chapter. But that doesn't mean we are in a hopeless spot—quite the opposite. We do many extraordinary things as educators and make such a personal impact on our students. In fact, some of the students you work with will have a special place in their heart for you, their influential teacher, until the day they die. That's amazing. And as you already know, the validation of our work is not always seen in the classroom. It may come years later when a student reaches out to let you know how something you said briefly in the hallway along with a random hug helped them more than you ever guessed.

Of course, I realize that we have to abide by federal, state, and district guidelines. I am not trying to say state standards or educational policies should go away. I believe that schools, for the most part, function extremely well and that standards and accountability have an upside to them. I also realize that standardized tests and quantitative metrics are probably not going anywhere any time soon either. And that's okay because they do provide content accountability. As educators, we can work with all of that. But our approach in the classroom can be different. Data from all the chapters in Part 1 suggest that it *has to be* if we want to meet the actual needs of our students and prepare them for success outside of a perfect ACT score.

Part 1 has shown us that some Gen Zers, the very kids we adore in our classrooms, have some significant vulnerabilities. These vulnerabilities have hit some groups harder than others. And in Part 2, I am about to show you that the global pandemic of SARS-CoV-2 preyed upon these shortcomings and exacerbated their already tenuous mental health state. Please, hang in there. I wouldn't be writing this if I didn't see an enormous amount of evidence that schools can turn this trend around. I promise you that. Much of the proposed strategies in Part 3 of this book will use data-driven science to fill in the gaps for Gen Zers and help them strengthen their protective factors. And from a teacher's perspective, these strategies ask you to prioritize what you **love to do as an educator**: make a positive impact on a child that is so profound, they never forget it.

Chapter 4 References

1. Hattie, J. (2015). The applicability of Visible Learning to higher education. *Scholarship of Teaching and Learning in Psychology*, *1*(1), 79–91. https://doi.org/10.1037/stl0000021

2. U.S. Department of Education. (n.d.). *College- and career-ready standards*. https://www.ed.gov/k-12reforms/standards

3. Epstein, D. (2011, September 6). *Investing in education powers U.S. competitiveness*. Center for American Progress. https://www.americanprogress.org/issues/education-k-12/reports/2011/09/06/10376/investing-in-education-powers-u-s-competitiveness/

4. U.S. Department of Education. (2020, October 1). *National Blue Ribbon Schools Program*. https://www2.ed.gov/programs/nclbbrs/eligibility.html

5. Morse, R., & Brooks, E. (2020, April 20). *How U.S. News Calculated the 2020 Best High Schools Rankings*. US News & World Report. https://www.usnews.com/education/best-high-schools/articles/how-us-news-calculated-the-rankings

6. Niche. (2021). 2021 Best School Districts in America. https://www.niche.com/k12/search/best-school-districts/

7. College Board. (2021). *Qualifying for an AP Scholar Award – AP Students*. https://apstudents.collegeboard.org/awards-recognitions/ap-scholar-award

8. National Merit Scholarship Corporation. (2020). *Guide to the National Merit Scholarship Program*. https://www.nationalmerit.org/s/1758/images/gid2/editor_documents/guide_to_the_national_merit_scholarship_program.pdf?gid=2&pgid=61&sessionid=7a8778c0-772d-4faf-b3c6-bae7327d2767&cc=1#:~:text=Currently%2C%20over%201.5%20million%20students,scholarships%20for%20college%20undergraduate%20study

9. U.S. Department of Education. (2020, October 28). *U.S. Presidential Scholars Program: Eligibility*. https://www2.ed.gov/programs/psp/eligibility.html

10. McFarland, J., Cui, J., Holmes, J., and Wang, X. (2019). *Trends in High School Dropout and Completion Rates in the United States: 2019* (NCES 2020-117). U.S. Department of Education. Washington, DC: National Center for Education Statistics. https://nces.ed.gov/pubs2020/2020117.pdf

11. Gallup, & Northwest Evaluation Association (NWEA). (2018). *Assessing soft skills: Are we preparing students for successful futures?* https://www.nwea.org/content/uploads/2018/08/NWEA_Gallup-Report_August-2018.pdf

12. National School Boards Association. (2019). *A Report of the Commission to Close the Skills Gap.* https://www.nsba.org/News/2019/Skills-Gap-Commission-Report

13. Gallup. (2018). *U.S. adults report graduating students are unprepared for college and the workplace.* Communities in Schools. https://www.communitiesinschools.org/media/filer_public/c2/66/c266eddc-3979-438a-9a33-ee358f5bb2e1/final_gallup_poll_survey_college_and_career_readiness.pdf

PART TWO

Cough, cold, and collapse...The impact of COVID-19

The impact of SARS-CoV-2 is not limited to the millions of people it infected. It has also changed the outlook and operations of the BILLIONS of people it isolated.

5

The mess of stress... Pressure points during the pandemic

Take a journey down a **hypothetical** path with me. A while ago, I had an idea for a large-scale research project that was ambitious and intriguing. I was confident it had never been attempted. I bounced the idea around in my head for quite some time, considering the potential resources needed, personnel demands, time requirements, and outside support it would likely require. It was a lot to manage. And to be honest, it seemed a little beyond the scale of what I am comfortable with, but I was also at the point of my life where I needed a new challenge. So, I put in an application to the Institutional Review Board (IRB), requesting permission to conduct this research project, and anxiously awaited their reply. This idea had the potential to be groundbreaking.

Now, if you don't know what an IRB represents, no worries, the IRB serves as a panel of experts at leading research institutions, such as universities, that review all research proposals to make sure they are safe, ethical, and purposeful. Seems like a wise idea. Yet, some people fear IRBs as they occasionally have some quirky reasons for turning down a research project. But, I am not one of them. I've never had an issue with an IRB review with the limited research I have done. Until...

Until they rejected my research proposal! The fuddy-duddies on the review panel made some outlandish claims and comments, asserting that my proposal was wildly inappropriate. Furthermore, they claimed I did not present sufficient justification for the potential harm that this research project could bring to my intended subjects, who happened to be school-aged children. This seemed harsh to me—excessively harsh. And to be honest, I can't move past their decision. Was my idea really that misguided?

The intent of the proposed research project was to examine the adaptability, resilience, and mental health fluctuations of students amid a realistic, once-in-a-lifetime stressor that seemed unsolvable for the foreseeable future. To do that, I thought the instigator of this stressor should be something that students knew little about and in no way would be able to contribute to the solution, making them feel powerless—an infectious disease seemed like a perfect choice. All participating school districts would just need a predetermined day zero where the fictitious disease was "discovered," and our team could implement the experiment one step at a time from there.

To start things off, I proposed that within one week, the selected school districts change their mode of school immediately from in-person to an all-online format and cancel all school activities for the foreseeable future. I emphasized that there should not be any advance warning or time to prepare for this decision, testing the resilience of students upfront. Additionally, I proposed that the students enrolled in the study had to stay at home unless they were the most able-bodied family member for activities of daily living, such as grocery shopping.

While at home, I needed the participants to watch non-stop media coverage, which a few select actors would provide, that focused on a new, contagious, and ill-defined virus that was rapidly making its way around the world, causing both mild and severe illness. In my proposal, I was extremely flexible regarding the name or type of fictional illness our media actors would cover, but I knew enough to insist that scientists and health care providers poorly understand the infectious agent. This guideline was important, as it fostered an excellent environment for study participants to persistently worry about the health and well-being of themselves and their loved ones.

Finally, I requested that participants be given information that health care systems across the globe have been pushed to their limits amid an economic fallout and randomly have immediate family and friends create the appearance of job loss, financial problems, as well as food and housing insecurities. Oh! And one last thing, I wanted everyone involved in the research study to encourage our student participants to maintain the same pre-pandemic level of engagement in school. Yikes.

I think by now you see the point that I'm driving at. No one would allow a research project such as this. It sounds far-fetched, harmful to the study participants, and absolutely chaotic in terms of logistical operations. Any actual IRB would probably need to request the termination of the individual who dared to propose a study like this in the first place. Yet, here we are today, and the actual reality is that our school-aged children, along with the rest of the world, did endure this absurd situation. Wild, huh?

COVID-19 was the largest stress test that our modern society could have imagined. It caused physical, emotional, financial, psychological, and social harm, all of which impacted our communities, including Gen Z students. Each unexpected challenge of COVID-19 piggybacked on top of all the unique pre-pandemic stressors many Gen Zers, their families, and others around them struggled with. That's obviously relevant. And for this book, we are obligated to look at the pandemic through a wide-angle lens, establishing a few universal stressors that many of our students (and their families) experienced. To put it simply, the COVID era either worsened pre-existing problems, improved pre-existing problems, or made no impact. And, as educators, it's crucial that we know.

Economic impacts

COVID-19 had severe negative economic impacts on our country—few debate this. And, there is a lot of data out there that substantiates this claim. But let's spend some time with the information provided by the Congressional Research Service from April 2020. Why this specific choice? It has unique relevance. This report will share with you a part of the same information that our federal legislative branch mulled over as they considered stimulus decisions. You may recall that April 2020 was the same month the first stimulus checks were released. Thus, this data is particularly important.

During April 2020, unemployment increased faster than ever before and spiked to a lofty level of close to 15%.[1] This crisis impacted specific groups of people more than others. For example, the peak unemployment rate for workers with less than a high school degree was 21.2% compared to those with a Bachelor's degree or higher at 8.4%. Also, unemployment gaps were evident across genders and age groups; for those aged 25-54, unemployment rates for females and males were 13.7% and 12.1%, respectively. Particularly relevant for us educators to note is that teenage females experienced an unemployment rate of 36.6% compared to 28.6% for teenage males.[1] That is some additional weight on our kiddos' shoulders.

Additionally, students from single-mother households may feel this burden more profoundly. This recession, unlike most others, has impacted females more significantly than males in the United States.[2] Some reasons for this include that industries with high female employment, such as the hospitality sector, were hit particularly hard by the pandemic. On top of this, daycare and school closures forced some working mothers to stay home and care for their children if they could not find or afford another childcare option.[2] Also, racial and ethnic minorities experienced higher unemployment rates in April of 2020; Hispanic workers had higher unemployment rates (18.9%) compared to non-Hispanic workers (13.6%), and Black workers had higher unemployment rates (16.7%) compared to White workers (14.2%).[1] As Damian Barr stated, "We are not all in the same boat. We are all in the same storm." All families were certainly impacted, but some more so than others.

Keep in mind that unemployment is only one aspect of the pandemic's associated economic crisis. Those who kept their jobs may have had to strain their resources by supporting family or friends who were struggling financially or even taking a pay cut at work. Pew Research Center conducted a survey that explored this further and discovered that one-in-four adults had trouble paying their bills since the pandemic began, one-third dipped into their savings or retirement funds to make ends meet, and about one-in-six of those surveyed borrowed money from friends or family and received food from a food bank.[3]

So much for only worrying about our health and our families during a pandemic, huh? The unfortunate reality is that I can *almost* assure you that in your immediate circle of friends and family, you know someone that is struggling as a direct result of the pandemic's economic crisis—whether they have shared this with you or not.

So, what do you take away from this? A lot. The economic crisis associated with the pandemic was a profound event and impacted a wide bandwidth of people. In some job sectors, those with six-figure salaries were almost as vulnerable to being laid off or furloughed as hourly workers with part-time employment. As such, most working individuals, including our Gen Z students, were vulnerable to some unemployment risk during the pandemic. As corporations and small businesses reorganize and assess the damage, this will likely continue to be a stressor in many families' lives. It's unlikely the economic downfall from COVID-19 will be righted by a few stimulus checks or one good summer.

The negative economic impacts of SARS-CoV-2 on parents, guardians, and teens will be around for years to come. These setbacks will be apparent in schools in both obvious and subtle ways. New students may arrive in your class because of parental job changes. Kids that used to be on your cross-country team may now need to work after school. PTO support for the school, especially grants, might disappear for some time. Be mindful of it all. Some of the unexpected changes around you involving students may harbor economic pressure as their driving force.

Health impacts

Like the economic implications of the pandemic, health outcome data illustrates that certain populations have been impacted more so than others. The June 2020 CDC Morbidity and Mortality Weekly Report (MMWR) examined the distribution of SARS-CoV-2 infections across demographics. The results revealed the following regarding the distribution of COVID-19 infections: 33% of individuals were Hispanic, 22% were Black, and 1.3% were American Indian/Alaskan Native.[4] Given that these populations account for 18%, 13%, and 0.7% of the United States population, respectively, the data suggests they have been disproportionately affected by COVID-19.[4] However, this health disparity goes beyond contracting the virus and testing positive. Take a look at the following data compiled from February of 2021:

- American Indian, Alaskan Native, and non-Hispanic persons have been hospitalized at 3.7 times the rate of White, non-Hispanic individuals and died from COVID-19 at 2.4 times the rate.[5]

- Eerily similar, Hispanic/Latino persons have been hospitalized at 3.2 times the rate of White, non-Hispanic individuals and died at 2.3 times the rate of White, non-Hispanic individuals.[5]

- Black or African American persons have been hospitalized for the virus at 2.9 times the rate and died at 1.9 times the rate of White, non-Hispanic individuals.[5]

- Nearly a third of the nurses who've died of coronavirus in the United States are Filipino, even though Filipino nurses make up just 4% of the nursing population nationwide.[6]

To state the obvious, these numbers are unsettling. The health disparity seen between races in terms of hospitalization and deaths adds another layer of emotion to the pandemic. This is critical to understand and acknowledge.

As of May 2020, the most common underlying conditions associated with an increased risk of severe COVID-19 included cardiovascular disease, type 2 diabetes, and chronic lung disease.[4] If an individual had just one of these conditions, their chance of hospitalization with COVID-19 was 12 times higher than it would be if they didn't have the condition at all.[4] That's obviously significant. But does this knowledge connect to the demographic distribution we just mentioned? The vital link would be if the subpopulations with higher rates of hospitalization and death also had higher rates of cardiovascular disease, diabetes, and lung disease.

Here is what we know. The average adult in the United States has a 40% chance of developing type 2 diabetes.[7] However, if you are African American, Hispanic or Latino, American Indian, Alaskan Native, Pacific Islander, or Asian American, you are at higher risk of developing type 2 diabetes at some point in life.[7] More specifically, Hispanic or Latino American adults have a greater than 50% chance of developing this disease.[7] And then, there's cardiovascular disease. Between 1999-2017, non-Hispanic Blacks were more than twice as likely as non-Hispanic Asian or Pacific Islanders to die of heart disease.[8] Additionally, hypertension (high blood pressure) is a form of cardiovascular disease and continues to be a serious problem for non-Hispanic blacks, more so than non-Hispanic whites.[8] So, what does this all mean? Race is a social construct, but there is more to consider from a medical perspective. Disease processes can demonstrate a higher prevalence in given subpopulations based upon genetics or a host of other potential reasons. The evidence is clear—SARS-CoV-2 definitely hit some families harder than others. And again, this is something to remember for your classroom.

All that said, it's not just genetics and principles of pathophysiology that determine the level of a given disease. Social determinants of health (such as access to employment with living wages) significantly impact health outcomes. We could spend an endless amount of time looking at minority communities' rates of exposure to the virus, illness severity, and hospitalization data that may lead us to the same conclusion—historic structural inequities in social determinants of health notably impact these groups and were exacerbated by the pandemic. Think about this. We already know that type 2 diabetes tends to be more prevalent in Hispanic and Latino populations, but equally important, patients in this demographic often experience a greater severity of disease due to uncontrolled diabetes. As of 2016, Hispanics were 2.6 times more likely to be hospitalized for end-stage renal disease treatment associated with diabetes compared to non-Hispanic whites.[9] Why is this?

If you are thinking about the social determinants of health, then you guessed it. A combination of relevant factors such as lower income and decreased access to quality health care can all impact disease management. Now, add the logistical constraints that some people experience. A few to consider: i) does the patient have access to transportation for a doctor's appointment? ii) does the patient have enough income to access healthy foods and/or a modified diet for diabetes? iii) does the patient have a safe place to exercise, and iv) does the patient hold a job that allows them time to exercise? These are just four considerations, and there are likely 400 more. And keep in mind, we are only talking about one disease—diabetes. Nevertheless, are you starting to see the link between social determinants and disease processes?

Let's strengthen our understanding with another example. *The New England Journal of Medicine* (NEJM) analyzed the hospitalization and mortality data among Black and White patients with COVID-19. It was found that Black patients with COVID-19, as compared to White COVID-19 patients, had higher rates of obesity, diabetes, hypertension, and chronic kidney disease, as well as a higher likelihood of having a fever, cough, or labored breathing at the time of testing.[10] So, in short, Black Americans demonstrated a greater chance of getting a SARS-CoV-2 infection and, once they did, were more likely to have a more serious form of the disease. Why? Many of the same reasons as we saw with increased severity of diabetes in Hispanics or Latinos in that there is some underlying genetic risk compounded by social determinants that may intensify the disease severity.

And so, to no surprise, this NEJM study went on to point out that factors such as Black race, public insurance, living in a low-income area, and obesity were *all* associated with a greater chance of hospitalization. Social determinants had once again compounded the problem, impacting peoples' COVID-19 experience. Admittedly, the last few paragraphs offer only a few examples of how populations in the United States were disproportionately affected by COVID-19, but the template of how it happens is there. It's crucial to realize that other groups such as immigrant and refugee communities have also suffered tremendously. In fact, our team could write at least another book on this alone. For now, please take to heart that some of your students are a part of these communities and have seen and experienced the worst with COVID-19. This is worth keeping at the forefront of your mind.

Before we close out this section of Chapter 5, just a few more thoughts on disparities associated with the social determinants of health and the stress that comes with them. Keep in mind that health disparities are typically studied at the large-scale population level. That involves large groups and cohorts. However, don't forget that examining individual situations in this pandemic is also crucial. Hear me out, please: the virus is already frightening enough for a student, but imagine knowing that your mom is currently undergoing chemotherapy for breast cancer, and therefore severely immunocompromised. Getting COVID-19 could be a life-or-death situation for someone like this. How terrifying is that?

We need to acknowledge that many of our school-aged children are living with people who have conditions that make them at increased risk for severe illness with COVID-19. The earlier discussion pointed out that cardiovascular disease, diabetes, and chronic lung issues were significant risk factors, but there are obviously more. Add in Down syndrome, sickle cell disease, obesity, and all of the other risk factors on the CDC website. A lot of Americans have family members with at least one of these medical conditions. I cannot imagine the constant state of fear that some of our Gen Zers have been living in over the past year or so, worrying about loved ones. It's unlikely those worries will dissipate quickly offering new challenges as the world reopens.

And furthermore, please don't forget that some of our school-aged children have these conditions themselves. As of December 2020, the American Academy of Pediatrics reported that over 2 million children had been infected with SARS-CoV-2. And even though school-aged children only represent 1.8% of COVID hospital admissions, all should be aware that roughly 33% of those children end up in the ICU, and some did not survive.[11]

How is a higher-risk child supposed to cope with this looming threat? As we return to the classroom, we need to be cognizant of the wide array of health-related experiences our students have faced, or are facing, due to the pandemic. Do not forget that this has not been a pandemic that has affected us all equally. Those families that felt the full ferocity of COVID-19 will struggle, especially as others dismiss their fears and long for swimming pools to open and unrestricted travel to hurry up. Educators need to be aware and willing to listen to high-risk student concerns, offer a kind smile, and talk about it.

Life stressors in 2020

2020 was historic for many reasons beyond the pandemic. Dr. Arthur Evans, CEO of the American Psychological Association (APA), did an excellent job summarizing 2020's challenges: "Not only are we in the midst of a global pandemic...we are also facing increasing division and hostility in the presidential election. Add to that racial turmoil in our cities, the unsteady economy and climate change that has fueled widespread wildfires and other natural disasters."[12] To put his words into context, note that 7 out of 10 Americans in May of 2020 thought that the United States was at its lowest point in the nation's history.[13]

Here are a few life stressors that may have contributed to the aforementioned belief: discrimination, police violence towards minorities, polarized impressions regarding the federal and state responses to COVID-19, expedited vaccine timeline that made some question its safety, and the 2020 presidential election.[13] That's a lot for one year to throw at people. And that's only the domestic stressors specific to America. From my point of view, 2020 was a complete dumpster fire. You might feel the same. However, opinions are clearly not as important as facts. As such, allow me to share some data regarding 2020

Election year stress

All election years generate stress, and for that matter, arguments. That is supposed to happen. Discussion and democracy are two foundational principles that make our country a wonderful place to live. That said, 2020 seemed to have an extra flare of political controversy. Regardless of where you fall politically, everyone was exposed to the same tense political climate. All you had to do was turn on the TV or take a scroll through social media—it was everywhere you looked.

In 2020, it was found that 68% of adults believed that the political climate or 2020 presidential election was a significant source of stress, up from 52% for the 2016 election.[13] Something to note is that heightened stress due to the presidential election wasn't only associated with one party affiliation; Democrats, Republicans, and Independents alike reported increased stress at 76%, 67%, and 64%, respectively.[13]

The majority of our Gen Z students can't yet vote. So, you may be wondering, why does this matter? Keep in mind that Gen Z is brilliant, and like Millennials, curious about world events and their impact. Most of your students, particularly the secondary school crowd, are acutely aware that the elections and decisions made in politics now affect Gen Z's *future*. They are engaged and aware.

Furthermore, elections are important. They emerge as a topic of conversation among adults at home, and these conversations often trickle down to kids. Our kids are listening, even when we think they are not—trust me! Otherwise, where did my eight-year-old get the creative phrase "That answer is literally crushing my soul"...which may or may not have been a proposed motivational phrase I wanted to paint on my classroom wall one year. Thanks for stopping that idea, my lovely wife! Children capture the words, syntax, and emotion from these conversations. If the people around our kiddos are stressed about the election, they will likely inherit some of these emotions as well. So, let's be tactful but honest. This election was particularly divisive—even causing friction for many of us within our inner circle, as 40% of Americans say the political climate has caused strain between them and their family members.[14] And although the election is over, we all know that the political division isn't going away anytime soon. Some students may carry the emotions associated with this challenge into your classroom.

Racial tension

On top of the political stress in America in 2020, the United States also experienced heightened racial tension. The outcomes of which continue to be significant, impacting several populations across the country. The Center of the Study of Hate and Extremism at California State University, San Bernardino examined hate crimes in 16 U.S. cities and found that Anti-Asian hate crimes increased by 149%, while overall hate crimes dropped 7% in 2020.[15] During this same year, among people of color, more than 44% reported discrimination as a major source of stress in their life, compared with 38% of people of color who answered the same in 2019.[13] When you break it down by race, Black Americans were the most likely to report discrimination as a stressor (48% Black vs. 43% Hispanic, 42% Native American, 41% Asian, and 25% White).[13]

Discrimination was not the only racial stressor, though. Deaths such as those of George Floyd, Breonna Taylor, and Jacob Blake sparked outrage and subsequently increased support for the Black Lives Matter Movement among people from every walk of life—no matter their age, race, ethnicity, socioeconomic status, spoken language, etc. Movements like this are fighting for racial equality, which I want to point out refers to society providing equal opportunity and treatment for all races (Black, Asian, American Indian, etc.). Following these tragic events, there were protests in over 2,000 U.S. cities (and more than 60 countries around the world) against systemic racism and police violence.[16]

Collectively, these protests mark what scholars are calling the largest movement in our country's history. To give you some context, the Women's March of 2017 drew in around three to five million people. According to leading research institutions, such as the Kaiser Family Foundation and Pew Research Center, anywhere from 15-26 million people participated in protests during the summer of 2020—that is 6-10% of the **entire** United States population.[17]

Pause and think about the enormity and weight of these events. Discussion and action towards racial equality has existed since the birth of our nation and is currently at the forefront of various calls to action among the American public—as it should be. Like us, our Gen Z students have experienced all of the emotions that come along with a historical moment in time such as this one. And, it's critical to realize, some of our students are *experiencing* the oppression fueling these movements.

As if we didn't endure enough...other notable events

It seems fitting to finish this chapter with other historical events in 2020 that garnered media coverage and may have caused stress among the American public. Please keep in mind that these events would have likely been *the* leading story in most other years, but with the chaos of the pandemic, they appeared for many as a transient blip on the proverbial radar of life.

- The Dow Jones industrial average experienced the worst single-day point drop on March 9th, 2020.

- An explosion at a port in Bierut, Lebanon, killed 200 people, injured 7,500 people, and destroyed a part of the capital city.

- More than 10 million acres burned as a result of fires across several U.S. states, including California, Idaho, Montana, and Oregon.[18]

- Donald Trump was impeached then acquitted on both articles of impeachment in February 2020.

- The United Kingdom officially left the European Union.

- Bushfires were rampant in Australia, while fires in the Amazon burned an area more than eight times the size of London.[19]

- Antarctica reached the highest temperature ever recorded.[15]

- America experienced the loss of many influential figures, including civil rights leader John Lewis, women's rights activist and supreme court justice Ruth Bader Ginsburg, and basketball legend Kobe Bryant.

- The 2020 Tokyo Summer Olympics were canceled and postponed until 2021.

Take a deep breath—it's all part of the mess of stress. While 2020 was a dumpster fire, I want to recall some bright moments associated with the pandemic. Health care workers worldwide shared data, strategies, and all sorts of clinical pearls to decrease the severe impact of COVID-19, leading to highly effective results. Grocery store clerks, Amazon workers, and gas station attendants all rose to the occasion to make sure our communities received what they needed to function. Teachers reached out to students and families with driveway chalk art, signs and balloons, and air hugs for their students. Virologists, clinicians, and public health experts launched one of the most rapid and efficacious vaccine efforts ever implemented in the history of humanity. It's impressive—all of it. And it reminds me of one of the most important lessons I ever learned about humanity. Fred Rogers used to teach us Gen Xers, back in the day, that when bad things happen, don't look at the mess, instead look for the helpers. You can always see good in the helpers.

Life doesn't stop...and so, neither will we. Please know that my goal with Chapter 5 was *not* to stir the pot within your heart and mind or add to your personal stress level—quite the opposite. My goal was to inspire understanding and empathy. This is what we will need to focus on if we want to meet the needs of our students over the next few years. And to do that well, we need to be aware and have insight into those potential stressors. The world events did impact most of our Gen Zers. They will continue to do so. That is a reality we all need to address in our own unique and caring ways.

As we transition to Chapter 6, we will dive into the stress that school closures and other cancelations added to our students' lives. This is important. While educators are normally part of the helpers that Fred Rodgers alluded to, circumstances around COVID-19 may have distanced us from our students' lives for various reasons, likely out of our control. That's not anyone's fault; it's just a reality that we need to accept. I would suggest that we also need to learn how to make corrections for this deficit. All of this is possible. We just have to move one step at a time. Because, before you can implement strategies that lead to improvements, you have to understand the problem fully.

Chapter 5 References

1. Falk, G., Carter, J. A., Nicchitta, I. A., Nyhof, E. C., & Romero, P. D. (2021, January 12). *Unemployment rates during the COVID-19 pandemic: In brief.* Congressional Research Service. https://fas.org/sgp/crs/misc/R46554.pdf

2. Alon, T., Doepke, M., Olmstead-Rumsey, J., & Tertilt, M. (2020). *The impact of COVID-19 on gender equality.* National Bureau of Economic Research. https://www.nber.org/papers/w26947

3. Pew Research Center. (2020, September 24). *Economic fallout from COVID-19 continues to hit lower-income Americans the hardest.* https://www.pewresearch.org/social-trends/2020/09/24/economic-fallout-from-covid-19-continues-to-hit-lower-income-americans-the-hardest/

4. Stokes, E. K., Zambrano, L., Anderson, K., Marder, E., Raz, K., ... Fullerton, K. (2020). Coronavirus disease 2019 case surveillance-United States, January 22–May 30, 2020. *Morbidity and Mortality Weekly Report, 69,* 759-765. https://doi.org/10.15585/mmwr.mm6924e2

5. Centers for Disease Control and Prevention. (2021, March 12). *Risk for COVID-19 infection, hospitalization, and death by race/ethnicity.* https://www.cdc.gov/coronavirus/2019-ncov/covid-data/investigations-discovery/hospitalization-death-by-race-ethnicity.html

6. National Nurses United. (2020, September). *Sins of omission: How government failures to track Covid-19 data have led to more than 1,700 health care worker deaths and jeopardize public health.* https://www.nationalnursesunited.org/sites/default/files/nnu/graphics/documents/0920_Covid19_SinsOfOmission_Data_Report.pdf

7. Centers for Disease Control and Prevention. (2019, September 15). *Hispanic/Latino Americans and type 2 diabetes.* https://www.cdc.gov/diabetes/library/features/hispanic-diabetes.html

8. Centers for Disease Control and Prevention. (2019, April). *Health, United States spotlight: Racial and ethnic disparities in heart disease.*

National Center for Health Statistics. https://www.cdc.gov/nchs/hus/spotlight/HeartDiseaseSpotlight_2019_0404.pdf

9. Office of Minority Health. (2021, March 1). *Diabetes and Hispanic Americans.* U.S. Department of Health and Human Services. https://minorityhealth.hhs.gov/omh/browse.aspx?lvl=4&lvlid=63

10. Price-Haywood, E. G., Burton, J., Fort, D., & Seoane, L. (2020). Hospitalization and mortality among black patients and white patients with Covid-19. *New England Journal of Medicine, 382*(26), 2534–2543. https://doi.org/10.1056/NEJMsa2011686

11. Jenco, M. (2020, December 29). *COVID-19 cases in children surpass 2 million.* American Academy of Pediatrics (AAP) News. https://www.aappublications.org/news/2020/12/29/covid-2million-children-122920

12. American Psychological Association. (2020, October 7). *2020 Presidential election a source of significant stress for more Americans than 2016 presidential race* [Press release]. http://www.apa.org/news/press/releases/2020/10/election-stress

13. American Psychological Association. (2020). *Stress in America™ 2020: A national mental health crisis.* https://www.apa.org/news/press/releases/stress/2020/sia-mental-health-crisis.pdf

14. American Psychological Association. (2020, November 19). *Outcome of Presidential election offers little stress relief, according to new survey* [Press release]. http://www.apa.org/news/press/releases/2020/11/post-election-stress

15. Center for the Study of Hate & Extremism CSUSB. 2021. *Fact sheet: Anti-Asian prejudice March 2021.* https://www.csusb.edu/sites/default/files/FACT%20SHEET-%20Anti-Asian%20Hate%202020%20rev%203.21.21.pdf

16. History.com editors. (2020, December 21). *2020: The year in events.* History. https://www.history.com/topics/21st-century/2020-events

17. Buchanan, L., Bui, Q., & Patel, J. K. (2020, July 3). *Black Lives Matter may be the largest movement in U.S. history.* The New York Times. https://www.nytimes.com/interactive/2020/07/03/us/george-floyd-protests-crowd-size.htm

18. Insurance Information Institute. (2021). *Facts + statistics: Wildfires.* https://www.iii.org/fact-statistic/facts-statistics-wildfires

19. Goodman, J., & Giles, C. (2020, August 29). *Amazon fires: Are they worse this year than before?* BBC News. https://www.bbc.com/news/world-latin-america-53893161

6

Getting schooled by school... Educational challenges of 2020

ake a moment to Google "COVID school closures." What did you find? More than you could read in a year? The pandemic was an enormous topic, accompanied by emotion, fractionated opinions, and at times, ferocity. To no surprise, the logistics of running a school during COVID-19 became quickly debated. Everyone seemed to have a goal, and therefore, a unique motivation behind their argument. And to say that a few side conversations evolved from every single decision that state or local school boards made may be *the* understatement of the year. There was an uncountable number of issues in 2020 associated with students, staff, and parents as we all tried to navigate education through remote, hybrid, and full in-person instruction, and every variant in between.

The decisions of 2020 are now behind us. You may agree with many of them. And alternatively, you may despise some of them. That's your choice and your journey. I respect that. However, what Chapter 6 of this book aims to do is straightforward but not simple: educators need to examine how some of these widespread changes implemented by most school districts impacted students and, subsequently, whether some students will need additional support.

Why? Remember that for every decision, there is an outcome. This life truth hasn't changed since SARS-CoV-2 wreaked havoc on schools. As such, it's worth our time to see what the long-term outcomes will be when it comes to common decisions that school districts made. Some choices will turn out to be beneficial for students, and others may have left children in a void or with a new set of problems. But in the end, it was a year of "survive and advance." And that, admittedly, is never ideal and the one statement that I think all sides would agree with.

Before we dive in and examine how school adjustments impacted Gen Zers, I want to take a moment to discuss the faculty that led them. Teachers and administrators often felt caught in the middle during this challenging time. Operational plans for learning were often a battleground in 2020, occasionally involving politics, community influence, and pressure from unions and parents. That's an unsettling situation. It can certainly make one feel like a pawn in a game of something much, much bigger. And I suppose, quite naturally, it creates an impression that your individual needs and concerns as an educator may not matter. But that is not what I'm aiming for in this discussion. There is nothing to be gained from stirring the pot and drumming up anger when this year needs to be about healing, repair, and reconnection.

As a fellow educator, I would like to acknowledge how incredibly difficult it was (and still is) to teach during a worldwide pandemic. Staff across the country were asked to put aside personal concerns, fears, and political beliefs so that they could continue placing the needs and wants of others first—more specifically, the needs of children. In a time where you could have just been selfish (because plenty of people were), you did the opposite. Case reports and news articles from around the nation illustrate how teachers sought to go above and beyond to help students. Whether it was teaching out of the back of a pickup for students that didn't have Wi-Fi or making desks with glass dividers to look like pick-up trucks for apprehensive kindergartners, educators did all they could to provide additional love and support in 2020.[1] And during all of this, educators were often scrutinized in the public eye. Schools were constantly evaluated with daily headlines and hourly social media posts as to whether or not they were doing a good job, while a virus that took thousands of lives continued to march across the nation. It was almost like a never-ending teaching evaluation during the worst of conditions. I acknowledge that. Please know that I was right there with you, serving as a teacher and health advisor for 25,000 students and staff and taking more emotional phone calls than I could have ever imagined.

I think we need to acknowledge and accept the stress, tears, nervous laughs, and everything else that faculty had to navigate. Why? Because the sheer fact that you're reading this now confirms that you did survive and you did advance. You are now stronger. And in many ways, you are likely more resilient than ever as an educator and a human. Few challenges remain in your career that could rival instruction in the midst of a lethal pandemic. Think about that. Really take a moment to internalize it. I find it all surreal.

In an effort to help put one more foot forward, would you kindly give me the chance to formally evaluate your hard work? Do you mind as a fellow educator if I offer my limited feedback regarding the love and support you offered your students during the worst of times? I think you may need this for closure. And although I am far from an expert in anything and certainly don't have all the answers, I do understand a lot of the clinical, public health, and curriculum-related challenges you experienced this year. It's a one-question evaluation. Please see the flowchart below and determine your performance.

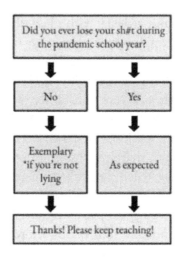

And that, my friends, pretty much sums up the emotion around school since the first case of COVID-19 crept into each one of our communities.

It's time to get into the nitty-gritty of some common adjustments that transpired at districts all across the country. The most universal and likely most impactful involved canceling in-person school for a duration of time. With this came the rapid implementation of remote learning and all the associated challenges. Now, please know that this chapter is not intended to persecute school leadership or public officials in any way—quite the opposite. Superintendents, school boards, nursing coordinators, principals, and lead custodians were all frantically following science at breakneck speeds while keeping up with new information and guidelines that were tossed in their faces each week. Much of what schools did was inherently reactionary. And that's fine. It's the reality of life in a pandemic. Nevertheless, decisions around COVID-19 unintentionally stripped away a lot of the support systems and resources students depend upon at school, which can lead to negative outcomes for students—some more profound than others. As caring educators, we need to be aware of these setbacks and the deficits they may have created. Let's investigate some school-specific and pandemic related challenges of students across America: i) loss of relationships, ii) educational disparities, iii) continued academic pressure, and iv) a forgotten future.

Loss of relationships

COVID-19 took an entire world of possibilities and reduced them to whatever was available in a student's bedroom. That's quite a reduction of space. But what's far more important than the reduction of cubic volume is the absence of people who generally fill that space, our friends and family. All students need connections to special people in their lives in order to stay healthy. These chosen few people form the meaningful connections and relationships we rely upon when good and bad events occur in our lives. As such, we value friends and family throughout every stage of our life. And if you want a visual representation of this concept, take time to observe a kindergarten class and high school seniors within weeks of graduation. What you'll see is fairly similar; relationships are the driving force in both settings when it comes to emotion and behavior.

As parents and educators, we spend countless hours focusing on healthy relationships and the work it takes to develop and maintain them. And we are not alone. Experts in psychology and child development share the same opinion. Although, their beliefs may be more data-driven than my own, which can be seen through my parenting this morning as I navigated a syrup-in-the-hair debacle... "Well, it's my job to make sure you don't grow up mean, it's bad for the world, and we already have enough going on! So please, go help your sister wash the syrup out of her hair, and you're not allowed to cut it this time!" Sorry, still working out some feelings from breakfast today.

At any rate, the National Scientific Council on the Developing Child made it clear how much they valued relationships when they posted on page one of their 2004 report that "young children experience their world as a collection of relationships, and these relationships affect virtually all aspects of their development—intellectual, social, emotional, physical, behavioral, and moral."[2] In short, developmental psychologists have argued for years that one of the foundational determinants for success or hardship in all areas of a child's development is relationships. That seems pretty important.

There are certainly many different types of relationships that are fostered, maintained, or ended during a typical school day. Some have names, such as best friends, girlfriends, boyfriends, close friends, favorites, and many more. Others do not have official titles but still have value—like the janitor that waves each morning as students enter the building, the teacher whose room is always a safe haven, or the secretary that leaves out candy for surly students and staff. Even recess has a role in important relationships. The American Academy of Pediatrics states that children develop intellectual constructs and cognitive understanding through interactive, manipulative experiences they can only get through play with their peers.[3,4] But what's most important to understand is that all of these relationships matter. All of them make school a second home.

Now, enter SARS-CoV-2 and the pandemic lockdown. Gone are the days of normal. Relationships now become relegated to whatever tech devices a student may have available and the comfort level of their parents and guardians allowing them to interact with friends. Most kids lost their second home in a fraction of a newscast, and school quickly became a blur. The relationships that made school worth rolling out of bed for at 6:30 a.m. were placed on hold. In-person conversations and hugs were replaced with Zoom, a platform most of us didn't know existed before March 2020. Yep, pixels on a laptop represented the new forced relationship that staff, students, and parents all had to enter into. And to no surprise, things changed. Relationships changed. It was no longer school as we knew it. Why? Because the remote learning experience lacked the relationships that kids craved and came to expect in their daily life. Eileen Wood, a first-grader teacher in Stoneham, Massachusetts, spelled this out quite nicely in a Washington Post article, "[Kids] come to school and they know what to expect. It's the stability, the repetition. They have art, they have gym, they have lunch, and they have teachers they know. And now it's all taken away."[5]

COVID-19 obliterated the relationships and routine of school. To no surprise, what remained was a shell or hollow construct of what school should be. Teachers and principals saw Zoom attendance dwindle and missing assignments increase. The interest in school was gone. Why? Because the relationships were gone. Dr. Beth Doll, a professor of educational psychology at the University of Nebraska-Lincoln, believes that it's relationships and the extracurricular connections of school that supports student engagement in the classroom.[6] As such, student overall well-being and academic interest stems more from relationships, including with the teacher, far more than the genius design of a lesson plan or how exciting content may be. And we know this. Ever chatted with a five-year-old about dinosaurs? Of course, you have! Once you mention the size of a T-rex tooth, you can't get them to stop talking about it. But have you ever seen a five-year-old pursue independent learning about dinosaurs? Nope. There is no one to share the excitement with. The relationships are lacking. And that makes dinosaurs, well, way less cool.

I mention all of these considerations around student relationships for a host of reasons. In the end, I suppose there is one primary takeaway for us educators: kids are not used to learning in isolation and rarely benefit from it. Instead, we find students learning in groups, interactive discussions, and collaborative endeavors. As educators, we know our students need to experience the relationships that come with learning, talking, and play. That's what school should be.

I think it's fair to say that there may actually be mountains of journal articles about the topic of relationships before the pandemic and even more added since COVID-19 began. Most of these additional contributions hit around April 2020, warning educators and parents that staying connected in relationships was necessary to navigate the pandemic. The authors were wise to say so. And in the end, schools did all they could to maintain those relationships. Teachers often visited students in their communities after working hours. Principals helped organize socially distanced drive-by experiences for students. Band directors taught music outdoors on the warm days of fall and spring, and coaches recorded workout plans as podcasts for their athletes, just so they could still hear their voice. Despite all of these heartfelt attempts, a lot of relationships disappeared in 2020. That's the reality of learning in a pandemic. We can't control that. But, as educators, we can control making it a priority to bring relationships back to the forefront of school.

Educational disparities

Working from home is TOUGH. Especially when my "office" includes leftover pancakes, a five-year-old that cries out while struggling with an iPad app, and a third-grader that insists on having an entire floor to herself so she can concentrate on math. And then, there is our puppy. Our sweet little golden retriever was inspired by the commotion and loved to bark during Zooms and chew on power cords for laptops. But she's not all bad. While I was setting up a science activity for my oldest, our cute little golden retriever sent two emails from my laptop. I have no idea how, but they were short and to the point, which I appreciate.

Comical, right? At times it was. But other times, it wasn't. I fully admit there were mornings where work was blowing up, and my daughters were feeling sassy, where I responded with anger or quiet tears. Keep in mind that's from an adult's perspective (at least chronologically) that handled substantial commotion in large emergency departments. What about the perspective of a child? I can't imagine what some of our students went through to try and concentrate on classes for eight hours a day and then do homework. It's almost laughable. And some students did not have the luxury of a living situation where the family could spread out. Many children report not having a quiet space for class, along with distractions such as assisting younger siblings with their school and completing household chores while their guardians did all they could to work from home and maintain their tenuous job status. But step back for a moment. All of these prior considerations assume that students' family members are healthy. The reality is that some high school and middle school students were often at home caring for sick family members. Trust me, I helped our health department with contact tracing...and at times, it was gut-wrenching to learn about the responsibilities some of these **children** took on.

Now, there are too many variables and factors to name in each child's home life that can produce disparity in remote learning. Adult supervision, emotional support, and teacher effort are just a few that scratch the surface. Deeper concerns might involve worries about eviction, increased divorce rates among couples, or escalation in domestic violence, which rose

10-20% in most urban environments during 2020.[7] These are all very real concerns. And then there are the fundamental needs for living life. Take food. In 2019, the National School Lunch Program (NSLP) provided free and reduced-cost lunches to 29.4 million children across the United States every day.[8] Closing schools without access to these meals suddenly introduced a critical issue that had to be solved for many families in dire circumstances. Sadly, all of these variables were part of a significant number of children's lives during remote "learning." It's extremely important to acknowledge that. And if those realizations sadden you, well, they probably should. Fixing the fallout from these issues is something that public health programs in every state should budget for, in my opinion. I encourage you to do your part in your local community to make that happen.

When COVID-19 hit, school districts set forth a plan that hinged upon one foundational component: internet access. Although 95% of teens have a cell phone, for schools, the pandemic highlighted that internet access is not as vast as we may have thought—cue the digital divide.[9]

Online school is not feasible for many students. To be exact, 4.4 million households with children don't have consistent access to a computer, and 9.4 million children ages 3-18 don't have internet.[10,11] Just like the SARS-CoV-2 virus itself, the digital divide disproportionately impacts low-income students and students of color.[10] These students are at higher risk of receiving no online instruction or low-quality instruction. In turn, students may experience a loss of learning and disengagement. Such educational loss may widen the achievement gap, heighten school dropout rates, and even create economic loss; McKinsey and Company predicts that current K -12 students could lose between $61,000 and $82,000 in lifetime earnings solely based on COVID-19's impact on learning.[12] And sadly, in some areas of the United States, this issue seemed to be swept under the rug and ignored.

So, what did these families do? How can students engage in learning when they don't even have access to the solution schools created? Well, they got creative. For some, this meant sitting outside school buildings, government buildings, or any place that had public Wi-Fi—often in the sweltering heat, or bitter cold, just for internet access to complete their lessons. Check out the CNN story that highlights the issue, sharing the experience of a fourth-grader in New Mexico, who walked to his elementary school each day to participate in his online work.[13] Keep in mind that CNN chose to air this story because this fourth-grader's situation was tragically common. But sadly, that shouldn't have been a surprise.

The digital divide was present pre-pandemic. However, students who lacked access to a computer or internet may have had other options, such as going to a library, community center, or after school program. But, when the pandemic hit, nearly all of these options were eliminated due to public building closures and social distancing guidelines. Many facilities still have not reopened to their fullest extent, and it will be some time before they do. I take time to point this out because those 9.4 million students we identified earlier had a very limited experience with remote school. This means that for many of them, little appreciable or contiguous learning took place during the remote or hybrid stages of instruction.

Take the spring of 2020 as an example. While limited data is available at this time on learning loss, the Northwest Evaluation Association projected that students returned to school (in any of its forms) in the fall of 2020 having made 70% gains in reading and only 50% in math; this means students may have entered our math classrooms close to an entire year behind.[14] As educators, we need to be ready for this reality. Students will, no doubt, feel apprehensive about their lost year. Educators will need to be flexible and creative to help children feel academically capable, regardless of their starting point.

Another topic regarding disparity involves special education. In 2018-2019, the percent of students ages 3-21 who received special education services under the Individuals with Disabilities Education Act (IDEA), was 7.1 million students.[15] This is approximately 14% of total public school enrollment, in case you were curious. These numbers include students with a specific learning disability, speech or language impairment, autism, developmental delay, intellectual disability, and more.[15] All of these students, just like their general education peers, have unique personalities, strengths, and areas for improvement. The difference is that students enrolled in special education often require unique support or scaffolding to optimize their educational journey. And to no surprise, a lot of these supportive measures occur in-person, in small groups and one-on-one settings. As you might imagine, COVID-19 presented a massive problem for this operational model.

School districts and administrators frantically worked with parents to solve these SPED support issues to the best of their ability. There were a lot of creative solutions. A short list includes:

- Zoom sessions for behavioral and academic support

- Using glass partitions and special transparent masks that were still OSHA compliant and CDC recommended for speech therapy

- Converting books and assignments to podcasts for those that struggled with dyslexia

- Opportunities to practice activities of daily living (ADLs) through socially distanced obstacle courses, adding an element of fun to the experience

These are just a few ideas out of the thousands of ingenious solutions that special educators drummed up. My heart and appreciation go out to all that tackled these challenges. I respect them for their effort, as do most parents of those children. All that said, every one of these solutions felt like the next best option. To be honest, during the pandemic, the "next best option" was the theme to most accommodations that special education students qualify for. This includes test accommodations, reading support, organizational skills, and addressing developmental exceptionalities. There's nothing wrong with this approach in terms of practicality. When you take the emotion out of it, the reality of the pandemic is that you are forced to balance individual needs against the concerns and needs of the population at large. A fast-moving and highly contagious virus that is lethal for specific subpopulations is a daunting counterweight on the see-saw of student needs, that's for sure.

And so, schools did the best they could. Survive and advance, choose the next best option...or however you want to describe it. But instead of using time and energy to critique their operational plans, I suggest that we focus on the future. Students in special education may require more support than ever as we emerge from this pandemic. We need to be honest with parents and students that it may take a while to get them back on the paths we strive for. Furthermore, there is only so much time in a school day. We need to prioritize the skills that these students need *ahead of content*. If there were ever a time to do that, I would argue it's now. Please don't create a false sense of pressure for these students that they need to relearn what's behind them. Rather, please teach them the skills they need to move forward. To quote my brother, who has a delightful and high-functioning autistic son, "I can teach my son everything about fractions at any time in his life. But I sure would love help getting him to chat with others and maintain eye contact while he has experts beside him." That seems to make a lot of sense to me. And by the way, my nephew agrees.

Grades and grit…while everything else quit

Despite all of these factors and changes in learning modes, the academic emphasis on grades did not change. While schools may have afforded students some latitude in the spring of 2020, that grace period did not necessarily carry into the fall semester of 2020 and beyond. The reality is that most school districts expected our secondary students to perform as if the world hadn't been flipped upside down. College applications still marched on, justifying the need for competitive GPAs, class rank, and selections for student honors. Yep. Grades did not go away, even as the pandemic raged on. And as educators, we were still expected to teach to our state standards and, as a result, expect our kids to progress academically at the same pace—although most educators knew this wasn't realistic, let alone possible.

So, was the pandemic school year all about optics with no substance? Tough to say. I certainly can't answer that. But, regardless of how you or I interpret it, grades still produced stress and impacted students. Many mental health and developmental experts are pouring over data to determine how academic pressure influenced students during the pandemic. One example is Active Minds, a nonprofit that partners with over 15 national organizations to support young adult's mental health. The staff at Active Minds conducted a survey in April 2020 that garnered 3,239 high school and higher education students. Keep in mind that this was early in the pandemic when some schools were broadcasting that grades would be frozen or that students could only improve their semester grades. Despite those reassurances, 38% of students reported that academic studies were their most stressful concern.[16] Furthermore, when asked what the most important student mental health topic school leadership should be thinking about, the answer wasn't depression, maintaining connections, or suicide risk—it was "academic leniency." Wow. That says a lot about the obsession regarding grades. The world is falling apart, isolation has become the new norm, and concerns about grades trump them all. To top this off, remember, not all school districts were as lenient with grading during this time as I described above.

Many students see school as their best way out of tough situations. Family issues, impending financial stressors, or living situations complicate their lives. Think about that. What if a student had a slide in their academics and no opportunities to showcase any extracurricular achievements? It fuels a lot of anxiety for students and, to no surprise, creates the erroneous impression that a student needs a 4.0 to make up for their remote learning performance. And truthfully, do any of us know if they're right or wrong? I hope not. But trade schools, the military, allied health programs, junior colleges, and more like to use cut-offs. Right now, I can't look a student in the eye and let them know for sure the impact of low grades in a pandemic year. Could you? That genuinely makes me sad. These kids have enough insight to know that even though they are much more than a grade, those letters open and close doors for them. That's a lot of weight on your shoulders if school is your only way out as a child in a tough situation.

And what about our university-bound students? Look at the apprehension many older Gen Zers experienced as they applied to college during a pandemic. What a mess. Robert Franek, editor-in-chief of the Princeton Review, points out some of the stressors for university applicants that have accentuated in the past year.[17] It comes down to the culmination of all components of the application process. Did you manage to take the ACT or SAT? Does the school you dream about claim that these standardized tests are optional this year? Do you exercise that option, or does it appear academically sheepish? How do you explain the sudden drop-off in grades that occurred in 2020? Is a C with depression equivalent to an A before depression? And hey, one more, do you and/ or your parents still have enough money to afford a college degree after job changes in the pandemic? There are a lot of moving parts to apply to college to begin with, but even more so this past year. As such, many students are paralyzed about how their academic performance will influence their future.

Forgotten future

CANCELED. It's a word that the world heard all too often during 2020. It seemed to apply to so much: vacations, concerts, family reunions, birthday celebrations, sporting events, religious gatherings, and more. In a student's life, the word "canceled" took on a heavier meaning when it started impacting the aspects of school they enjoy the most. Think back to your elementary school days. How amazing were class birthdays, the Daddy-daughter dance, field days, and so forth? All of the surprises and end-of-the-year hugs that elementary students missed this year seem almost uncountable. Additionally, do you recall how important it was to live out your last day as a kindergartener before becoming a big kid and moving to first grade? Well, kids in 2020 just had to imagine it. Now, jump to adolescence. Some of my happiest moments (that were parent-approved) included running track with my friends, Friday night football games, after-school band practice, prom, and the opportunity to laugh about the week's events at school. All of those things involve school and related activities.

Researchers have discussed the value and benefit of participating in extracurricular activities for quite some time. There is a plethora of quantitative and qualitative evidence linking improved physical, emotional, academic, and social well-being to participation in extracurricular activities. In fact, there is even research on how school activities improve emotional regulation and grades.[18] Adding to this list of benefits is something else that all educators see and observe; extracurricular activities often help troubled students turn the corner, sparking excitement for school and developing a critical sense of belonging. In many ways, these activities create a sense of identity. For young students, extracurricular activities expand who they are as a person and often impact their self-esteem and self-efficacy, two critical protective factors for resilience and life satisfaction.

Both schools and outside activities, such as dance and taekwondo studios, did their best to adapt to the circumstances and still provide students with the opportunity for involvement. However, involvement during the pandemic is different. Dance class may occur through Zoom. Indoor swim may require a lap lane reservation and no teammates. And while music is audio-driven, playing the clarinet for your laptop as your band teacher stares back at you is kind of weird. As students continue to remind us, everything is just different. Individual accommodations for specific activities are not the issue. Rather, it appears that society is worn down by the totality of these changes and their cumulative effect. It appears that SARS-CoV-2 canceled normalcy, and it has not been courteous enough to let us know when we all get to return.

The short-term impact of this uncertainty, with cancelations and accommodations, is typically frustration and boredom. However, the long-term outcome of multiple cancellations yields more profound results. Going back to the Active Minds student survey, 74% of college students struggled with maintaining a schedule and routine in life because so many things were canceled. This disturbance, in turn, led to a drop off in confidence and only 69% of students feeling hopeful about their future. These feelings can spiral into depression, which is why 20% of college students admitted their mental health took a nosedive by April of 2020.[16]

Now, let's go one step further. Look at the physiological changes that occur from ambiguity. When the future is uncertain, it often leads to anxiety and a heightened perception of threat and fear.[19] Why? There are many reasons, but the bottom line is that escalating uncertainty triggers concerns about an individual's needs being met. Sometimes these may be emotional. Sometimes these may be more biological, such as securing food, water, or sleep. Either way, persistent ambiguity and concern trigger a neuroendocrine response that releases adrenaline and cortisol, often called stress hormones. This combination of hormones increases the brain's utilization of glucose, increases heart rate and blood pressure, and releases products needed for body repair. It sounds like a good thing at first, and in short-term fight or flight situations, it is. However, maintaining this physiology over weeks to months can become exhausting, as your body is rapidly consuming resources and, subsequently, your internal organs are taking the heat over time.[20] Seems like a cycle you want to break, right? Agreed. But that's tough to do when one thing after another is canceled or rescheduled, and your routine for life has exploded.

Conclusion

When it's all said and done, educators and administrators made operational decisions with the best intentions. Many times, politics or other confounders may have blurred the issue, but I still believe that those who entered education did so because they care about children. Nevertheless, the entire educational system had to find its role in the community effort to navigate COVID-19 while still trying to meet the goals and directives of schools at large. This challenge encompassed all schools, regardless if they were well funded, scraping by, positioned in rural settings, or centered prominently in the middle of a city. And although some districts had more financial means or support to wade through the COVID mess, the dilemma was present for all.

It's in that same spirit that school officials, policymakers, and teachers need to move forward. All educators need to acknowledge the loss students experienced when schools were remote or in modified learning settings. Students took a huge hit. They lost their second home. And while there is no need to point fingers or assign blame, there is significant value in anticipating the deficits created and how to ease kids back to the schedules, opportunities, and intangibles that our brick-and-mortar buildings provide.

Chapter 6 References

1. Belleville, D. (2020, August 19). *Teacher turns desks with shields into tiny trucks to make first graders comfortable with social distancing.* 13 News Now. https://www.13newsnow.com/article/news/health/coronavirus/teacher-desk-trucks-social-distancing/67-dbd9e0ff-6daf-4eed-9d6 7-60a0e13e42df

2. National Scientific Council on the Developing Child. (2004). *Young children develop in an environment of relationships.* Working Paper No. 1. http://www.developingchild.net

3. Council on School Health. (2013). The crucial role of recess in school. *Pediatrics, 131*(1), 183. https://doi.org/10.1542/peds.2012-2993

4. National Association of Early Childhood Specialists in State Departments of Education. (2002). *Recess and the importance of play: A position statement on young children and recess.* https://eric.ed.gov/?id=ED463047

5. Strauss, V. (2020, April 22). *How relationships between teachers and students are being tested in covid-19 crisis.* The Washington Post. https://www.washingtonpost.com/education/2020/04/22/how-relationships-between-teachers-students-are-being-tested-covid-19-crisis/

6. Stringer, H. (2020, October 13). *Zoom school's mental health toll on kids.* American Psychological Association. http://www.apa.org/news/apa/2020/10/online-learning-mental-health

7. Boserup, B., McKenney, M., & Elkbuli, A. (2020). Alarming trends in US domestic violence during the COVID-19 pandemic. *The American Journal of Emergency Medicine, 38*(12), 2753–2755. https://doi.org/10.1016/j.ajem.2020.04.077

8. U.S. Department of Agriculture – Economic Research Service. (2020, October 1). *National school lunch program.* https://ers.usda.gov/topics/food-nutrition-assistance/child-nutrition-programs/national-school-lunch-program

9. Anderson, M., & Jiang, J. (2018, May 31). *Teens, social media, & technology 2018*. Pew Research Center. https://www.pewresearch.org/internet/2018/05/31/teens-social-media-technology-2018/

10. USA Facts. (2020, September 28). *More than 9 million children lack internet access at home for online learning*. https://usafacts.org/articles/internet-access-students-at-home/

11. Camera, L. (2020, April 1). *Disconnected and disadvantaged: Schools race to give students access*. US News & World Report. www.usnews.com/news/education-news/articles/2020-04-01/schools-rush-to-get-students-internet-access-during-coronavirus-pandemic

12. Dorn, E., Hancock, B., Sarakatsannis, J., & Viruleg, E. (2020, June 1). *COVID-19 and student learning in the United States: The hurt could last a lifetime*. McKinsey & Company. https://www.mckinsey.com/industries/public-and-social-sector/our-insights/covid-19-and-student-learning-in-the-united-states-the-hurt-could-last-a-lifetime

13. Williams, D., & Zdanowicz, C. (2020, October 23). *A fourth-grader walked to school to use its WiFi because he didn't have internet at home*. CNN. https://www.cnn.com/2020/10/22/us/new-mexico-school-internet-trnd/index.html

14. Kuhfeld, M., & Soland, J. (2020). *The learning curve: Revisiting the assumption of linear growth across the school year*. (EdWorkingPaper: 20-214). Annenberg Institute at Brown University. https://doi.org/10.26300/bvg0-8g17

15. National Center for Education Statistics. (2020, May). *The condition of education: Students with disabilities*. https://nces.ed.gov/programs/coe/indicator_cgg.asp

16. Active Minds. (2021). *The impact of COVID-19 on student mental health: April 2020 survey data*. https://www.activeminds.org/studentsurvey/

17. Anderson, J. (2021, February 18). *Harvard EdCast: College admissions during COVID*. Harvard Graduate School of Education. https://www.gse.harvard.edu/news/21/02/harvard-edcast-college-admissions-during-covid

18. Roopesh B.N. (2018). All work and no play: The importance of extracurricular activities in the development of children. In: Deb S.

(Eds.), *Positive schooling and child development*. Springer, Singapore. https://doi.org/10.1007/978-981-13-0077-6_15

19. Grupe, D. W., & Nitschke, J. B. (2013). Uncertainty and anticipation in anxiety: an integrated neurobiological and psychological perspective. *Nature Reviews Neuroscience, 14*(7), 488–501. https://doi.org/10.1038/nrn3524

20. Mayo Clinic Staff. (2019, March 19). *Chronic stress puts your health at risk*. Mayo Clinic. https://www.mayoclinic.org/healthy-lifestyle/stress-management/in-depth/stress/art-20046037

7

The last straw...Accelerating mental health concerns

Assuming I drank the perfect amount of caffeine, Chapters 5 and 6 should have provided a clear picture regarding the powerful stressors school-aged youth encountered inside and outside of school during much of the disruptive pandemic. Individually, these stressors have the potential to influence daily life, adding burdens for an unknown amount of time. Cumulatively, these burdens carry the possibility of forever changing a child's perspective, dreams, and ability to navigate life. That's undeniably powerful. And in a way, I think it's fair to make the claim that many Gen Zers (and for that matter, many adults) experienced the greatest mental stress test of their life thus far.

As it stands right now, the term "stress test" is merely two words stacked side by side with ample room for interpretation. For this discussion, you and I need to have the same level of understanding. It's important for you, the dedicated reader, and me, the over-caffeinated author with a golden retriever chewing on my desk, to lock in the same concept of what a stress test truly is. It will enhance our understanding, interpretation, and discussion of the next round of data this book offers. So, without further delay, let's explore the concept of a stress test in depth by examining one of the most common ways it's implemented in our modern world—the cardiac stress test, a frequently used assessment to screen for signs of an impending heart attack. Seems pretty important. That's because it is. And, if you allow me some latitude, I'll show you how cardiac stress tests have a good amount in common with the mental health "stress test" our students just experienced.

To start, it's important to understand a guiding principle of medicine: heart attacks are weird and scary. For most patients, heart attacks seem to present suddenly and without notice. Yet, in reality, the build-up to a heart attack is a rather lengthy process, often requiring decades of cholesterol build-up on the inner walls of the artery. Along with other malfunctions, cholesterol, platelets, and inflammation can lead to a complete blockage of an artery on one fateful day. In that regard, a heart attack seems like an unexpected event. However, per the process I just described, there is nothing unexpected about it at all...well, assuming the patient and health care provider know the process is occurring. Weird, huh?

Now, the bright side of this cardiac conundrum is that health care providers can screen for heart attacks using cardiac stress tests. So, what does this test entail? Do nurses and doctors ask your heart to do some high-level math with a timer in the background, all while yelling at it? Does the stress lab ask your heart to design a presentation for your boss in less than two hours while 263 coworkers pop into your office to ask irrelevant questions? Obviously, not. How do we stress the heart? Simple. Ask it to work harder. Sounds a lot like what all of us went through in 2020.

There is obviously more to it, though. At a closer level, stress tests are scientifically and thoughtfully designed moments of increasing labor for the heart over timed intervals. Each interval correlates with increasing exercise demands. How? The test's stages ask the heart to meet the exercise demands by either: i) increasing how fast the heart beats, ii) increasing how hard the heart contracts, or iii) increase heart rate and contraction strength together. But how do health care providers know if a patient handled the cardiac stress well or not? The answer is straightforward. For each age group of individuals, there is a well-defined average regarding how long able-bodied patients, presumably without cardiac disease, can exercise without complications or need to stop. Health care providers will examine the performance of a patient in reference to these averages and factor in other important metrics such as EKG changes, vital sign changes, and patient symptoms. And there you go, that's the basics of understanding a cardiac stress test!

However, wait a second. For those of you that really paid attention, I am guessing a few things are still confusing when it comes to stress tests. Perhaps, even unsettling. For starters, the whole idea of a cardiac stress test is to look for abnormalities and problems with the heart...by piling additional stress and work on top of normal "stress." Seems a little cruel, huh? Take a relaxing breath and enjoy the peace of knowledge to know that it's actually not. Cardiac stress tests need to discover previously hidden problems, issues critical to the heart's performance, and survival, that need to be identified. So, the heart is incrementally put to increased levels of demands in a controlled, monitored, and safe environment. Stress tests afford health care providers the opportunity to discover life-threatening issues with minimal risk and address them before they produce an unexpected and weird heart attack. This makes cardiac stress tests quite valuable.

Now, I suspect you know where I'm going with this. The COVID-19 pandemic, with all its external pressures and challenges, served as a profound mental health stress test. It enrolled billions of patients without consent and put their resilience, coping mechanisms, and zest for life to the test. In many ways, the pandemic stress test was analogous to the cardiac stress tests we are familiar with.

- Stress tests demand increasing the performance of their subject in an effort to see if the subject can meet the demands as well as most people in their peer group. Meeting the norm makes it less likely there is a problem. Both a cardiac stress test and the pandemic stress test do that.

- What about the escalating challenges? As individuals progressed through the pandemic, they piled on one incremental stressor after another, similar to the increased exercise demands of a cardiac stress test.

- Finally, did the pandemic stress test help identify problems? Did it discover those with subclinical mental health challenges? Tough to say. This pandemic was clearly not a scientifically approved study, which I wrote about somewhat glibly in Chapter 5 to make a point. All that said, there are plenty of credible institutions that monitor metrics of mental health strain on an annual basis. As such, we can turn to their data to see if there was an uptick in mental health visits and diagnoses during the mayhem of COVID-19.

We can find some good from this challenge. Just like a cardiac stress test, we should expect those with pre-existing challenges or fragility to show signs of that burden. It may not have been exactly like running on a treadmill, but I can assure you that this pandemic exercised our mental health resilience. And as such, one would expect there to be signs of increasing decompensation for those with mental health challenges. The rest of this chapter examines how, if any, the pre-pandemic trends in mental health changed amidst one of the world's most profound mental health experiments.

Focus #1–Trends in mental health visits

"During these uncertain times..." This phrase. I'm not sure how to put into words how I feel about it. Is it even possible to estimate how many times the average American heard these words during 2020? I'm not sure if I could go back and figure that out. However, I am confident that this set of buzzwords became seared into the frontal lobe of my brain. So much so that I avoid using them at all costs, as they seem cold, distant, and inadequate in terms of grasping the emotional magnitude of the pandemic. To be honest, I would have preferred that my boss used an alternate word choice, one that added a human element—verbiage that staff could truly internalize and relate to when discussing all the uncertainty around COVID-19. Perhaps, something like the following. "During this dumpster fire of a year...." or more poignantly, "while traversing this sh#t hot mess..." Sadly, I think those would have connected with me far better.

Nevertheless, the words I don't care for are an accurate description of 2020. Public health guidelines rapidly evolved, media reports often conflicted with each other, and moods at home and work seemed to follow Disney's Space Mountain roller coaster's path, jumping in every direction in the dark. It was truly an uncertain time. And in many ways, I recognize that it still is because the pandemic represented an experience that everyone who wasn't alive in 1918 hadn't encountered before. But for now, let's just concentrate on the 2020-2021 school year and how that ambiguity impacted our students.

While most of us like having choices in our life, wide-open uncertainty can lead to significant setbacks. Aoife O'Donovan, PhD, is an associate professor of psychiatry at the UCSF Weill Institute for Neurosciences. Dr. O'Donovan's area of expertise includes ways persistent psychological stress can lead to mental disorders, such as post-traumatic stress disorder (PTSD).[1] Most of us are aware that ambiguity can force us to expend time and effort to predict potential outcomes of a situation and how we will deal with them. Depending upon the circumstances, this can be fantastical fun or utterly exhausting. For example, I love thinking about how our family will spend our first day when we make it back to Disney World. What rides will we take? How should we use fast passes? What character meals will bring the biggest smiles to my kids' faces? The flip side is not as enjoyable. What would we do if my wife lost her job in the pandemic? If the grocery store shelves go empty, will there be violence over food? Should we scrape together a trust fund for our girls in the incredibly slim chance that something happens to both of us in the pandemic? These are just a few examples of millions of moments of uncertainty and how they exercise our brains.

Dr. O'Donovan points out that the stress of uncertainty, especially when prolonged, is one of the most insidious stressors we experience as human beings.[1] It's also capable of generating a substantial amount of anxiety. If you're wondering why this is the case, there is an intriguing evolutionary explanation. Uncertainty forces our brain to make a decision, occasionally without sufficient information. That, in itself, forces the human mind to invest energy and rapidly consider what venturing into the unknown might result in. And, there are innumerable possibilities to consider. That can be mentally exhausting.

To no surprise, your brain is hard-wired in numerous areas to scan for potential threats, as danger can impact longevity, reproduction, and survival. This is an evolutionary trait that animals, including humans, utilize throughout life for protection. This pathway in your brain doesn't just look for known threats; it also considers potential harm. Any time a course of action is not definitively safe, your brain may perceive the situation as potentially dangerous. This perception in our consciousness can lead to anxiety for many of us, which tells a more primitive part of our brain, known as the hypothalamus, to release stress hormones that prepare the human body for fight or flight. That's a profound neurologic response to the unknown. In case this still doesn't make sense, or you are more of an experiential learner, think back to the first time you: i) jumped off a high dive into the pool, ii) tried skiing fast down a steep mountain, iii) delivered a speech to a large crowd, or iv) showed up for your first day at a new job. Did your heart race? Did you feel nervous? Maybe even nauseous? These are all physiologic responses from your neuroendocrine system, and as you know all too well, they are very real. But the key point is this: all of these manifestations can be triggered by making a decision with insufficient information that forces you to move into the unknown.

Combine this insight regarding uncertainty and multiply it by all the unknowns Americans dealt with at the federal, state, local, and individual level last year. Yep, our good ole friend 2020 really tossed us into a whole new version of life in the unknown. Jokes aside, that's an awful lot of presumptive decisions and chronic stress for people to navigate. As such, one might expect an increase in mental health strain during the pandemic. Specifically, anxiety, excessive worrying, obsession, compulsion, irrational fear, and other thought disturbances might have seen an increase over already escalating trends pre-pandemic.

The Centers for Disease Control and Prevention published a compelling review in November of 2020. Focusing on youth under 18 years of age, the report utilized National Syndromic Surveillance Program (NSSP) data, which identified mental health visits to emergency departments across the United States between January 1, 2020 and October 17, 2020.[2] This resulted in an enormous data set, encompassing 47 states and representing 73% of all emergency department visits. That's a lot of kiddos. What the CDC found was quite concerning when it comes to the mental health of school-aged children.

- The average reported number of children's mental health-related ED visits overall was higher from January 1-March 15, 2020, than in 2019.[2]

- The number of children's mental health-related ED visits decreased sharply from mid-March 2020 through early April and then increased steadily through October 2020.[2]

- During the same time, the overall proportion of reported children's ED visits for mental health-related concerns increased and remained higher through the end of the reporting period in 2020 than that in 2019.[2]

- The proportion of mental health-related ED visits among children increased 66%, from 1,094 per 100,000 during April 14-21, 2019 to 1,820 per 100,000 during April 12-18, 2020.[2] (Note: the increase in volume per 100,000 goes against the thought that the increase in mental health cases was based upon percentages only and a shrinking number of ED cases.)

Now, a reminder here that emergency departments are often the first point of care for children undergoing an unexpected (or new) mental health crisis. This is true in most years, but especially during 2020, when mental health services were reduced and offices were temporarily closed. This is particularly relevant if you wonder why mental health visits rose proportionally in the emergency departments during the pandemic. Was it because emergency departments were one of the few remaining sites to receive care? If limited availability was the issue, we should have seen an increase in many areas of patient services, such as wound care, medical management, and surgical issues.

A report in *The Journal of the American Medical Association* from August 2020 confirms that's not the case. This study looked at 24 emergency departments across five states, spanning rural and urban settings, and noted a decrease in emergency department visits ranging from 41.5% to 63.5% over a four-month period.[3] Furthermore, data from the NSSP found that between March 29-April 25, 2020, when widespread shelter-in-place orders were in effect, ED visits for the general population (all ages) declined 42% compared to 2019 volumes.[2] Both of these sources suggest that the overall volume of emergencies fell during the pandemic, making the rise we see in mental health cases even more significant.

It's important to keep in mind that there is no pause on disease. Pandemic or not, all the traditional ailments that communities deal with still exist, meaning that the worldwide prevalence of problems such as asthma, diabetes, and arthritis probably held quite steady. And, individuals with these conditions are expected to have emergencies and ED visits at a fairly steady rate. Yet, we saw a drop in emergency visits and emergency care. This suggests that many individuals, particularly between March and April 2020, when public health authorities stressed shelter in place, hesitated to seek medical care. The hospital was seen as a place where you might run into COVID-19, which evoked a good amount of fear. Thus, the increase in mental health cases is potentially underreported, given that some affected individuals hid at home, bravely trying to navigate the challenge without medical care.

Focus #2—Assessment of anxiety in youth

The number of issues to worry about during the height of COVID-19 was genuinely remarkable. Chapter 5 discussed some of the economic fallout, health-related concerns, social polarization, and racial tension that most communities dealt with during the pandemic. I fully admit the discussion represents a small fraction of what was out there and, in many ways, is *still* out there. A series of books could be written on one of those factors alone. It's staggering to try and internalize all the pressures these issues present. I think about it from time to time and feel somewhat ashamed that the totality of COVID-19 makes me feel overwhelmed, and I'm not even part of one of the age groups or demographics that absorbed the greatest risk from the virus and marginalization from the social response. It's a lot to ponder.

But for many people, the biggest stressor was not the pressure points we knew about but rather what we did not know. Don't forget that uncertainty is in close proximity to anxiety at all times. Venturing out into the unknown, where results can only be predicted, and harm is a possibility, forces the deepest parts of our brain to worry. This is the way humans are built, and it's not a terrible response. A healthy dose of periodic fear is probably what kept me alive during my teen years (especially when packed into a car with music blaring, friends screaming, and curves on backcountry roads calling). However, excessive amounts of fear or situations where ambiguity and uncertainty persist for too long can obviously be a problem. Those factors create the right environment for pathologic anxiety to creep in and take hold.

So, did anxiety prey upon the abundance of worry and ambiguity in 2020? Did anxiety sneak its way into a large portion of our student's daily routines, insidiously altering their self-esteem, self-efficacy, and hope for the future? Based on the widespread stressors and the loss of school as students knew it, I would be shocked if anxiety didn't grab a foothold in many of our students' lives. And, how could it not? We are built to worry at specific times, enhancing our fight or flight abilities and increasing our evolutionary chances of survival. However, we are not built for the anxiety pathway in our brain to be persistently triggered over long periods of time, and there is definitely data to support this realization.

The Kaiser Family Foundation (KFF), a nonprofit organization that has focused on national health issues since the 1920s, released a report in February 2021 that demonstrates a spike in the perception of anxiety amongst the United States population.[4] KFF sends an annual survey in January that solicits questions that screen for generalized anxiety, using two proven scales known as GAD-2 and PHQ-2. In 2019, they found that 11% of household respondents met the criteria for anxiety and/or depression. In January 2020, which was the beginning of America's involvement with COIVD-19, these numbers soared to 41.1% of household respondents, almost four times greater than their previous assessment.[4]

Kaiser is not alone in their findings. A large-scale German study examining over 1,100 general practices and 1.9 million patients also found similar results, noting a monthly increase in respondents' anxiety when comparing the first six months of 2019 to the first six months of 2020.[5]

January	February	March	April	May	June
Increase 4% compared to January 2019	Increase 4% compared to February 2019	Increase 34% compared to March 2019	Increase 8% compared to April 2019	Increase 2% compared to May 2019	Increase 19% compared to June 2019

Source: Jacob et al., 2020

Now, it's important to know that both of these studies focused on participants 18 years of age and over; however, this information is still relevant to children. Why? *The Journal of Abnormal Child Psychology* addressed this in 2010 with an impressive review of multiple data sets that confirm the following: parental anxiety disorders facilitate increased chances for symptomatic anxiety and depression in children.[6] Thus, for the foreseeable future, there are many families across the nation that will send children back to schools with a higher propensity for anxiety.

Further, and perhaps more compelling, are the trends insurance companies began to see with telehealth visits. Numerous private practices, outpatient facilities, and hospital-based practices were asked (or forced) to use telehealth for much of 2020. The thought was to reduce the risk of SARS-CoV-2 transmission in health care offices, especially around patients that might be medically fragile. And in turn, mitigating risk factors for health care workers increased the chance that these providers would remain healthy and continue to provide care. These decisions boosted telehealth to a place of prominence in terms of routine yet important medical care across the globe. Telehealth has become so important that insurance companies are furiously combing through data to see where and how the platform can persist following the pandemic. Patients can use this format to receive care and sometimes at a fraction of the cost of a traditional office visit. With all that in mind, The Child Mind Institute launched a massive investigation into telehealth, all of which can be seen in their 2020 online report. Two impressive pieces of outcome data regarding telehealth include:

- Anxiety (40%) and depression (37%) are the most common mental health challenges leading parents to seek telehealth services for their children.[7]

- More than two-thirds of parents who sought help for their child since the start of the pandemic said they had witnessed a decline in their child's emotional well-being (72%) and behavioral changes (68%). This is what prompted them to request assistance.[7]

The final piece of data I'll share regarding pediatric anxiety during COVID-19 comes from a study published in January 2021 for *Psychological Medicine* that serves as the leading research journal for the Cambridge University Press Public Health Emergency Collection. The inquiry took a look at 451 youth (ranging from 12-22 years old) in the New York City area between March and May 2020, when America's largest city was experiencing the full force of COVID's destructive elements.[8] Various mental health metrics were assessed and then compared to data from the Screen for Child Anxiety Related Disorders between December 2014 - July 2019. The study confirmed a large number of predictions with the following[8]:

- Anxiety intensifies as one moves from late childhood through early adulthood.

- Findings suggest that the COVID-19 pandemic contributed to increased symptoms of generalized anxiety by roughly 17% and social anxiety by approximately 10% compared to 2019 values of similar age groups.

- Females experienced increased depression, panic attacks, and physical symptoms such as a fast heart rate and sweating.

The widespread pressures and worries associated with COVID-19 clearly exacerbated individuals with pre-existing anxiety and pushed a fair number of individuals to a new anxiety diagnosis. It's fair to assume that there will be mountains of data released in 2021 and beyond that further accentuates and validates the early publications. Even as I write this, Germany has released some troubling mental health data regarding the 13.7 million youth they want to protect.[9] More countries, including the United States, will follow with large-scale analyses. I encourage you to keep up with the data and the reports. It's wise to be informed as time goes on. That said, I also encourage you to trust the initial results and begin making adaptations to your classroom that will help those anxious Gen Zers in need. Because friends, if 2020 was truly the dumpster fire many of us refer to, then think of anxiety as the gasoline that fueled it.

Focus #3—Depression trends in the pediatric population

It would be wonderful if there were a silver lining to mental health challenges in 2020. For example, I wish I could tell you that anxiety was the only diagnosis to worsen, and somehow other issues were held in check. But sadly, that's not the case. Evidence suggests that depression also expanded its grasp upon individuals, as many were severely impacted by the trials of the pandemic and the subsequent challenges of lockdown. Although this phenomenon struck most age groups, school-aged children were among the population cohorts that took the brunt of the psychological and depressive impact during the pandemic. This holds true for many nations across the globe.

- An expansive study in China investigated 3,613 school-aged children, ranging from ages 7-18, and found that the prevalence of clinical depression symptoms in children and adolescents was 22.28% during the COVID-19 outbreak, which was much higher than the widespread estimation of 13.2% for China's youth during a former study.[10]

- Turning to Europe, a combined study from Italy and Spain surveyed parent perception of 1,143 children, 3-18 years, regarding behavioral changes during the pandemic. Overwhelmingly, 85.7% of parents reported disruptive changes in their child's emotional stability and behaviors during shelter at home directives. Behavioral changes observed included: difficulty concentrating (76.6%), boredom/lack of engagement (52%), irritability (39%), restlessness (38.8%), nervousness (38%), loneliness (31.3%), and excessive worry (30.1%). Of note, the study also points out that children were more likely to experience behavioral changes if their parents modeled observable setbacks from stress as well.[11]

- Within the United States, a group of researchers under the direction of Dr. Maria Loades jump-started discussions by searching for prior information on how isolation and loneliness affect mental health in youth. Their rapid review focused on validated research over the past few decades, encompassing more than 63 studies and 51,000 participants, with a mean age of 15.3 years. In the end, Loades and colleagues found that duration of loneliness was more predictive of depression than intensity of loneliness, and that social isolation could increase the risk of depression for the following nine years.[12]

Admittedly, the bulleted information only represents three scientific inquiries across the globe. There are clearly far more. Nevertheless, this small sample size suggests that the novel pressures and challenges pertaining to COVID-19 were universally felt by school-aged children virtually everywhere. And to no surprise, many behavioral changes that correlate with risk factors for major depressive disorders were observed. Data such as this foreshadows the increasing need for addressing childhood depression in our schools, homes, and communities. However, as good as this information is, it's still predictive. Much of what has been published about 2020 thus far limits the discussion to *predicting* how COVID-19 influenced the perspective and mental health of many Gen Zers and what that might look like for the foreseeable future. So, let's go one step further and examine outcome data.

To truly see what happened to the prevalence of youth depression during the pandemic, we need to follow the money trail. Quite literally. Insurance claims offer insight into the frequency of a particular diagnosis, as well as associated demographic information. And one of the most profound assessments of the medical happenings of 2020 is a report from Fair Health. We utilized this report before in Part 1 of this book and will do so again, examining the report from March 2021. This monumental effort investigated 32 billion private health care claims filed between January and November 2020, representing an enormous data set and an equally large opportunity to assess the frequency of youth depression. Here are some highlights[13]:

- First and foremost, Fair Health states that medical health insurance claims for United States teens doubled early in the pandemic compared to the same time span in 2019.

- The study was able to assess how mental health needs progressed throughout the year. For patients aged 13-18, mental health insurance claims took a monumental jump in March 2020 (97.0%) and even more so during April 2020 (103.5%).

- Keep in mind that while youth mental health diagnoses rose substantially, medical claims fell 53.3% in March and 53.4% in April, probably because shelter in place orders were in effect and communities feared that hospitals and clinics were an easy location to pick up COVID-19.

- The pattern of increased mental health claims and lower medical claims held through November 2020 but to a lesser degree. Mental health claims remained at least 19% higher in 2020 than in 2019.

So, it appears that anxiety is not alone in creating mental health mayhem for Gen Zers during the era of COVID-19. Depression also significantly spiked. Recall that this is in addition to the persistent rise in depression demonstrated since the early 2000s, compounding issues for many of our current students. In fact, before the pandemic, depression was one of the top five leading causes of disease and disability amongst individuals 15-19 years of age, and in the top 15 for ages 10-14.[14] As such, many students already had a pre-existing mental health challenge, but may have experienced more severe symptoms, or took on additional mental health challenges that are linked (ex. anxiety and depression or anxiety and ADHD) during the pandemic. Other students who may have encountered their first mental health setback during the pandemic now return to school. Some of these children will choose to mask their symptoms in an attempt to maintain the pre-pandemic image they believe their friends and family expect. That's a difficult journey and can lead to further isolation.

The CDC reports that around one in five students aged 3-to-17 years will not seek treatment for major depressive disorders.[15] That's not only 20% of your class, but millions of children across the nation. Educators need to be cognizant of that as we scan the room and work with our second family.

Focus #4—Substance misuse and abuse

When it comes to the adult population, there have been several memes that sarcastically point out, "many people will survive COVID-19, but many livers may not." I fear there may be some truth to this claim. Once the pandemic hit, alcohol consumption spiked. An article from *The Journal of the American Medical Association* cites that in the week ending March 21, 2020, in-person sales of alcohol rose 54%, and online sales skyrocketed 262% compared to the same period in 2019. Furthermore, the CDC reports that as of June 2020, 13% of Americans reported starting or increasing substance use as a way of coping with stress or emotions related to COVID-19.[17] And, for some, their method of escape extended beyond beer, wine, and shots.

The Overdose Detection Mapping Application Program (ODMAP), which examines overdose frequency and precipitating causes, found that the early months of the pandemic brought an almost 17% increase in overdoses across the United States when compared to the same time period in 2019.[18] And, the American Medical Association confirms that this trend continued to the end of 2020, as 40 states saw an increase in opioid-related deaths when compared to 2019.[19,16]

Sadly, very little of this is surprising. Individuals often turn to drugs or alcohol to escape difficult and unrelenting aspects of life or feel emotions that differ from their troubled baseline. However, the question educators need answering is whether or not America's youth followed the same trend as many of their adult peers. Some answers can be found through the Monitoring the Future (MTF) survey, implemented by researchers at the University of Michigan and funded through the National Institute on Drug Abuse. The survey has been utilized annually since 1975, and this year captured 11,821 students from 112 private and public schools. What they found was unsettling, but not surprising [20,21]:

- The number of 12th graders in 2020 that reported consuming alcohol at some point in their life rose from 58.5% in 2019 to 61.5% in 2020. More significantly, the daily consumption of alcohol in youth is on the rise. Daily drinkers represent a small cohort of overall adolescent alcohol use yet demonstrate a concerning early dependence upon alcohol. MTF found that the number of 12th-grade respondents who consume alcohol daily doubled when comparing 2018 data to 2020. This also held true for the number of daily drinkers in 8th grade.

- Binge drinking appears to be increasing. Data from the 8th, 10th, and 12th grades all demonstrate a small increase in those that admit to consuming five drinks or more in a row.

- Vaping nicotine at the 8th, 10th, and 12th-grade levels increased by at least 2%. However, vaping marijuana either held relatively steady or decreased in those same age groups.

- Hallucinogen users represent an admittedly small fraction of the respondents. However, the MTF demonstrates a 30% increase among 8th grade students that used them in the past year and a 15% increase among 12th graders.

- Prescription drugs that contained opioids varied, with most holding steady, but there was a small rise in oxycontin use in 12th graders compared with 2019. It is impossible to know if this was legitimate or inappropriate use, but one has to wonder.

In addition to the raw data, it's interesting to consider how students were using alcohol and illicit drugs during this unique time. None of us can peer into homes, so in many ways, that's a tough question to answer. However, a Canadian study of 1,054 adolescents published in 2020 revealed that the largest group of adolescent respondents (49.3%) engaged in solitary use, with no social component.[22] This is perhaps the most concerning avenue for drug use, as it has strong ties to negative coping strategies and longer-term addiction. Not to say that we endorse the 31.6% that used substances with underage friends, but it's more likely their activity was tethered to the social aspects of drug use.[22]

One final piece of data to consider regarding youth substance abuse in the pandemic concerns claims related to death by overdose. In December 2020, the CDC published that a little more than 81,000 drug overdoses resulted in death in the United States between May 2019 and May 2020.[23] That is the highest 12-month period to date, based upon their provisional data. If you look a little deeper, it appears that opioids seem to be the driving force behind most of these fatalities, as 37 of the 38 U.S. jurisdictions with reliable synthetic opioid data reported increases in synthetic opioid-related overdose deaths.[23] Not good.

All of these numbers are tragic. However, do we know for sure if these deaths are truly pandemic-related? It's tough to say. I'm not sure anyone can prove that definitively. I certainly don't claim that this book will. There are many possible explanations for many of these overdoses. For example, it's absolutely plausible that numerous individuals overdosed accidentally with prescription medications because the caretaker overseeing their meds no longer felt comfortable coming to their house due to COVID-19. Also, don't forget that there was a worldwide shortage in acetaminophen (Tylenol) and ibuprofen products for a period of time, which ironically drove some practitioners to write for more opioids in an attempt to treat pain.

It's exceedingly difficult to apply the information regarding overdose mortality to school-aged children. All we know at this point is that multiple credible sources suggest that youth drug use increased in many areas in 2020. And from an outcome perspective, there is reason to be concerned. The report from Fair Health makes it clear that compared with March and April 2019, overdose-related health insurance claims among secondary students, aged 13-18-years, climbed 94.9% in March 2020 and 119% for April 2020. Along the same continuum, substance use disorder claims in secondary students rose in March 2020 (64.6%) and April 2020 (62.7%).[13] Presumably, the lockdown and restrictive environment of the pandemic had some part in these hospital visits.

In the end, all we can say is that both children and adults felt a substantial increase in pressure and demands from issues associated with the pandemic. And at the same time, they also experienced a loss of support from schools, extracurriculars, and potentially their parents or guardians. That's certainly an ideal set of circumstances for a child to want to escape reality and turn to drugs and alcohol. Hence, we see evidence of upticks in the use of many substances. And I would guess that many of these students began experimenting with substances innocently, simply searching for a way to navigate the ridiculous circumstances surrounding them. And to be honest, I can completely see why. Allow me to pick on myself. While I never abused drugs during the pandemic, I certainly engaged in a daily "relay race" where two cups of coffee during the workday would hand off to one (large) glass of wine at night...and pretty much stuck to that daily operation for several months.

It will be essential to acknowledge the totality of that situation and not infer judgment toward students over the next few years. I suspect some will show signs of substance abuse in the coming years. Hopefully, these students will ask for help before their situation gets out of hand. I can't imagine how hard that will be for them. To break character and admit what lies beneath...what a daunting task for anyone. We need to form a relationship and build trust. And, we need to remember why we went into teaching in the first place. It wasn't for the lesson plans or the ridiculous number of assessments. It was to listen, to acknowledge, and then point a student in the right direction. None of that requires a clinical license or expert knowledge of substance abuse. We *are* trained to help our students with this. Please don't forget that.

Focus #5—Suicidal ideations and self-harm

If you look at a list of protective factors and determinants associated with positive mental health, most of the items on the list require meaningful human interaction. An interaction that forms a connection and fosters trust. This leads to future interactions, building an ever-increasing layer of connections. The CDC illustrates this point quite nicely on their website. They emphasize the following when it comes to valued protective factors: i) connections to friends, ii) connections to community, iii) supportive relationships with care providers, iv) connections to cultural and religious elements that discourage suicide, and v) access to physical and mental health facilities.[24] None of this should be a surprise. Humans have always sought strength and safety in numbers. And beyond our biological drive, recent research papers about social media (several hundred pounds worth it seems) validate that authentic human connection is superior to other forms of interaction when it comes to security, trust, and support. All of which seem like critical elements to positive mental health.

As we know all too well, COVID-19 took away most face-to-face smiles and in-person interactions— even in the health care arena. Elective surgeries were canceled. Outpatient health clinics that served both physical and mental health needs closed for various spans of time, at least until more was known about the transmission of SARS-CoV-2. This, in turn, forced a lot of individuals with mental health challenges to pivot to other treatment options quickly. Most were reassigned to telehealth services, which have their benefits, but definitely stray considerably from established in-person care. Additionally, due to the logistics of both internet service and insurance reimbursement, some mental health patients had to switch providers or suspend their services for an interim amount of time. In short, many of these modifications added challenges to an event that was designed to do the opposite—provide counseling, support, and calm. That's an irony that ended in tragedy for some.

As of March 2021, data is beginning to pour in regarding patients that engaged in self-harm and suicidal ideations. I would caution you that this data remains somewhat limited, at least in establishing a clear and confident trend. It might take a while before that information is clearly sorted out. Perhaps by the time you read this book, we'll know more. But as of publication, it does appear that some of the prognostic indicators are concerning when it comes to youth:

- To begin, the Fair Health report from March of 2021 reveals that self-harm (which included cutting, crashing a vehicle intentionally, and other acts of attempted suicide) for 13-to-18-year-olds, exploded upwards by 333.93% in August 2020 as compared to 2019 values for Northeast America.[13]

- Looking outside the Northeast region to the entire United States, self-harm insurance claims rose 90.7% in March of 2020, as compared to March 2019, for 13-to-18-year-old students. They remained high for the same age group, nearly doubling in April 2020 compared to April 2019.[13]

As you think about the above data, please keep in mind that the Fair Health report reviewed **32 billion** private health care claims. Those are likely to be extremely high-powered numbers, leading to greater accuracy. However, I would argue there is still more to this. What are the clinicians and foot soldiers in treatment centers noticing? For that answer, we turn back to our friends in health care.

A recent publication from *Pediatrics*, the official journal of the American Academy of Pediatrics, took a detailed look at suicide ideation and attempts before and during COVID-19.[25] Like many others, the investigators chose to examine a time period in 2020 and compare it to previous trends from the same period in 2019. The group did an excellent job reviewing suicide risk screens from January-July 2019 and then completed the same review for suicide screens applicable to January-July 2020. The ages of patients spanned from 11-21 years with a mean age of 14, and the total number of screens reviewed surpassed 9,000. More importantly, this pediatric emergency department served a diverse population, with 47.7% of the patients representing Hispanic and/or Latino populations, 26.7% represented non-Hispanic Whites, and 18.7% identified as non-Hispanic Black. The outcome data was unfortunately grim.

- Screening results indicated that February, March, April, and July 2020 showed a higher rate of suicidal ideation. The most notable increases were associated with March and July.[25]

- Specifically, the statistics revealed that the odds of recent suicide ideation were 1.6 times higher in March 2020 compared with March 2019 and 1.45 times higher in July 2020 compared with July 2019.[25]

- Interestingly, this data impacted school-aged children fairly equally across demographics. The study reports that the "interaction between year and race and ethnicity was not statistically significant, indicating that no racial or ethnic group reported a greater increase in the likelihood of recent suicide ideation from 2019 to 2020."[25]

All of those numbers are telling. They hurt me deeply as an educator, physician, and dad. Data, perhaps more encompassing, will follow in the coming months to years. While I don't know exactly what it will show, I am concerned that there will be some worrying aspects to it and validation of the preliminary information we are digesting in 2021.

Before we leave this difficult topic, it's important to acknowledge the following. Teachers work to better the lives of children and prepare them for a long journey through life. It's our calling. And for many of us, our students are like a second family...even if they add to the dysfunctional elements of our actual family. I mention this because losing a student in your school or classroom is an abysmal event. One you can't put into words. I know this because it happened at one of my teaching sites. Not just once, but twice. And as others who have experienced this can verify, the sadness never *really* goes away. Rather, it just becomes a feeling you get better at pushing aside each day. Based on our research, if we do not alter the trajectory of youth suicide and address mental health fallout in school-aged kids, more teachers will experience this first-hand.

Part 3 of this book demonstrates that educators have the unique talents, abilities, and training to be meaningful contributors to improving youth mental health. Admittedly, we will need to make some adjustments to do it; however, none of them will be half as daunting as the adjustments we were all asked to make for this pandemic.

Chapter 7 References

1. Reynolds, B. (2020, November 1). *There's a lot of uncertainty right now – this is what science says that does to our minds, bodies.* University of California San Francisco. https://www.ucsf.edu/news/2020/11/418951/theres-lot-uncertainty-right-now-what-science-says-does-our-minds-bodies

2. Leeb, R. T., Bitsko, R. H., Radhakrishnan, L., Martinez, P., Njai, R., & Holland, K. M. (2020). Mental health–related emergency department visits among children aged <18 years during the COVID-19 pandemic - United States, January 1–October 17, 2020. *Morbidity and Mortality Weekly Report*, 69, 1675–1680. http://dx.doi.org/10.15585/mmwr.mm6945a3.

3. Jeffery, M., D'Onofrio, G., Paek, H., Platts-Mills, T., Soares, W., Hoppe, J., Genes, N., Nath, B., & Melnick, E. (2020). Trends in emergency department visits and hospital admissions in health care systems in 5 states in the first months of the COVID-19 pandemic in the US. *JAMA Internal Medicine*, *180*(10), 1328–1333. https://doi.org/10.1001/jamainternmed.2020.3288

4. Panchal, N., Kamal, R., & Garfield, R. (2021, February 10). *The implications of COVID-19 for mental health and substance use.* Kaiser Family Foundation. https://www.kff.org/coronavirus-covid-19/issue-brief/the-implications-of-covid-19-for-mental-health-and-substance-use/

5. Jacob, L., Smith, L., Koyanagi, A., Oh, H., Tanislav, C., Shin, J., Konrad, M., & Kostev, K. (2020). Impact of the coronavirus 2019 (COVID-19) pandemic on anxiety diagnosis in general practices in Germany. *Journal of Psychiatric Research*, S0022-3956(20)31088-8. Advance online publication. https://doi.org/10.1016/j.jpsychires.2020.11.029

6. Burstein, M., Ginsburg, G. S., & Tein, J. Y. (2010). Parental anxiety and child symptomatology: An examination of additive and interactive effects of parent psychopathology. *Journal of Abnormal Child Psychology*, *38*(7), 897–909. https://doi.org/10.1007/s10802-010-9415-0

7. Martinelli, K., Cohen, Y., Kimball, H., & Sheldon-Dean, H. (2020). *2020 children's mental health report: Telehealth in*

an increasingly virtual world. Child Mind Institute. https://childmind.org/our-impact/childrens-mental-health-report/2020-childrens-mental-health-report/

8. Hawes, M. T., Szenczy, A. K., Klein, D. N., Hajcak, G., & Nelson, B. D. (2021). Increases in depression and anxiety symptoms in adolescents and young adults during the COVID-19 pandemic. *Psychological Medicine*, 1–9. Advance online publication. https://doi.org/10.1017/S0033291720005358

9. Grieshaber, K. (2020, February 27). *Experts notice pandemic's mental health toll on German youth*. ABC News. Retrieved April 5, 2021, from https://abcnews.go.com/Health/wireStory/experts-notice-pandemics-mental-health-toll-german-youth-76151234

10. Duan, L., Shao, X., Wang, Y., Huang, Y., Miao, J., Yang, X., & Zhu, G. (2020). An investigation of mental health status of children and adolescents in China during the outbreak of COVID-19. *Journal of Affective Disorders*, *275*, 112–118. https://doi.org/10.1016/j.jad.2020.06.029

11. Orgilés, M., Morales, A., Delvecchio, E., Mazzeschi, C., & Espada, J. P. (2020, April 21). Immediate psychological effects of the COVID-19 quarantine in youth from Italy and Spain. *PsyArXiv*. https://doi.org/10.31234/osf.io/5bpfz

12. Loades, M. E., Chatburn, E., Higson-Sweeney, N., Reynolds, S., Shafran, R., Brigden, A., Linney, C., McManus, M. N., Borwick, C., & Crawley, E. (2020). Rapid systematic review: The impact of social isolation and loneliness on the mental health of children and adolescents in the context of COVID-19. *Journal of the American Academy of Child and Adolescent Psychiatry*, *59*(11), 1218–1239.e3. https://doi.org/10.1016/j.jaac.2020.05.009

13. FAIR Health. (2021, March 2). *The impact of COVID-19 on pediatric mental health: A study of private healthcare claims* [White paper]. https://s3.amazonaws.com/media2.fairhealth.org/whitepaper/asset/The%20Impact%20of%20COVID-19%20on%20Pediatric%20Mental%20Health%20-%20A%20Study%20of%20Private%20Healthcare%20Claims%20-%20A%20FAIR%20Health%20White%20Paper.pdf

14. Kessler, R. C., Angermeyer, M., Anthony, J. C., DE Graaf, R., Demyttenaere, K., Gasquet, I., DE Girolamo, G., Gluzman, S.,

Gureje, O., Haro, J. M., Kawakami, N., Karam, A., Levinson, D., Medina Mora, M. E., Oakley Browne, M. A., Posada-Villa, J., Stein, D. J., Adley Tsang, C. H., Aguilar-Gaxiola, S., ... Ustün, T. B. (2007). Lifetime prevalence and age-of-onset distributions of mental disorders in the World Health Organization's World Mental Health Survey Initiative. *World Psychiatry, 6*(3), 168–176.

15. Centers for Disease Control and Prevention. (2020, June 15). *Children's mental health: Data and statistics.* https://www.cdc.gov/childrens-mentalhealth/data.html

16. Pollard, M. S., Tucker, J. S., & Green, H. D. (2020). Changes in adult alcohol use and consequences during the COVID-19 pandemic in the US. *JAMA Network Open, 3*(9), e2022942. https://doi.org/10.1001/jamanetworkopen.2020.22942

17. Czeisler MÉ, Lane RI, Petrosky E, et al. (2020). Mental health, substance use, and suicidal ideation during the COVID-19 pandemic - United States, June 24–30, 2020. *Morbidity and Mortality Weekly Report, 69,* 1049–1057. http://dx.doi.org/10.15585/mmwr.mm6932a1

18. Alter, A., & Yeager, C. (2020, June). *COVID-19 impact on US national overdose crisis.* Overdose Detection Mapping Application Program (ODMAP). http://www.odmap.org/Content/docs/news/2020/ODMAP-Report-June-2020.pdf

19. American Medical Association. (2021, March 3). *Issue brief: Reports of increase in opioid and other drug-related overdose and other concerns during COVID pandemic.* https://www.ama-assn.org/system/files/2020-12/issue-brief-increases-in-opioid-related-overdose.pdf

20. National Institute on Drug Abuse. (2019, December 4). *Stats & trends in teen drug use with interactive chart.* https://teens.drugabuse.gov/teachers/stats-trends-teen-drug-use

21. National Institute on Drug Abuse. (2020, December 17). *Monitoring the future study: Trends in prevalence of various drugs.* https://www.drugabuse.gov/drug-topics/trends-statistics/monitoring-future/monitoring-future-study-trends-in-prevalence-various-drugs

22. Dumas, T. M., Ellis, W., & Litt, D. M. (2020). What does adolescent substance use look like during the COVID-19 pandemic? Examining changes in frequency, social contexts, and pandemic-related

predictors. *The Journal of Adolescent Health, 67*(3), 354–361. https://doi.org/10.1016/j.jadohealth.2020.06.018

23. Centers for Disease Control and Prevention. (2020, December 21). *Overdose deaths accelerating during COVID-19: Expanded prevention efforts needed.* Press Release. https://www.cdc.gov/media/releases/2020/p1218-overdose-deaths-covid-19.html

24. Centers for Disease Control and Prevention. (2021, January 25). *Risk and protective factors.* https://www.cdc.gov/suicide/factors/index.html

25. Hill, R. M., Rufino, K., Kurian, S., Saxena, J., Saxena, K., & Williams, L. (2021). Suicide ideation and attempts in a pediatric emergency department before and during COVID-19. *Pediatrics, 147*(3). https://doi.org/10.1542/peds.2020-029280

PART THREE

Immunity through community...Strategies for students and staff

Part Three of *After the Mask* offers evidence-based implementations that focus efforts upon specific mental health determinants within the licensure and capacity of teachers **in a manner that educators desire**. This allows school districts to proactively make a contribution to the overall effort to improve youth mental health.

8

Pick your battles wisely... Schools and the mental health crisis

At the tender age of 12, I learned a phenomenal lesson about life—one that could never be pulled off in a classroom. It took a crisp fall day in my backyard with friends, family, and a pickup football game to master this learning target. But if you knew me as a kid, this nontraditional setting for instruction really wouldn't have been a surprise, as I definitely prefer to learn through experience. Hands-on activities engage my attention, senses, and memory far better than any form of direct instruction, and they are undoubtedly superior to "death by worksheets." Anyway, I got one heck of an experience that sunny afternoon.

The life lesson began while guarding my 18-year-old brother on the final play of a close and somewhat contested football game. Despite him being a nice guy, my other friends refused to guard him. Not sure why. But I'm guessing it had to do with his height, athletic frame, and the 220 pounds of muscle that came with it. Fortunately, I was willing to step up to the challenge. Now, knowing that my brother was faster, stronger, and able to jump higher than all of us, I anticipated the final throw of the game would go to him. What can I say? I was a regular detective. Luckily, I was also a planner. I quickly formulated a brilliant strategy to negate his ability to score the last touchdown. In true Karate Kid form, I intended to "sweep the leg" and take my brother to the ground before he could catch the ball. It would work. It had to work. Seconds after making this decision, "hike" left the quarterback's mouth, I sprang into action, and my shoulder took out one tree trunk of a leg. My brother fell hard, and as a result, our team won. It was glorious! Until, it wasn't.

My brother ignored the pain in his knee, hopped up, and twirled me around with such ferocity that even roller coaster engineers would have been mesmerized. All of this, of course, was so that my nose could become intimately familiar with his fist. And, to make sure they really knew each other, my nose and his fist got to make contact five or six times...I think. It's still a little hazy. Anyway, blood joined the party moments later, pouring out of my nose and mouth like a firehose. I believe this was around the time where this spectacle became a full-on gong show, as my brother expertly reshaped my face over the next 20 seconds. My friends stood in slack-jawed horror. However, those 20 seconds, which seemed like 20 years, ended abruptly when my father yanked my brother off of me and offered the comforting words of "Stop! Both of you! Oh sh#t. Honey...where are you? Chris might need a new face." And, there it was. That was the exact moment I learned that emotion is powerful but not particularly wise. So, be better than me. Pause. Reflect. And know the reasons and potential outcomes associated with where and how you apply your emotion.

Now, picking your battles wisely seems like a straightforward idea. And in some ways, exceedingly simplistic. I suppose in certain scenarios it can be. Let's look back at the vignette of my brother and me playing football. I chose to engage in a confrontation the moment my shoulder collided with my brother's knee, risking significant injury to his leg. And for what? To appease my competitive nature? Regardless of the origin of my actions, I'm pretty confident that 99.9% of you reading this book would assess my decision to attack my brother as somewhere between reckless and stupid. Perhaps you think I even deserved the 20 second attitude adjustment my brother offered me. Either way, we are looking at this story from a superficial level. What's far more important is not what I did, but what motivated me to take the course of action I selected. In short, what was the determining factor or factors that propelled me into battle? To this day, I still don't know.

Questions regarding motivation launch us into areas of the human brain that are absolutely fascinating. The physiology of intrinsic and extrinsic motivation involves diverse areas of the brain, depending upon the situation at hand. For example, humans are hard-wired in the hypothalamus and amygdala to be aggressive when we aren't meeting physiological needs such as sleep, thirst, or hunger. That's an unconscious battle that we are often forced to fight. I remind my kids of this when I'm sleep-deprived, as I typically need five minutes of silence until coffee has touched my soul.

More complex than our survival instincts is our long-term memory. Deep within our frontal and temporal lobes, we store information pertaining to the events of a situation. We can also recall the emotion we experienced with those events. Let's take a pleasant example like baking cookies with your grandmother. Do you remember how everything looked, sounded, and smelled? Me too. That's because the human mind often links emotion to the other five senses when a meaningful event occurs and then, loosely speaking, stores that package of information in your long-term memory. This also holds true for negative events.

A not-so-pleasant example might be recalling an 8th grader making fun of your glasses when you were 13—the same glasses that were the best your parents could afford. I can tell you that I remember exactly where I was standing, what the hallway looked like, and how I felt when this happened to me. So, is it any surprise that in my classroom, I unconsciously protect kids with glasses and support their self-esteem? Probably not, because those students navigate a battle I can relate to, and I am motivated to help them. The point is that the human mind has both unconscious and conscious pathways that allow emotion to influence our decision-making.

All of that is interesting, but let's go one level higher in the hierarchy of conscious thought and really examine the governance of our actions. We need to discuss one of the strongest motivators in the human brain. One that I consider paramount to this book and all that we have discussed thus far. What about the moral imperative? What about causes that are so exceedingly close to our hearts and the personal concept of what life **must** be? These are the determinants that have the greatest influence on us. They shape our view of the world and play into our daily lives by dominating both the conscious and unconscious areas of our brain. We often refer to these moral imperatives as our values. But whatever term you prefer, I think it's fair to say that these beliefs make life exceedingly complex for us because when they come under attack, we find ourselves aggressive and willing to go to battle for them in one way or another. And as a generally non-confrontational person (ignore what I did to my brother in the backyard), I don't like to rise up and fight. I don't relish the thought of getting riled up and expending non-productive energy. I'm not the only one. For most, there is far too much going on in life to add unnecessary drama, especially if it appears that our individual efforts will have little influence on the problem at hand.

However, something happens to most of us when our deepest values and visions of how the world should operate are shattered. These are moments that attack the moral imperative behind much of what we do. When that attack occurs, we often surprise ourselves and break natural tendencies. The thought of NOT doing something seems like the worst option of all—at least, far more detrimental and ill-advised than engaging in the situation at hand. It's in these moments we all come alive. And to no surprise, we do this in different ways. Some of us lash out with inflammatory comments. Others take to social media to wage a different kind of war, applying peer pressure to the one that offended us. In reality, there are endless options once the battle has been picked. But for me, who doesn't want to make the same mistake I did at the age of 12, I curb emotion for a moment, take a deep breath, and look for solutions that are supported by evidence. That doesn't seem like much of a battle at first, does it? I assure you that it is. Like most educators, once I know a strategy will positively impact students, staff, or both, AND I'm convinced my effort will yield results...well, at that point, I can take on a level of tenacity and persistence that rivals no other. That, my friends, is why my most thoughtful responses, albeit slower, have always been my most successful.

I mention all of this for a reason: to establish buy-in. I need to earn it from you. Part 1 of this book laid out a substantial amount of data to demonstrate the mental health challenges our current students have faced since the early

2000s. Please also remember that Part 2 of the book demonstrated that the pandemic threw an inequitable, unethical, and unrelenting stress test at Gen Zers, which only made things worse. Data from the CDC, American Academy of Pediatrics, American Psychological Association, and leading clinical studies are compelling regarding the erosion of mental health in school-aged children. In fact, the information and trends regarding youth mental health are so profound that ignoring them as an educator might be considered some form of negligence.

Now, take a breath, please. I am not trying to use a scare tactic or over-embellish the situation here, I assure you. Rather, I simply want to point out that numbers this powerful left unaddressed would be unheard of in any career path outside of education. Here are a few examples to illustrate the point:

- Cardiovascular disease is a frequent problem for individuals in the United States and can lead to blocked blood vessels, eventually manifesting in heart attacks. To avoid this, America allocates around $2 billion to heart research each year.[1] This has produced clear and decisive evidence that demonstrates the best options for treating cardiovascular disease and preventing heart attacks, creating a standard of care for cardiovascular disease. And, this standard of care is so compelling and agreed upon that any health care provider that deviates from it without an excellent reason (ex: allergies to a medication) is considered negligent or engaging in malpractice. With that in mind, let me ask a quick question. Would you be fine sending your loved ones to a doctor that acknowledges cardiovascular data but doesn't follow it? I think I know the answer.

- Boeing, the enormous Seattle-based aerospace company, recently underwent a prolonged investigation regarding their 737 Max aircraft. At the time, the plane demonstrated some concerning instabilities, particularly during take-off, due to a design modification that changed the center of lift. It resulted in two crashes and several other incidents.[2] When examined, the evidence regarding the engineering flaws was substantial. As such, Boeing addressed the issue, taking the appropriate steps to stabilize the aircraft. But what if they hadn't? What if they just stared at those safety reports and said, "Wow. That's tragic," and then took no action? Would you fly in their airplanes? Would you trust their integrity in the future?

Let those examples above soak in for a moment. Both represent two authentic situations where scientific evidence became overwhelming enough that they generated an immediate need for action, so profoundly clear that not acting would have been negligent. Many of us would call a situation like that the moral imperative. If you agree with that line of thought, the next important question is this: do you see some similarities between these examples and the data regarding youth mental health trends?

I would suggest that Parts 1 and 2 of this book established enough data from trusted authorities that we find ourselves in a situation similar to cardiologists and leaders at Boeing. What do I mean? Based upon the recent trends for youth anxiety, depression, substance abuse, mental health visits, and suicidal ideations, we are staring down an important crossroads regarding how we take care of students at school. For some, the evidence from Part 1 and Part 2 will function as the moral imperative to take action and reach out to students in need. For others, the evidence may inspire empathy for the situation, but no action will take place. Either way, the ball is in our court, and the public is watching.

Allowing schools to gravitate to pre-pandemic "normal" operations does not offer a solution. It does not address the problems at hand. As demonstrated in Part 1, there was a disconnect between the best-laid plans and measurable improvements when it comes to student mental health initiatives. Schools were working hard, yet the downward spiral in student mental health persisted. The data we reviewed makes that undeniable. As such, why would we ever go back to an inadequate approach? Of course, the daunting question is where and how to make upgrades in a school district's plan for mental health stressors? And, to what extent do schools put themselves into the process of fixing youth mental health? Is that decision impacted by legal responsibility, motivation of staff, outside influences, or all of those things? It's tough to say.

Like it or not, perception often dictates reality. And the perception of many communities across America is that schools need to fix the mental health problems in school-aged children. The National Education Association highlights some of these parent expectations in a 2018 article, where it's evident that the public's natural response is to demand more mental health initiatives in schools to help with the fallout.[3] And given that around 50% of significant mental health challenges start by age 14, schools should focus on younger children as much as secondary students.[4] So, there you go, schools. Please let us know when you fix it... the clock is ticking.

Sarcasm aside, there is plenty of evidence to suggest that schools are, in fact, perfectly positioned to make an effective impact in the battle against eroding mental health. In a 2017 article in *Children and Schools*, Susan Frauenholtz and colleagues point out that schools function as the bridge between home and the community, serving as a valuable (and logical) site for identification and intervention with children experiencing mental health distress.[5] Schools also represent a natural environment where students feel comfortable working on skills and trying new strategies for problem-solving. However, any interventions or strategies that a school district takes need to be appropriate for the staff members involved. Frauenholtz confirms that "research has indicated that many teachers and other school staff have limited knowledge of children's mental health and are unprepared to support students in distress."[5] This is important to acknowledge. Teachers can't be more than teachers. Additionally, principals aren't counselors, paraeducators don't possess the skills of social workers, and coaches are not school psychologists. This stark reality can't be lost or swept under the rug when schools select strategies to respond to the mental health crisis.

So, here we are. Educators are clearly in an unenviable spot. Credible evidence points to deeply concerning trends in mental health, establishing the need to take action on behalf of these students. Community pressure makes it clear, right or wrong that schools have to be involved in the solution, and in some ways, should lead the charge. And finally, there is the critically important realization that staff are already exhausted and lack the extensive training it takes to make skilled mental health interventions. This sounds like a mess. That's because it is—no way to sugarcoat it.

So, what do school districts do? Is there any way out of this debacle? Absolutely. Follow the evidence. That's what was needed to establish a call to action. However, it's now time to shift our focus to the causes that led to those problems. By mitigating or modifying the causes, you can often reduce the severity of the problem and occasionally eradicate the issue altogether.[6] The diagram below reminds us of the process.

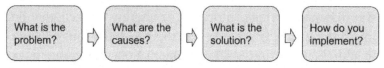

Source: CDC Introduction to Public Health

So, what causes seem to be precipitating the youth mental health crisis? Chapters 1 and 2 shared some compelling evidence, along with expert insight, that suggested there are some predictable and fairly prevalent vulnerabilities in current school-aged children. To start with, many Gen Zers live with heightened parental expectations and involvement in their lives, leading to reduced opportunities to make independent decisions. Now add a deep reliance upon technology to solve everyday problems, which amplifies screen times and diminishes in-person encounters and emotional feedback. Like it or not, that's the world that many of our students live in. And for some, this framework can lead to a life where the number of likes, shares, and retweets determine their impressions of self-worth instead of dialogue with family and friends. All of these elements discussed in Chapter 1 seem to play a substantial role in the downward spiral of Gen Zer's self-esteem, self-efficacy, and life skills. Evidence suggests they serve as some of the causes contributing to the problem of erosive mental health in this age group. That's valuable to know because to solve this dilemma correctly, any solution that school districts look to should address these causes and improve self-esteem, self-efficacy, and develop life skills for any future roles.

Before we jump in with proposed solutions, it would be wise to assess what resources school districts have to fight this battle in the first place. Doing so will provide quick insight as to what schools can do and what they can't do. Now, it's important to acknowledge that schools have a vested interest in preparing students for life after graduation and have a responsibility to keep children as safe as reasonably possible. But like most complex problems, it's highly unlikely that one institution, such as schools, has the capability and resources to address the entirety of this problem alone. It's going to take a team effort. And school districts need to know their role on that team.

School district resources for mental health

Right from the start, it's vital that you are aware of a huge deficit regarding mental health services in the United States. To say that mental health services are stretched thin does not give the situation justice. How bad off are we? Allow me to put it into perspective for you: nearly 60% of United States counties don't have a single practicing psychiatrist.[7] Let that become more than a number, as it geographically represents more than half of the country. And as you might have guessed, rural communities experience a higher deficit, with only 20% benefiting from a licensed psychiatrist.[7] That situation becomes more dire when examining the availability of child psychiatrists. The Child Mind Institute, in conjunction with Blue Shield of California, estimates there are only about 8,300 child psychiatrists available to support over 17 million kids in need.[8] And, a study from *Pediatrics* in 2019 confirmed that despite a 21.3% increase in child psychiatrists between 2007-2016 in the U.S. there remains a substantial deficit of child psychiatrists, particularly in parts of the country with lower levels of income and education.[9] Friends, that's a shortage of *epic* proportions.

I mention the above information to set the framework for what we are diving into. If the health care sector is struggling to provide enough mental health support for communities at large, how do we think schools will compensate? That's a tough question, but it needs consideration before any other plans can be made. Furthermore, what level of mental health care fits within the responsibilities of a school district? Educators across the country are charged with many expectations. At the very least, schools need to provide students with the knowledge, skills, and resilience to succeed in the world. To do that effectively, social and emotional understanding and development need to take place. Situational awareness, practicing professionalism, displaying appropriate empathy, and navigating complex emotional responses are necessary for adulthood in general and represent an unwritten requirement for any form of employment. I don't think many educators would challenge those claims. So, in a sense, school districts do seem to carry a portion of the responsibility to develop children with stable mental health. However, that does not make school districts a mental health clinic capable of complex diagnosis and multivariable treatments.

To better understand the potential interventions schools can offer for mental health, let's look at what school districts currently have in terms of mental health support. At a superficial glance, it appears schools have some options. Schools maintain skilled staff members, ranging from school psychologists, licensed counselors, to well-trained social workers, all of which can be integrated into a school system rather seamlessly and offer tremendous support for students. Those are huge assets. However, the reality is that these skilled providers are limited in number and obviously have a cost associated with them. School-based mental health professionals may be underpaid in some communities compared to private practice, but from the school perspective, they are still expensive. Additionally, the availability of these skilled providers can be limited, particularly in more rural environments. These two factors combine forces to result in a notable deficit when it comes to providing licensed mental health care for students, as seen below:

- The National Association of School Psychologists (NASP) recommends a staffing ratio of 1 school psychologist per 500-700 students, allowing for comprehensive school psychological services.[10] National data demonstrates that most schools can't meet that recommendation, estimating a national ratio of 1:1381. In some states, it's even worse, with a ratio of around 1:1500. Keep in mind that this deficit existed in 2014-2015 before the pandemic made some mental health challenges worse.[10]

- In some areas of the country, budget is not the issue. There simply aren't enough interested applicants. Back in 2017, the Kansas Association of School Psychologists reported that their survey of school districts and special education agencies in Kansas identified 38 school psychologist positions that remained open and presumably unfilled during the first semester of the 2016–2017 school year.[11]

- The Health Resources and Services Administration (HRSA), a division of the federal government, states that as of 2018, there are only around 700,000 social workers in the United States. The HRSA estimates that as the total number of social work jobs continues to grow and qualified personnel lag behind, there will likely be a shortfall of 10,000 full-time employees by 2025.[12] These represent positions that will presumably not be filled.

Admittedly, that data is far from reassuring. Math does not lie. And right now, there is an apparent shortage of psychologists and social workers in general, as well as in school positions. While these numbers can improve over time, it will take at least a decade to make an impact. These individuals have to undergo education, training, and often some sort of mentoring experience before they hit the ground running. This creates lag time. And that's assuming there are enough qualified individuals that want to change the course of their life and jump into a job where they are guaranteed to be overworked for quite some time. As such, school psychologists, at least as a group, may not be able to address the short-term spike in student mental health challenges in the ways we would hope.

So, what other options are out there? School counselors represent another type of skilled provider. They undergo specialized training within their licensure that allows them to engage in effective prevention strategies, specific interventions, and identification of students that need additional support, generating a referral to a higher level of care outside the school district. This, among other reasons, makes counselors a valued commodity for schools. However, this is only *one* of the assignments given to counselors. There is much more to their job than addressing student mental health concerns. The reality of school building operations, which I affectionately refer to as "the front lines," requires counselors to perform a wide array of additional administrative duties and fulfill educational responsibilities:

- Need someone to organize the ACT, SAT, and AP exams? How about a counselor?

- Register classes? Even ones outside the school district? Yep, counselors can do that.

- Deal with parent concerns, sudden class adds or drops outside the registration period, and contact any students that are failing...how about counselors?

- Implement a drug and alcohol program? Teach sex education? Oooh....vaping is a problem? Let's get counselors to look into that as well.

All sarcasm aside, you can see that counselors are spread thin. I have never worked as one, but it took me just six short weeks as a new teacher to realize the similarities between their role and my former life in the emergency department. Effective counselors know how to triage all matters into severity, scope, and timing. They also have a wonderful way of intervening in multiple ways at once. Now, I'm not trying to say that every day is this chaotic for counselors, but many are. That's the reality of their job.

So, is there data to suggest relief is on the way for school counselors? Well, I'm not going to lie. It looks pretty rough at this time. The American School Counseling Association (ASCA) recommends that schools maintain a ratio of 250 students for every counselor. In reality, ASCA reports that schools nationally demonstrate a ratio closer to 482 students for every 1 counselor.[13] That is almost double the recommended volume. If that data represents your school building, I'm sorry. But, know it can get much worse. The Education Trust claims that nearly 1 in 5 students, which is about 8 million children, "do not have access to a counselor in their school at all, and nearly 3 million of those students do not even have access to other school support staff, such as school psychologists or social workers."[14] And where do we see these shortages most often? The ASCA makes it clear that schools serving students of color and/or low-income families have been underserved for many years. Counselors in these demographic settings typically have higher caseloads and less funding. This leaves many students in jeopardy and without access to support while at school. That's a sad reality. In some ways, it's unforgivable. But what makes it far more devastating is that this demographic is similar to the cohort populations that took the brunt of the pandemic in terms of severity of illness. These districts deserve the greatest support, but as it stands now, they will receive the least.

One persistent suggestion is that school districts offer more money for these critical mental health positions in an attempt to find solutions. The logic is that sufficient compensation might attract more candidates to school districts and justify the long hours counselors, social workers, and school psychologists provide. It's a reasonable thought. However, this idea has been floating around for a long time as there has continually been a substantial salary gap between schools and the general community when it comes to skilled providers. Take school psychologists again, for example. According to an inquiry by U.S. News and World Report, school psychologists average $23,500 less compensation than community psychologists, which can be around a 25% income differential per year.[15]

Frustrating, right? Agreed. But truth be told, no matter what kind of passionate argument regarding funding goes before local municipalities or state education leaders, I don't see salary differentials changing anytime soon. All 50 states found themselves dealing with unexpected financial strain due to the COVID-19 pandemic. Many individuals undergoing lockdown earned less income and spent less in the open market, dropping state revenue from sales tax and income tax. The Brookings Institute claims that state and local government revenue will likely decline $155 billion in 2020 and $167 billion in 2021, which is about 5.5%-5.7%, respectively.[16] Now, combine this drop in revenue with an increase in expenditures, as many states understandably hemorrhaged cash in an effort to support COVID-19 related setbacks. It's a rough set of circumstances and does not seem like the right time for anyone in state-funded education to ask for a substantial salary increase.

Before we close this section, there's one more relevant point regarding the economics of education. If you're aware of the CARES Act legislation, then you know that it offered school districts across the United States around $13.2 billion in 2020.[17] That figure seems like a substantial amount of support. Can't we draw from that pool of money to boost the level of mental health professionals in schools? "Maybe" is the most optimistic answer I can provide. Although the CARES Act offered districts a great deal of help with PPE costs, substitute teacher coverage, and other COVID expenditures, it's unlikely that it will fully address our mental health needs. Quite simply, the dedicated K-12 funds within the CARES Act represent only 2% of total public education funding associated with the 2020-21 school year. Furthermore, this funding must be used to address the additional costs of dealing with SARS-CoV-2 and cannot be used to fill budget holes.[18] That's obviously unfortunate. It also adds to the forecast that restrictive budgets will continue to be a problem for some time.

These financial constraints are a lot to process. I suspect they always have been—hence, the never-ending disagreements about school funding and the factors that impact it. However, the information we explored during this section still has immense value because it highlights what resources we currently have and confirms that it's unlikely that schools will receive a significant increase in funding for mental health concerns over the next five to ten years. That could change, of course, as life is never static. But, as of now, any strategies created and/or implemented for mental health support in schools should not plan on additional funding being there for long term. We may not like that. But we are wise to accept that reality as we strategize what evidence-based improvements are realistic for school districts.

Given the limitations of budget and availability, schools will never be able to address all of the mental health fallout that we see in Gen Zers. And you know what? They shouldn't. Schools are not medical facilities. They lack inpatient services. They do not offer pharmacies. Most of all, schools are largely filled with educators, who, because of their kind hearts, have already overstepped their training in many areas, trying to do the right thing. The reality is that these selfless individuals don't have clinical insight to consistently know what the "right thing" is when it comes to student mental health. That's a glaring and undeniable fact. I would argue that school districts be proactive and establish within their community what they *can* offer and where the limitations lie. By doing this, school districts can move from a reactionary role to a leadership position in the community, forcing a discussion regarding the *collective effort* that needs to take place to fill all the gaps. That, my friends, is a lesson that every community member would benefit from. And hey, who better to teach it than schools?

Realistic improvements for student mental health

So, what options remain to address the mental health crisis in America's youth? The evidence we covered thus far demonstrates a profound shortage of skilled mental health providers for children. Furthermore, districts fortunate enough to have access to school psychologists, social workers, and licensed counselors are currently overwhelmed with case volumes. Yikes. It seems as though there is a nebulous and stormy cloud hanging over any tentative improvement regarding mental health support for schools. That said, there is one option that has been deliberately withheld until this point in the book. It involves leveraging the strengths found within the heart and backbone of education. Teachers.

Please let me immediately reaffirm that teachers are **NOT**, and never will be, skilled mental health providers. That's not their role, and frankly, it never should be. Any strategies implemented to improve mental health in students that involve teachers have to respect that fact and never ask teachers to perform outside the capacity of their licensure and training. Doing so would be dangerous and put students, parents, and staff members at risk. As a former emergency medicine physician, I can promise you that hospitals would never let a provider offer services far outside their licensure, so why would we consider it for schools? The answer is that we shouldn't—ever. The last thing we need is a well-meaning educator making ill-advised decisions with a child that results in a bad outcome.

I highlight the limitations of teachers for a reason. Some legislators and community leaders intermittently suggest that teachers should be cross-trained for various roles in order to fill gaps in community coverage. Interesting idea. I suppose if the cross-training naturally fits with the role of a teacher, it might be worth considering. However, the problem is that many individuals making these cross-training suggestions have seemingly lost sight of the fact that teachers are not a catch-all for community needs. Should you need a meaningful example, take school shootings. Not long ago, I was asked by a politician, "how should we design a program for teachers to carry handguns so that we can address school shootings?" Hmm. Pretty sure that regardless of your political opinions, that may not be such a good solution. Unless, of course, I was the only certified teacher in the building that missed the in-service training on tactical firearms and hand-to-hand combat.

But, back to the issue at hand...the erosion of Gen Zers mental health. It still needs to be addressed. If we take the approach that educators should not function as mental health providers in schools, then how can they possibly be part of improving the situation? And perhaps more importantly, from an evidentiary vantage point, anything teachers do should be well supported in terms of scientific efficacy. It can't be an intervention that is superficial, or worse, built upon fluff. The health and stability of the children in America's classrooms should not be addressed with whimsical ideas or initiatives that are merely for optics. Kids are precious, and a good chunk of them are mentally fragile right now. Should schools implement something with teachers, it should be evidence-based, and represent a high yield investment of time.

Unfortunately, there is another challenge that might curb teacher involvement. And, I want to acknowledge that it's a substantial one. Can we ask teachers to do one more thing right now? Staff across the United States have expressed quite clearly that the pandemic threw extra burdens and extraneous responsibilities into their laps, increasing their experience of stress and the risk of burnout. There have been a large number of news articles about this very topic. And keep in mind, there was already a national shortage of qualified educators before the pandemic, many of whom have deep-seated concerns about the future of education in general. Per CNBC's 2021 inquiry, around 27% of K-12 employees surveyed are strongly considering leaving their jobs.[19] That's not surprising. It's been a brutal year for most occupations. Teaching remotely while listening to all the polarizing views regarding schools amidst the pandemic has been, at a minimum, somewhat disconcerting. For some, the additional stress has been enough to exit education altogether. Clearly, these feelings are important to take to heart when considering potential roles teachers might play in improving the mental health of their students.

And so, for months, I thought about this dilemma. I continued to reach out to trusted friends and colleagues across the United States, listening to their perspectives regarding the upside and downside of education and where it may be going. I also watched plenty of wonderful people, far brighter than me, toss their arms up in the air during Zoom calls when asked how to best help Gen Zers with their mental health stressors. It's a complex and wide-reaching problem. We all acknowledge that. And, it can be a deflating problem to solve, as there is no single solution or perfect intervention. So, I continued to mull it over. And while I was feeling sorry for myself, the state of the world, and a few things our dog did to a relatively nice dresser, something hit me. Not all at once, but in a repetitive and somewhat insidious fashion. The following thoughts materialized:

- Teachers miss feeling invigorated about their job, and for some, morale is quickly eroding.

- Educators are often pulled in many different directions with poor guidance on prioritizing the tasks given to them. This creates a lack of clarity when identifying the role of a teacher in some schools unless the role of a teacher is as ill-defined as "fix everything."

• More and more, aspects of school seen as "red tape" prevent educators from connecting with kids in ways that genuinely matter. That further impairs teacher morale.

Now, I admit that the three above bullet points are all claims that we have heard for a while, correct? But do me a favor. Examine this situation from a different lens and connect the dots between students and staff. It now appears as the following:

What teachers WANT in their job right now is to: i) prioritize meaningful connections with students above other tasks, and ii) focus their efforts on projects within the scope of their licensure and training. This is also what students NEED to improve their mental health.

Pause for a moment. The observation above is a prognostic indicator for success that should not be ignored. The most ideal and productive partnerships occur when one party's needs directly align with the other party's desires. It's how the best business deals, marriages, and many other meaningful relationships are formed. As such, we need to leverage this reality for the success and health of BOTH our students and staff.

Educators worked their tails off to invest in a career in education. It wasn't for the financial reward. And it's not like teaching is the only job out there with eight weeks of time off. As you already know, most teachers and administrative leaders in education jumped headlong into this career path because they felt a calling and knew they had the skills to serve. So, let's give teachers what they want. Let's focus on using strategies that fall within their training and have evidence to demonstrate that their effort will make a measurable improvement for Gen Zers and the mental health of many generations to follow. Educators need an evidence-based plan with focused recommendations, appropriate scaffolding, and permission to leverage academic content to address critical determinants of mental health and build life skills in a way that falls within the scope of a teacher's current training. Chapter 9 is going to provide that in great detail.

But before we get too excited, let's clarify something. What I propose in Chapter 9 is *NOT* traditional Social Emotional Learning (SEL). While SEL has its role and looks great on paper, it also has some problems. See if these sound familiar:

- SEL lessons currently occur as an **adjunct** in the classroom. They are typically forced into a unit as opposed to being integrated into lessons in a seamless fashion. How many times has an instructor been asked to pause their lesson so that a counselor can pop in and discuss alcohol abuse? It doesn't really fit into the second act of Shakespeare's Macbeth. Unless, of course, you want an unhealthy way to cope with reading Macbeth.

- SEL is not standardized and, in some school districts, covers a wide array of topics, often at the discretion of the counseling staff or principal. This can be good or bad, depending upon the topic, delivery, and student interest. Based on the presentation, there may be little to no efficacy from that intervention.

  o Example: Many districts toss kids into a gym one afternoon, hire a speaker, and check the box required for a given topic. I know this because I've provided some of these presentations. And trust me, as much as I would like to claim that I can captivate 1,500 students in a gym, you and I both know I would be far more effective in a smaller classroom.

- Many SEL lessons are content-based only, almost as a form of direct instruction. Why does this matter? Here is an example. I can teach you how to care about someone who is anxious, but that is not the same as forming relationships with them, complimenting them when they handle a difficult situation well, promoting their self-esteem, and/or putting them through safe exercises every week that demonstrate to them that they do, in fact, have the resilience to manage anxiety.

- In most settings, academic content is emphasized *over* mental health, resilience, and skills for the future. Students are aware of this and, therefore, take SEL less seriously. In fact, depending upon the culture of the school, there can be a stigma attached to many breakout SEL lessons.

To be clear, I'm not trying to suggest that SEL learning is a bad thing. Quite the opposite, as I do see tons of value in it. However, I also know that the data we explored in Part 1 and 2 is telling, and numbers do not lie. SEL alone may have slowed the decline in mental health, but the decline still exists. That is an undeniable fact all educators and parents are forced to accept. And so, I share the following again to drive home the point:

Mental health trends in school-aged children were frightening before the pandemic. Please do NOT kid yourself and go back to "normal." Data from the CDC, American Academy of Pediatrics, National Institutes of Health, and leading research endeavors demonstrate that our earlier "solutions" will likely not improve the downward trend.

It's likely that SEL suffered in some districts due to the scattered implementation and varying levels of use in classroom settings. But in the end, that's admittedly an educated guess. Whatever the precise cause, educators can't afford to ignore the trends for anxiety, depression, mental health visits, and suicidal ideation from 2000-2019. That data exposes the shortcomings of the prior operational constraints within schools in general. And in the end, SEL can still offer students a great deal of value. I would argue it should remain for a long time. However, the data you have reviewed demonstrates that SEL alone is clearly not sufficient.

Enter a teacher-led initiative, driven by the evidence cited in this book, which can be layered on top of current SEL programs. This creates a supportive integration, and it will become more apparent in Chapter 9. But for now, know that the value of teachers leveraging their innate skills is a proven commodity for academic proficiency, extracurricular success, and other priorities in a school district. It's time to grant teachers permission to let go of some educational red tape and tradition that have served as roadblocks for decades. Students need teachers to have time to generate inspiring moments that make the following clear: self-esteem, self-efficacy, and life skills are high priorities in their school.

Evidence behind improving self-esteem

Back in Chapter 2, we took a deep dive into the importance of self-esteem and self-efficacy. Both are potent determinants of mental health, serving as either protective factors or risk factors. This makes our work with self-efficacy and self-esteem a high yield area of intervention. Consider the tremendous shift in mental stability when someone pulls a child out of a negative self-esteem environment into a place where they believe they can navigate problems and know that others see value in them. That's quite the change, as it negates considerable risk factors in their life and literally replaces them with protective factors. I wish we could do that for other areas of health! Think about it. I would happily replace specific areas of flabbiness (courtesy of cortisol stress hormone during 2020) on my abdomen for some muscle—a positive replacement that should boost my amateur triathlete status from semi-decent to average.

I would like to further the broad concepts from Chapter 2 by exploring some data that specifically applies to education. Why? Because educators deserve to know that there is evidence, not just opinion, that confirms a teacher's ability to positively impact both self-esteem and self-efficacy with a high degree of effectiveness. This isn't just a feel-good, fluff-based, pendulum swing in education, where we all awkwardly high-five each other at the end of the presentation. Rather, if used correctly, this is science that will make us want to jump up and hug each other for what we did for our students and our career satisfaction.

To begin, the American Psychological Association has a portion of its website dedicated to itemized ideas on how educators can build student self-esteem.[20] Why? Because ever since Dr. Nel Noddings, professor of education at Stanford University, explored the ethics and impact of caring for students in schools way back in the 1980s, there have been countless articles validating the impact teachers play on students' self-esteem. Well, to be truthful, they are countable. Google seems to think there are 778 million related possibilities. "Sorry, not sorry" that I didn't cover them all. But the point is that educational researchers have looked into this intently and consistently found that teachers have the time, setting, and skills to positively impact students' mental health through boosting self-esteem.

As this research evolved, it became more focused. By 2011, Dr. Martin Seligman, the director of the clinical training program in the Department of Psychology at the University of Pennsylvania, isolated five critical factors that increase the probability of positive flourishing and mental stability.[21] Seligman called his approach to these factors the PERMA model, and they were quickly considered the foundational concepts of a field now known as positive psychology.[21]

- P= positive emotion

- E= engagement

- R= relationships

- M= meaning

- A= accomplishment

Interesting list. I want to ask you a simple question. Who is better trained to implement these concepts in a child's eight-hour day than a highly effective teacher? Honestly, I can't think of anyone. But as insightful as Dr. Noddings and Dr. Seligman are, it's also nice to see some raw numbers and quantitative evidence. Let's explore a peer-reviewed article that *Teaching and Teacher Education* published in 2020. The research article does a wonderful job rehashing observational work related to student self-esteem, citing more than 30 other academic sources. The authors, Dr. Shiri Lavy and Eman Naama-Ghanayim, then share quantitative data from their multilevel study of 675 secondary students. Using statistically valid tests, they proved a mathematical correlation (p-value <.05) between a student's perception of high teacher engagement, which manifested as caring, and elevated student self-esteem.[22] Even though educators already suspected this, it's nice to verify. The practical and critical takeaways from t Lavy and Naama-Ghanayim's analysis include:[22]

- Teacher caring was positively associated with students' self-esteem, well-being, and school engagement.

- Teacher-student relationships mediated these associations.

- *Teachers' sense of meaning at work was associated with students' reports on their teachers being caring.*

The last bullet point is particularly insightful and extremely important for the post-pandemic classroom. Intervening to boost student self-esteem doesn't just save the student. Allowing teachers to focus on how to better a student's life as much as academics generates a true win for both parties.

Strategies to improve self-efficacy

I've often thought that self-efficacy is a buzzword bounced around educational environments so much that we are desensitized to how important it is. Self-efficacy drives a student when the process or pathway to reach that goal is difficult or tethered to long hours and extra work outside of class. If students have high self-efficacy, they are willing to leverage the skills they have to solve problems and accomplish tasks. Perhaps more importantly, students with a high degree of self-efficacy are willing to chase down new knowledge or skills to overcome unexpected roadblocks because they believe that they can accomplish the task at hand once they have that piece of the puzzle. That's a wonderful approach to life. It's also an economic asset, as employers look for problem-solving skills, confidence, and solutions-driven thought patterns in their applicants.

To no surprise, a wide bandwidth of interested parties have taken a look at the value of self-efficacy because it represents a key element of success in their environment. Various business journals and corporate executives argue the link between high self-efficacy and successful entrepreneurship, career advancement, and wealth acquisition.[23] Health care, which is largely data-driven, invests time and effort to optimize patient self-efficacy for improving long-term health outcomes.[24,25] And to no surprise, medical training requires nurses, physicians, and other providers to model high levels of self-efficacy throughout their medical training. And then, there are the armed forces. The United States military spends a lot of time, effort, and money sending high-ranking officers through graduate education at the Command and Staff College, where self-efficacy is a foundational pillar of their leadership curriculum. And, it should be. Well-developed self-efficacy seems like an unspoken requirement if you're responsible for leading human lives into unpredictable and sudden conflicts.

Self-efficacy is a valued attribute for life after graduation. It's essential for navigating life's challenges, whether work-related, personal, or both. However, what's the best way to promote self-efficacy in students? How do we create a positive perception of self-efficacy in our classrooms, allowing students to practice one of the most important gifts a teacher can give them? Good news. There are a plethora of good resources on the internet from respected institutions to turn to for advice. Allow me to share four strategies that the American Psychological Association recommends specifically for teachers.[26]

- Share experiences on decision making and managing emotions

- Acknowledge brilliant performances (success breeds more success)

- Frame student feedback to promote encouragement over unintentional discouragement

- Promote situations that allow management of psychological factors (ex: student gives a speech to friends with the teacher out of the field of view, conquering a small part of the student's anxiety)

As you might imagine, there are plenty of other strategies beyond the APA suggestions. Goal setting with feedback and creating daily problem-solving activities are also efficacious ideas.[27] But the point is not to persuade you to pick one self-efficacy resource over another. Instead, it's to demonstrate one essential concept—the importance of teachers. Enthusiastic teachers are the perfect role models to implement these self-efficacy strategies because each one of them plays to their training, creativity, and calling. Educators and administrators know this. However, sometimes school districts can get distracted with hot topics or community initiatives that detract from this. Try hard to avoid that from happening. Taking the time to teach a student that they can persevere through a problem and reach the goal on the other side has never been more critical. And that, my friends, is true inside and outside the classroom.

Skills uncertainty

The final focus for educators should be dealing with uncertainty. What exactly do I mean by that? A few things. First and perhaps foremost, the wild events of 2020 reminded us again that we live in a time of enormous uncertainty and volatile change. The political, economic, social, and even health-related landscape can all change overnight, and all of us are asked to adapt. Some do this well. Others struggle. What's one of the major determinants that sets those two cohorts apart? Skills. More specifically, the type of skills that are universally applicable to all sorts of environments, allowing an individual to have the confidence that they possess the ability to succeed in their current situation and whatever the world morphs to next.

Now, as you might guess, these are not content-based skills. Technology and information are evolving so fast that it would be impossible to teach a secondary student industry content in 2021 that would likely be relevant in 2025 when they graduate from college. And if they pursue trade school or seek out a career in the military, those institutions are prepared to provide the high-level content they need for that particular role. So, what better way to use the time in K-12 than to teach universal skills that will be ingrained in the mindset of our students before they take their first job.

All that said, what are some of these specific skills that apply in any uncertain situation? Oh, just ones that teachers would be outstanding at implementing in their classroom. Here are some skills that *Forbes* advertises as ideal for career development and success during 2020 and beyond.[28]

1. Complex problem solving

2. Critical thinking and analysis

3. Creativity, innovation, ideation, originality, and initiative

4. People management

5. Coordinating with others

6. Emotional intelligence

7. Judgment, reasoning, analytical thinking, and decision making

8. Service orientation

9. Negotiation

10. Cognitive flexibility

11. Active learning and learning strategies

12. Technology design and programming

13. Leadership and social influence

14. Systems analysis and evaluation

15. Cultural sensitivity and awareness

I can't think of a single skill in the above list that I couldn't work into a classroom setting. The state standards and district expectations provide plenty of opportunities to do so. And furthermore, give educators enough time, and they will inherently link these skills with self-esteem and self-efficacy. Need an example? Before a student turns in a social studies project, ask them how they negotiated with their partner regarding what topic they would select and what was hard about that negotiation? Want to go one level deeper? Ask the student if their partner's body language matched their words when making decisions about the project and which did they trust more? All of these dots can be quickly connected when placed in the hands of a motivated teacher.

Final thoughts

When I opened this chapter, I rehashed the painful lesson imparted to me in my backyard with brotherly love. As we discussed, that discrete moment in time taught me a lot about facial swelling, the velocity of venous blood, and how to pick your battles wisely. But clearly, there is much more that can be garnered from this lesson. For starters, it would be exceedingly difficult, if not exhausting, to cruise through life and pick battles left and right for emotional reasons—or, more accurately, for unbridled emotions that are not linked to data or careful consideration. This passionate and impulsive behavior may seem charismatic, but it's not guaranteed to improve the world around you. There is often little thought behind that passion and even less evidence to support it. As a bloodied 12-year-old, I sorted that out pretty quickly.

That said, there are also times in our life where battles *are* worth our time, effort, and emotion. Those times are rare for a multitude of reasons. First, there has to be credible evidence that suggests we are in the right and that someone is afflicted unjustly. If that's not validated, the cause we fight for may not be noble. Secondly, there has to be another set of evidence demonstrating that our efforts, if victorious, would result in a positive outcome. An outcome that is highly likely, if not guaranteed, to benefit the afflicted in measurable ways, which in turn will better their life. If both of those things are true, then we might be coming into contact with a moral imperative...meaning that NOT intervening would be inexcusable and potentially harmful. If that all holds true, then we come to the final point of consideration. Do we have the skills to engage in this specific battle and the perseverance to work toward a positive outcome? Rarely do all three of those things line up. But in the case of improving youth mental health, they do—they emphatically do.

Schools have hit a critical point. While their intentions have been good, they need to implement a more informed battle against youth mental health. They can't ignore the mental health fallout of Gen Zers. They also can't fix youth mental health on their own. But educators can wisely do their part. Students need someone that spends time with them, celebrates their authentic self, and establishes a connection. They also need someone who can assess their strengths and weaknesses and point out their growth and successes. And finally, students need someone that shows them the strategies, skills, and approaches that will allow them to solve problems in any future environment because they are confident that they **will** figure out the issues at hand. These are some of the critical elements that all school-aged children need—they are found in the hearts and minds of teachers.

Chapter 8 References

1. Nicholls, M. (2018). Funding of cardiovascular research in the USA: Robert Califf and Peter Libby – speak about cardiovascular research funding in the United States and what the latest trends are with Mark Nicholls. *European Heart Journal*, *39*(40), 3629–3631. https://doi.org/10.1093/eurheartj/ehy638

2. Schaper, D. (2021, January 8). *Boeing to pay $2.5 billion settlement over deadly 737 max crashes*. NPR. https://www.npr.org/2021/01/08/954782512/boeing-to-pay-2-5-billion-settlement-over-deadly-737-max-crashes

3. Walker, T. (2018, September 13). *Are schools ready to tackle the mental health crisis?* National Education Association (NEA). https://www.nea.org/advocating-for-change/new-from-nea/are-schools-ready-tackle-mental-health-crisis

4. World Health Organization. (2021). *Improving the mental and brain health of children and adolescents*. https://www.who.int/activities/Improving-the-mental-and-brain-health-of-children-and-adolescents

5. Frauenholtz, S., Mendenhall, A. N., & Moon, J. (2017). Role of school employees' mental health knowledge in interdisciplinary collaborations to support the academic success of students experiencing mental health distress. *Children & Schools*, *39*(2), 71–79. https://doi.org/10.1093/cs/cdx004

6. Centers for Disease Control and Prevention (CDC). (2014). *Introduction to Public Health*. In: Public Health 101 Series. Atlanta, GA: U.S. Department of Health and Human Services. https://www.cdc.gov/training/publichealth101/public-health.html

7. Child Mind Institute. (2020). *Highlights of the 2020 children's mental health report: Telehealth in an increasingly virtual world*. https://childmind.org/our-impact/childrens-mental-health-report/2020-childrens-mental-health-report/

8. Martinelli, K., Cohen, Y., Kimball, H., & Sheldon-Dean, H. (2020). *Children's mental health report: Telehealth in an*

increasingly virtual world. Child Mind Institute. https:// childmind.org/our-impact/childrens-mental-health-repor t/2020-childrens-mental-health-report/

9. McBain, R. K., Kofner, A., Stein, B. D., Cantor, J. H., Vogt, W. B., & Yu, H. (2019). Growth and distribution of child psychiatrists in the United States: 2007–2016. *Pediatrics, 144*(6). https://doi. org/10.1542/peds.2019-1576

10. National Association of School Psychologists (NASP). (2021). *Shortage of school psychologists.* https://www.nasponline.org/ research-and-policy/policy-priorities/critical-policy-issues/ shortage-of-school-psychologists

11. Kansas Association of School Psychologists. (2017, January). *Report on the shortage of school psychologists in Kansas.* https://www.nasponline.org/Documents/Resources%20and%20Publications/Resources/ KASP_Report_Shortages.pdf

12. Health Resources and Services Administration/National Center for Health Workforce Analysis; Substance Abuse and Mental Health Services Administration/Office of Policy, Planning, and Innovation. 2015. National Projections of Supply and Demand for Behavioral Health Practitioners: 2013-2025. Rockville, Maryland. https://bhw. hrsa.gov/sites/default/files/bureau-health-workforce/data-research/ behavioral-health-2013-2025.pdf

13. American School Counselor Association, & National Association for College Admission Counseling. (2015). *State-by-state student to counselor ratio report: 10 year trends.* https://www.nacacnet.org/ globalassets/documents/publications/research/state-by-state-ratio- report.pdf

14. The Education Trust. (2019, February 1). *School counselors matter.* https://edtrust.org/resource/school-counselors-matter/

15. U.S. News & World Report. (2019). *How much does a school psychologist make?* https://money.usnews.com/careers/best-jobs/ school-psychologist/salary

16. Sheiner, L., & Campbell, S. (2020, September 24). *How much is COVID-19 hurting state and local revenues?* Brookings Institution. https://www.brookings.edu/blog/up-front/2020/09/24/ how-much-is-covid-19-hurting-state-and-local-revenues/

17. U.S. Department of Education. (2020, April 23). *Secretary DeVos makes available over $13 billion in emergency coronavirus relief to support continued education for K-12 students*. https://www.ed.gov/news/press-releases/secretary-devos-makes-available-over-1 3-billion-emergency-coronavirus-relief-support-continued-education-k-12-students

18. Griffith, M., & Berry, W. (2020, September 24). *COVID-19 and state education budgets: The story behind the numbers*. Learning Policy Institute. https://learningpolicyinstitute.org/blog/covid-state-education-budgets-story-behind-numbers

19. Dickler, J. (2021, March 1). *More teachers plan to quit as Covid stress overwhelms educators*. CNBC. https://www.cnbc.com/2021/03/01/more-teachers-plan-to-quit-as-covid-stress-overwhelms-educators.html

20. American Psychological Association. (2021). *Students experiencing low self-esteem or low perceptions of competence*. https://www.apa.org/ed/schools/primer/self-esteem

21. The University of Pennsylvania Positive Psychology Center. (2021). *PERMA^{TM} theory of well-being and PERMA^{TM} workshops*. The University of Pennsylvania School of Arts and Sciences. https://ppc.sas.upenn.edu/learn-more/perma-theory-well-being-and-perma-workshops

22. Lavy, S., & Naama-Ghanayim, E. (2020). Why care about caring? Linking teachers' caring and sense of meaning at work with students' self-esteem, well-being, and school engagement. *Teaching and Teacher Education, 91,* 103046. https://doi.org/10.1016/j.tate.2020.103046

23. Prince, R. A. (2013, October 16). *Self-made millionaires = high self-efficacy*. Forbes. https://www.forbes.com/sites/russalanprince/2013/10/16/self-made-millionaires-high-self-efficacy/

24. Hoffman A. J. (2013). Enhancing self-efficacy for optimized patient outcomes through the theory of symptom self-management. *Cancer Nursing, 36*(1), E16–E26. https://doi.org/10.1097/NCC.0b013e31824a730a

25. Buzaglo, J. (2016, November 17). *Empowering Patients to Become Effective Self-Advocates*. Psychology Today. https://www.psychologytoday.com/blog/the-patient-s-voice/201611/empowering-patients-become-effective-self-advocates

26. Relojo-Howell, D. (2017, December 3). *Help your students believe in themselves: Self-Efficacy in the classroom*. American Psychological Association's Psych Learning Curve. http://psychlearningcurve.org/self-efficacy-in-the-classroom/

27. The Education Hub. (2018). *6 strategies for promoting student self-efficacy in your teaching*. https://www.theeducationhub.org.nz/wp-content/uploads/2018/03/6-strategies-for-promoting-student-self-efficacy.pdf

28. Beckford, A. (2020, July 2). The skills you need to succeed in 2020 and beyond. Forbes. https://www.forbes.com/sites/ellevate/2020/07/02/the-skills-you-need-to-succeed-in-2020-and-beyond/

9

SEAL Ambassador Program... Implementing strategies for students

A ny way you cut it, the demands that came with COVID-19 created unprecedented problems for all members of our community. Admittedly, some specific demographics and cohorts were hit harder than others when it comes to the physical and mental toll of this pandemic. That is undeniable. To no surprise, those severely afflicted populations will need additional support. But in the end, I have to believe that all of you reading this book experienced some level of stress and challenges from SARS-CoV-2. All the more reason each one of us should place empathy and kindness at the forefront of our minds for quite some time...because there are still plenty of Americans staggering around in a daze, perhaps wondering, "What next?"

I suspect that most educators feel disillusioned from this pandemic due to one reason or another. I know from the educators I collaborate with that exhaustion and burnout have never weighed more on their daily lives. Take time to reflect. Don't worry too much about the haze you might be in right now. It will eventually clear. And in the end, all of us will choose how we move forward with life and our careers.

But, before you make that decision, I want to selfishly share with you some wisdom I ran across. And, I say selfishly because my ulterior motive is to encourage you to remain steadfast in the world of education. To even consider that, you need to think about what education might offer you once the dust of COVID-19 has cleared. That may seem tough to do right now but try. For starters, do you still enjoy connecting with students? And hey, be honest...would you enjoy your role further if you could spend more time focusing on a child's long-term outlook for life, as opposed to memorization and test prep? And if you are willing, please go one step further. Consider this: do you still feel a calling inside you that working with children is what you are meant to do? If the answers to those questions stir up positive emotions for you, then please keep reading. I'd like to share an evidence-based operational framework that will allow you to run your classroom in a way that prioritizes time to better the life of a child while still respecting the state standards and district expectations.

So, how do we do that? What should be the next move for all of us that are currently disillusioned yet know we'll be supervising a significant number of students that are desperately struggling with mental health? That's a tough question, but here is my suggestion. What **HAS** to be next is a change in mindset. And to be more specific, consider the following shift:

"You're not here to survive this. You're here to take charge of it."

Definitely a call to action, huh? But here is the thing. I confess that I'm not one of those inspirational quote kinds of people. You won't see a poster in my office, classroom, or house that is there to pick me up on a rough day. However, this quote is powerful to me. Let me share why: it's the source of the quote that impacts me. This little pearl of wisdom comes from the U.S. Navy SEAL teams, who represent the most rigorously trained, most resilient, fearless group of individuals you could ever imagine. Need data to prove it? Candidates that apply for Navy SEAL training must prove themselves to be in exceptional shape in terms of mental and physical toughness with qualifying assessments, yet around 75% of these leaders will drop out before the initial training is complete. The physical duress, mental challenges, and persistent lack of sleep are so consuming that the human body often falls prey to utter exhaustion and collapses.

With all this in mind, I hope you can appreciate that Navy SEALs command a level of intensity and resilience that only a handful of people in the world possess. Impressive. Please do me a favor—go back and read that quote one more time and appreciate *who* is saying it as much as what's said. These brave and skilled individuals are put in the worst situations and at extremely high risk. Yet, it is not enough for them to simply survive a mission. They are looking to own the situation and take charge of it. That's one of many things that makes a Navy SEAL special.

As educators, we fought through the pandemic, doing our best to survive the challenges thrown at us. So did our kids. It's time to move from reactionary to proactive. We need to do this for the students as much as ourselves. I'm not saying there was anything wrong with the "survive and advance" mentality that governed school operations for quite some time. It was necessary for various reasons. However, I would argue that we are all now collectively in a different place, and it's time to rebuild our confidence and restore the value and joy in teaching that needs to be there. In short, friends and colleagues, it's time to take charge of things.

Before this chapter ends, you'll have the opportunity to explore the Social Emotional Academic Leader (SEAL) Ambassador Program. Consider it a call to action for educators who understand mental health trends and are willing to admit that Gen Zers were suffering well before COVID-19. We can't afford to go back to "normal" without expecting the same mental health erosion. The compelling data from the CDC, American Academy of Pediatrics, and Youth Risk Behavior Survey make that incredibly clear. Instead, I would argue that educators need to adjust and draw upon their natural talents. Allow teachers to prioritize mental health so high that it becomes a natural and integrated part of their daily classes, not a stand-alone video or assembly. And to do this well, in a way that allows the program to flourish and kids to benefit, we need implementations to be teacher-driven, not a directive from the district office. Rather, the SEAL Ambassador Program needs to function as a breath of fresh air that allows teachers to leverage academic content to teach more important lessons about self-esteem, self-efficacy, and universal skills that provide students the confidence to navigate life after graduation.

I fully admit that not every staff member will jump at this opportunity. Some individuals, quite understandably, may want to wait in the wings to see how the first round goes and what the initial teachers think. That's fine. There is nothing wrong with that approach. I am also confident that every school building contains some SEAL Ambassadors at heart, willing to be the first ones to dive in and lead the charge. Friends, the data is compelling. In fact, *not* addressing the mental health downfall in Gen Zers and future generations fits the medical definition of negligence. But as we talked about in earlier chapters, teachers have the innate skills to make an evidence-based impact, making this worth our time, our students' time, and allowing schools to contribute to an overall solution. But it all has to start somewhere. And just like the real US Navy SEAL teams, each building will need some heroes to lead the charge. I hope you're willing to be one of them.

Before we can begin, I need to give some insight into the process. To visualize how educators can take charge of mental health protective factors, we need a logical pathway. This pathway must provide evidence-based strategies that improve the mental health of school-aged children **without** moving beyond the scope of a teacher's licensure or skill set. Because, as we mentioned earlier, teachers are not mental health providers. No one in the community should expect them to be. However, teachers do have the perfect skills for this situation and can make a positive impact if districts give them the latitude to do so. To demonstrate this further, the remainder of this chapter will provide the following details:

- Logistical roadmap, providing the shift in mindset and operations of the SEAL Ambassador Program

- Strategies and resources for promoting self-esteem, self-efficacy, and life skills in students

- Specific examples for unit and lesson design that utilizes SEAL Ambassador Program integration

Introducing the SEAL Ambassador Program

Any time there is a shift in educational operations, it's likely that one of two possibilities is driving the change. The first possibility, and perhaps most common, occurs when the district office implements a new policy and the directive is seemingly forced upon teachers from the top down. This can be good or bad in terms of teacher buy-in, depending on the timing, delivery, and topic. The second possibility, which is more grassroots in nature, stems from teachers and building leaders proactively adjusting their practice to address a critical issue before them. The SEAL Ambassador Program is built to be the second. The pathway is teacher-initiated and teacher-led, two critical elements to its longevity and success. And throughout this chapter, you will see these principles represented in all six phases of its implementation.

Equally important, the SEAL Ambassador Program is a framework. It is a detailed scaffold with ample supporting material, but it is **NOT** a prescriptive document. I don't pretend for a moment to know the ins and outs of your district or building. As such, the operational choices within the framework need to be made by the SEAL Ambassador Team in conjunction with support from administrators. It's important for me to be clear with those facts upfront. Why? Because teachers are exhausted. They have been through an uncountable number of hardships during the pandemic. The last thing they need is for anything to impede one of their greatest joys—using their creative flair and teaching style to impact a child. That creativity is yours. It always should be. And I'm happy to relay that the SEAL Ambassador Program will draw it out of you even further, allowing you to focus on building kids into what they need to be for the rest of their lives: confident, resilient, loving, and *healthy*. I hope that's exciting and refreshing for educators reading this book and wondering, "what's next?"

With all that in mind, the SEAL Ambassador Program is meant to start small. For this upgrade to be a teacher-led process, it should start with a dedicated group of staff and move at a pace that those teachers deem to be manageable for their building, district, and community. Administrators, counselors, school psychologists, and social workers are there for guidance and support, but in the end, the success of the program and the positive change in students will be largely driven by the teachers involved. There are six distinct phases to guide the process, with each offering a well-researched scaffold. And keep in mind, changes can be made. The SEAL Ambassador Program is built to evaluate its own strategies, incorporate revisions, and recruit additional rockstar teachers along the way.

Phase 1: Establish common understanding and program goals

To begin any worthwhile initiative, there needs to be a common understanding. And in this particular project, I would suggest our understanding should focus upon the causes and vulnerabilities that precipitated the youth mental health crisis and what sustains it. By using that line of inquiry, educators are less likely to put a metaphorical Band-Aid on the *symptoms* of the youth mental health fallout and more likely to care for the *deeper issues* driving the crisis. As such, Phase 1 of the SEAL Ambassador Program takes time to share some powerful data regarding youth mental health trends to get everyone on the same page. This, in turn, fosters a deeper understanding of the SEAL Ambassador Program's overall goals before the operational details are discussed.

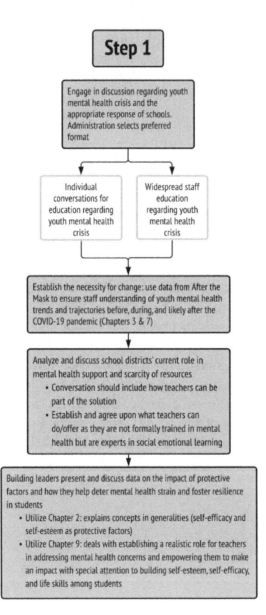

Step 1

Engage in discussion regarding youth mental health crisis and the appropriate response of schools. Administration selects preferred format

Individual conversations for education regarding youth mental health crisis

Widespread staff education regarding youth mental health crisis

Establish the necessity for change: use data from After the Mask to ensure staff understanding of youth mental health trends and trajectories before, during, and likely after the COVID-19 pandemic (Chapters 3 & 7)

Analyze and discuss school districts' current role in mental health support and scarcity of resources
- Conversation should include how teachers can be part of the solution
- Establish and agree upon what teachers can do/offer as they are not formally trained in mental health but are experts in social emotional learning

Building leaders present and discuss data on the impact of protective factors and how they help deter mental health strain and foster resilience in students
- Utilize Chapter 2: explains concepts in generalities (self-efficacy and self-esteem as protective factors)
- Utilize Chapter 9: deals with establishing a realistic role for teachers in addressing mental health concerns and empowering them to make an impact with special attention to building self-esteem, self-efficacy, and life skills among students

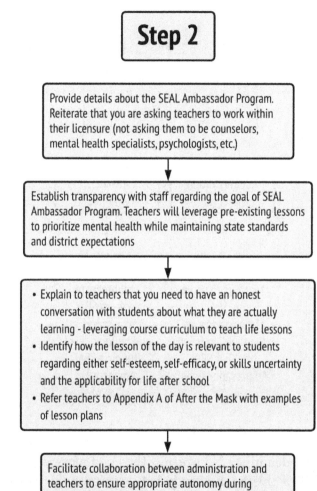

Step 2

Provide details about the SEAL Ambassador Program. Reiterate that you are asking teachers to work within their licensure (not asking them to be counselors, mental health specialists, psychologists, etc.)

Establish transparency with staff regarding the goal of SEAL Ambassador Program. Teachers will leverage pre-existing lessons to prioritize mental health while maintaining state standards and district expectations

- Explain to teachers that you need to have an honest conversation with students about what they are actually learning - leveraging course curriculum to teach life lessons
- Identify how the lesson of the day is relevant to students regarding either self-esteem, self-efficacy, or skills uncertainty and the applicability for life after school
- Refer teachers to Appendix A of After the Mask with examples of lesson plans

Facilitate collaboration between administration and teachers to ensure appropriate autonomy during program implementation

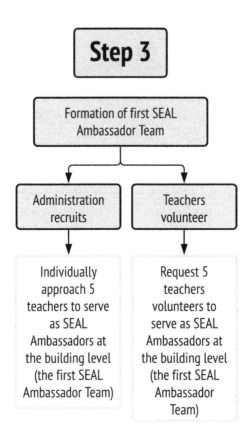

Seem daunting? No worries. The good news is that Parts 1 and 2 of this book already led you down this investigative path. You have all the information to get started. Recall that the first four chapters took a deep dive into the likely vulnerabilities, concerning predictions, and tragic outcome data regarding Gen Zers' mental health status over time. This established an unfortunate and concerning trend regarding youth anxiety, depression, substance abuse, and suicidal ideation, which seamlessly correlated with the rise in pediatric mental health visits and the use of professional services in the past decade. Knowing that the relevant data has been gathered for you, all that remains is for building leaders to share that information with other staff in the right setting and for the right purpose.

So, what is the purpose of sharing this information? Simple—establish the moral imperative for action and, equally important, reignite the fire in teachers' hearts. That flame dwindled significantly during the pandemic, and it needs to be restored with something that staff believe in and see as a real opportunity for success. This is good for students and restorative for staff. Furthermore, it's no secret that passionate individuals are typically the most productive workers, as their actions no longer seem like labor. Their time and effort correlate with a natural calling—teachers know that feeling. It's what drove us into the field of education and inspires us during the low points of our careers. So, I suppose, like many journeys, the first step of the SEAL Ambassador Program will be the most important. As such, please take time to establish the moral imperative. If you do, it will always remain.

All that said, great actions need to be planned and not driven by emotion alone. As I mentioned before, be wise when you pick your battles. Building leadership requires taking a moment to have a healthy discussion regarding the realistic role of school districts and individual educators when it comes to improving student mental health. This allows the discussion participants to acknowledge some boundaries and limitations before launching into the passionate initiative to improve the student mental health crisis. By doing this, educators can see their role in the larger effort to address the mental health crisis and confirm that schools do not have the skills or capacity to fight the battle alone. That is the reality of the situation. And, based upon the hundreds of discussions I have had regarding this topic with educators, I'm predicting you and your colleagues would come up with something close to the following:

- Teachers and administrators are **NOT** mental health professionals and should not act as such.

- There is already a scarcity of school specialists that can address complex mental health issues, and budget constraints will likely limit the future growth and development of this cohort.

- Teachers are professionally trained and possess skills that foster the academic prowess and life skills of a child, preparing them for life after graduation.

So, how can teachers be the heroes and heroines in this battle against erosive mental health in children? Simple. Play to the strengths of teachers. Allow qualified educators to work in a way that excites them by leveraging their current curriculum and lessons to enhance self-esteem, promote self-efficacy, and introduce critical skills that facilitate success in all job settings. This is what kids need. And they need it effective immediately. Teachers know this because there may not be a better person on earth to connect with a child outside of the home and prepare them for life. In some ways, educators hold more influence than parents. Anyone who has taught for a few years realizes this. Even my daughter has announced at the dinner table that "a growth mindset is important to solving this problem!" (Trust me... if I suggested some problem-solving strategies, an eye roll and groan would be in my future). Yet, in the chaos of test-taking, state assessments, and 2 million rolls of educational red tape, we collectively lose sight of this. Maybe not entirely, but frequently in terms of our day-to-day operations.

Teachers have begged to have their autonomy and creativity back. Sadly, they finally have an argument to "up the ante" when it comes to their request—students *desperately* need time and attention directed to their mental well-being. But, where will that time come from? How will it magically infuse into the classroom, our new battleground, to improve mental health? I would humbly suggest that time is generated from the creative minds of capable staff. Don't believe it's possible? Hear me out.

While state standards and district expectations are here to stay, they typically don't define the depth of understanding for each topic. This allows teachers to exercise discretion regarding what academic content requires more time and what content could/should be superficial in nature. As such, teachers need to stop concerning themselves with teaching every topic in every unit to the maximum depth. It's self-imposed pressure that does not need to be there. Please don't fall into the trap. Use your professional skills to seek out opportunities frequently and infuse memorable experiences that improve self-esteem, self-efficacy, and build life skills—the kind of skills that students actually believe they will use after they graduate. This shift in mindset has to happen in education. To say it's a game-changer for students is an understatement. To say that it's a lifesaver is actually realistic. You just need to pick the first group of SEAL Ambassadors that are willing to lead it.

Phase 2: Provide training and logistical support (first SEAL Ambassador Team)

NASA proved with their Apollo program that practice leads to perfection, or at least something close to it. And boy, did they practice. Thirty-eight thousand hours in a simulator, which called upon thoughtful planning, real-time revisions, and forming close bonds as team members, is what it took to get all of their Apollo astronaut crews to the moon and back.[1] Quite an impressive feat. Admittedly, 99.9% of projects in the world don't require that kind of time commitment. However, they should consider following a similar model when it comes to appropriate training and preparation. This is exactly what Phase 2 of the SEAL Ambassador Program is designed to do.

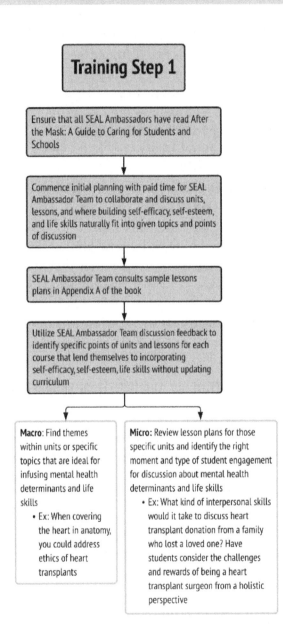

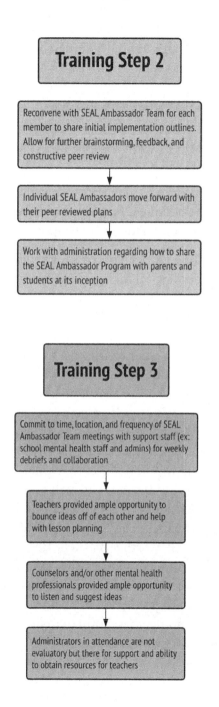

Training Step 2

Reconvene with SEAL Ambassador Team for each member to share initial implementation outlines. Allow for further brainstorming, feedback, and constructive peer review

Individual SEAL Ambassadors move forward with their peer reviewed plans

Work with administration regarding how to share the SEAL Ambassador Program with parents and students at its inception

Training Step 3

Commit to time, location, and frequency of SEAL Ambassador Team meetings with support staff (ex: school mental health staff and admins) for weekly debriefs and collaboration

Teachers provided ample opportunity to bounce ideas off of each other and help with lesson planning

Counselors and/or other mental health professionals provided ample opportunity to listen and suggest ideas

Administrators in attendance are not evaluatory but there for support and ability to obtain resources for teachers

As the logic charts demonstrate, Phase 2 exists to organize the timeline and appropriate personnel to support the first SEAL Ambassador Team. The major steps needed to move SEAL Ambassador Team 1.0 from a concept to a positive force in the classroom are as follows:

- Provide sufficient data regarding the mental health crisis and student vulnerabilities.

- Set up the recommended professional learning community for the building's first SEAL Ambassador Team and provide the full bandwidth of support teachers need.

- Scaffold the suggested process for reviewing current lessons and curriculum for opportunities to infuse teachable moments regarding self-esteem, self-efficacy, and skills uncertainty.

In the beginning, one of the most challenging elements for the first SEAL Ambassador Team will likely be familiarity and confidence. Teachers are certainly aware of the definition and applicability of both self-esteem and self-efficacy, but it will take some time before consistently infusing them into class discussions, projects, and various other forms of student engagement. This will undoubtedly require a shift from traditional teaching, and the students will notice. But that's also the point. When students feel a connection with their teacher and perceive compassion and caring toward them, it adds to their feelings of self-worth.[2] As such, Phase 2 of the SEAL Ambassador Program emphasizes the importance of *planning* for an honest and open discussion with students regarding the intent of the program (Phase 3 will explain *having* these discussions). By doing this, both the educator and student will enter this journey together.

That said, what about SEAL Ambassador Team member confidence? That's tough to predict. Confidence may come slowly, or it may be there on day one. But either way, you are now part of a *group* of SEAL Ambassadors, and that has tremendous value. It's rare when an individual alone can outperform an individual surrounded by brilliant minds. This is why school districts group talent together. Most schools operate under collaborative principles, maximizing peer review and brainstorming within buildings in an evidence-based manner. In fact, depending upon your age, you may recall that Dr. Richard DuFour, former high school principal and educational guru, stressed this concept when he argued for the creation of professional learning communities. Continuing along with this trend, we see team-based approaches driving projects in the corporate world with equally great success. This is a popular strategy because of its proven success. So, why deviate from it? The SEAL Ambassador Program does not. Initial plans and efforts created by SEAL Ambassadors are peer-reviewed for a reason. It adds to the benefit of all, inside and outside the classroom. Please embrace your SEAL Ambassador Team. Rely on each other. Learn from each other. Laugh and cry with each other. Because in the end, **you are not here to survive this. You are here to take charge of it!**

NOTE: If your SEAL Ambassador Team needs inspiration, please consult sample lesson plans in Appendix A that have been used in classrooms and received excellent staff, student, and counselor feedback.

Phase 3: Implementation of SEAL Ambassador Team 1.0

One of the first steps of Phase 1 was to spend time establishing teacher buy-in and motivation. Phase 3 mirrors that process with students. Yep, we will take time to pull students into the center of discussion and share with them the design, purpose, and motivation behind this program, and more significantly, the change in your classroom. Instead of something being about the students or happening to the students, the

SEAL Program is an initiative that occurs **with** the students. This places the Gen Zers in your classroom in a much more active role. And admittedly, that might seem strange for your students. Why? Think about how education usually unfolds. From a student perspective, someone in another building makes a compelling argument regarding instruction for the district. Teachers learn about this decision and the initiative at hand. A change in the classroom occurs, which may or may not be noticed by kids, but either way, minimal discussion is provided as to why the change took place. And in the end, education *simply happened* to students.

I understand why this bothers students. And honestly, I agree. While the process is not malicious, it seems to marginalize the role of the student and minimize their feedback. It almost gives the impression that the teacher or school doesn't care about their thoughts and emotions, which could slam some doors when it comes to making connections. Why don't we pull kids in from the beginning of an initiative and let them feel part of the process? What's the problem with allowing students to understand the reason for a classroom initiative and the benefits it's designed to offer? And most importantly, why can't students be a part of assessing a new initiative since they are ultimately the principal component in this effort? The soft grievances make sense. Students want to be involved in action plans just as much as educators do. It brings them relevance, understanding, and often, motivation. This is precisely what Phase 3 of the SEAL Ambassador Program emphasizes.

PHASE 3: SEAL AMBASSADOR TEAM 1.0
IMPLEMENTATION

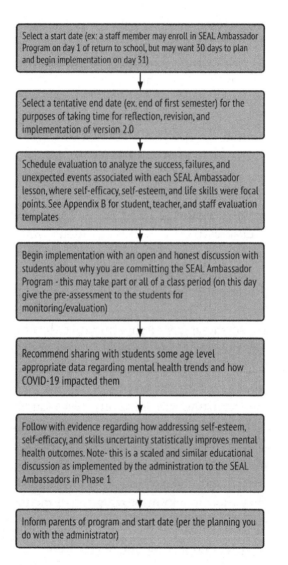

Select a start date (ex: a staff member may enroll in SEAL Ambassador Program on day 1 of return to school, but may want 30 days to plan and begin implementation on day 31)

Select a tentative end date (ex. end of first semester) for the purposes of taking time for reflection, revision, and implementation of version 2.0

Schedule evaluation to analyze the success, failures, and unexpected events associated with each SEAL Ambassador lesson, where self-efficacy, self-esteem, and life skills were focal points. See Appendix B for student, teacher, and staff evaluation templates

Begin implementation with an open and honest discussion with students about why you are committing the SEAL Ambassador Program - this may take part or all of a class period (on this day give the pre-assessment to the students for monitoring/evaluation)

Recommend sharing with students some age level appropriate data regarding mental health trends and how COVID-19 impacted them

Follow with evidence regarding how addressing self-esteem, self-efficacy, and skills uncertainty statistically improves mental health outcomes. Note- this is a scaled and similar educational discussion as implemented by the administration to the SEAL Ambassadors in Phase 1

Inform parents of program and start date (per the planning you do with the administrator)

As the graphic highlights, once the open and honest discussion occurs with students, it is quickly followed by a pre-program assessment for the teachers, counselors, and students involved. There are two reasons for this. The first is related to data. The second involves student voices and the need to integrate their thoughts from the very beginning. This way, the actions of SEAL Ambassadors match their words right from the start, which helps to build trust.

A few more words about data: it is not meant to be fluff or simply for optics—far from it, as that would be a waste of everyone's time. Rather, the SEAL Ambassador Program is built with the tools to assist teachers with qualitative and quantitative feedback that allows them to make week-to-week adjustments, analyze trends over time, and ultimately, create the next upgraded version of the SEAL Ambassador Program. This way, it ensures the program is a "living" initiative that responds to feedback and evidence. I suppose that means that a SEAL Ambassador program in northeast Kansas could end up looking different from those in Dallas, Texas, and Ocala, Florida. That's fine. In fact, it's more than fine. In many ways, it's one of the assets of this initiative. It allows teachers to flex the operational process to address specific mental health concerns in their building and district. And that, my friends, is what a teacher-driven process should look like. But for those that lean toward uniformity, rest assured that the framework and goals of the SEAL Ambassador Program are universal: use evidence-based strategies for the classroom that fall under the training and skill set of a teacher and optimize self-esteem, self-efficacy, and skills uncertainty, allowing schools to play their role in improving youth mental health.

Phase 4: Program monitoring and evaluation

As mentioned, SEAL Ambassador Teams need data. There is very little point in implementing a program unless you can make informed adjustments and upgrades for the future. Otherwise, an initiative becomes static and quickly outdated, potentially losing its applicability and/or relevance. I have already seen this occur multiple times thus far in my decade of teaching. Need an example? Several well-written vaping initiatives were too rigid in their design and put into practice well before consumers figured out how to add opioids and marijuana to e-cigarettes. These added drugs put a huge new spin on how schools should talk to students about the risks of vaping. So sadly, the programs became irrelevant. This could have been avoided if these programs utilized a platform that could undergo revisions and updates without compromising their end goals.

PHASE 4: SEAL AMBASSADOR PROGRAM MONITORING AND EVALUATION

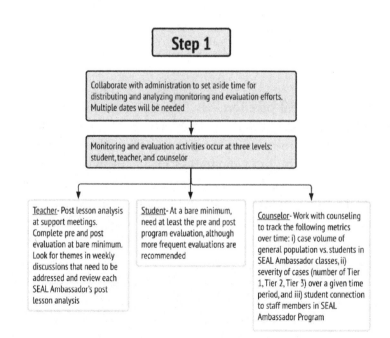

Step 1

Collaborate with administration to set aside time for distributing and analyzing monitoring and evaluation efforts. Multiple dates will be needed

Monitoring and evaluation activities occur at three levels: student, teacher, and counselor

Teacher- Post lesson analysis at support meetings. Complete pre and post evaluation at bare minimum. Look for themes in weekly discussions that need to be addressed and review each SEAL Ambassador's post lesson analysis

Student- At a bare minimum, need at least the pre and post program evaluation, although more frequent evaluations are recommended

Counselor- Work with counseling to track the following metrics over time: i) case volume of general population vs. students in SEAL Ambassador classes, ii) severity of cases (number of Tier 1, Tier 2, Tier 3) over a given time period, and iii) student connection to staff members in SEAL Ambassador Program

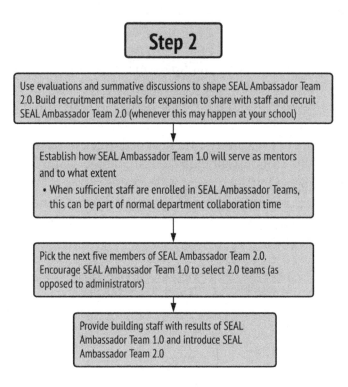

A great deal of effort has been spent to ensure SEAL Ambassador operations are NOT static. The goal of leveraging content to improve student mental health may remain constant, but the implementation mechanisms are meant to grow and improve. How does that happen? With meaningful data. In Appendix B, you will find templates and explanations regarding obtaining outcome data over short and long-term durations. This critical information allows SEAL Ambassadors to look for trends that highlight successful strategies along with unintentional shortcomings. Over time, these trends will grow and can lead to large-scale adjustments that help shape the initial approach of the next SEAL Ambassador Team. With this in mind, the SEAL Ambassador Program should inherently become more effective each semester to make a *measurable* positive impact with students in the specific areas of self-esteem, self-efficacy, and skills uncertainty. That's great information to collect and share with all involved, including the school community, when the time is right.

Finally, we all know that perspective matters. As such, the evaluations of the SEAL Ambassador Program provide a diverse set of information, adding to the perspective of feedback. It's no coincidence that evaluations regarding SEAL Ambassador Program strategies come from students, SEAL Ambassadors, and school-based mental health leaders. Each possess a unique perspective regarding this process and serve as invested stakeholders to improve youth mental health. The range of evaluations should only enhance discussions about the successes and setbacks of each week, month, and semester.

Furthermore, the data collected has to be meaningful and trusted. The quantitative evaluations of self-esteem come from the Rosenberg Self-Esteem Scale, which has been validated repetitively since its inception around 1965. The General Self-Efficacy Scale, created by Schwarzer & Jerusalem in 1995, provides the quantitative data for self-efficacy and has also been consistently validated in a variety of settings. These two metrics are concise, proven, and easy to implement. I strongly recommend that you hold to them, especially if you want to share data with outside sources. It adds to the validity of your information. But as far as the qualitative questions that elicit free response, they were authored by the *After the Mask* research team. We surveyed teachers, students, and counselors for feedback and designed a shortlist of free-response questions that investigated information all three of those cohorts were interested in knowing. We then created the survey instrument and trialed the questions through a peer-review process. Reviewers for the qualitative questions focused on determining if the questions collected meaningful information over time that could inspire action if needed. That being said, your district may have specific concerns that need to be investigated; therefore, these free-response suggestions could easily be replaced by questions that are tailored to the specifics of your school district and SEAL Ambassador Team. This allows further flexibility of the SEAL Ambassador Program.

Phase 5: SEAL Ambassador+ expanding operational capabilities

Although five educators can make a tremendous impact, the mathematical reality is that five people represent a small cohort. I mention that because the first SEAL Ambassador Team should not expect to solve all, or even a majority, of mental health challenges across the building. It's unlikely to see those kinds of results in the first few months or years of a scaled initiative. Growth needs to occur first—the type of growth that slowly evolves over time and eventually shifts the culture of a building and even a district. To do this, other teachers need to form upcoming SEAL Ambassador Teams and launch into the process with the same passion and curiosity as the initial group of leaders in SEAL Ambassador Team 1.0, which is now a group that enjoys a new set of positive bonds and closeness. And because SEAL Ambassador Team 1.0 has been through the process, learning much along the way, it seems fitting and wise that they should play the largest role in selecting the willing staff for SEAL Ambassador Team 2.0.

Looking ahead, each person who follows in the footsteps of SEAL Ambassador Team 1.0 will have their unique reasons. That's no surprise. Each one of us differs in our intrinsic and extrinsic motivation. But that diversity in thought should provide strength to the next SEAL Ambassador Team, increasing their bandwidth of purpose. Just consider some of the possibilities that could contribute to the creation of the next SEAL Ambassador Team:

- Increased motivation after discussing the success and challenges of SEAL Ambassador operations from peers they respect in the building or district

- Feeling drawn to student excitement—when students take a magical moment to put down their smartphones and share out enthusiasm for a school initiative, well... we all know that speaks volumes

- Impressed by the data points collected regarding self-esteem, self-efficacy, and skills uncertainty throughout the first implementation cycle...all of which improve mental health and inspire confidence in students

- Opportunities to understand youth mental health further while still staying within the capacity of their teaching license and role

- Increased willingness to join the program now that a group of mentors (SEAL Ambassadors 1.0) are available for extended support and leadership

- Seeing the opportunity to reignite their career with the same sense of purpose that called them to be a teacher in the first place

- Desire to reach out further and support cohorts of students that may have been marginalized before, during, and after COVID-19

It's for these reasons above, and hopefully many more, that the teacher-driven SEAL Ambassador Program will grow each implementation cycle. And to be honest, the first step in growth will likely be the most important.

PHASE 5: SEAL AMBASSADOR+ EXPANDING OPERATIONAL CAPABILITIES

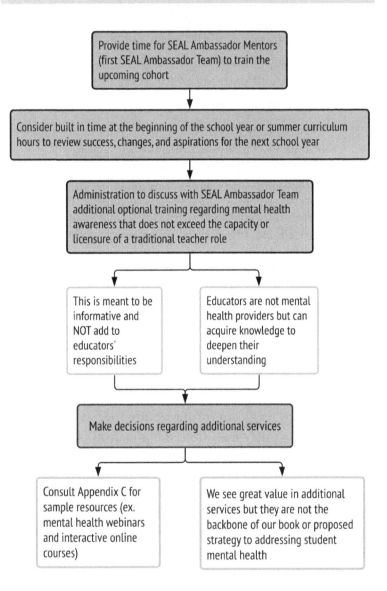

Provide time for SEAL Ambassador Mentors (first SEAL Ambassador Team) to train the upcoming cohort

Consider built in time at the beginning of the school year or summer curriculum hours to review success, changes, and aspirations for the next school year

Administration to discuss with SEAL Ambassador Team additional optional training regarding mental health awareness that does not exceed the capacity or licensure of a traditional teacher role

This is meant to be informative and NOT add to educators' responsibilities

Educators are not mental health providers but can acquire knowledge to deepen their understanding

Make decisions regarding additional services

Consult Appendix C for sample resources (ex. mental health webinars and interactive online courses)

We see great value in additional services but they are not the backbone of our book or proposed strategy to addressing student mental health

There is one more point of interest regarding Phase 5. As the graphic pointed out, there will hopefully come a time when the building of SEAL Ambassador Teams are on auto-pilot and incorporate enough faculty that optional training could be considered. I mention this now because schools are often bombarded with opportunities to cross-train educational staff with additional mental health knowledge, and it's important to be aware of it. I would encourage you to approach these opportunities with caution. Ask many questions. For starters, is the training meant to be informative for staff to deepen their understanding of common mental health challenges? Or, does the training create the impression that staff should act as something more than teachers? The latter is potentially harmful. As a former emergency medicine physician that saw thousands of patients, I can promise you that limited mental health training may seem useful, but it is **NOT** adequate to diagnose mental health disorders, let alone treat individuals correctly. Qualified health care professionals should do that. Asking a teacher to move outside their scope of practice is ill-advised and a potential legal disaster.

With this in mind, I would suggest schools *never* require or push SEAL Ambassadors to enroll in additional mental health training outside the school district. Accept the reality that any cross-training in mental health should simply be informative and not change the responsibilities or role of a staff member. I admit that some programs are well designed and offer potential benefits for staff who have the time and desire to engage. Just investigate them thoroughly and keep the following in mind. The SEAL Ambassador Program provides an approach to improving student mental health in an evidence-based fashion that does **NOT** require staff to be anything more than they are. The skills that teachers possess are the exact skills needed to enhance the mental health determinants we identified in our book—self-esteem, self-efficacy, and building life skills for uncertain situations. That's a great resource. And, it's what schools can offer in the wide-scale and multifaceted community effort to improve youth mental health.

NOTE: School districts that want to investigate responsible options for additional and voluntary instruction regarding student mental health can check out Appendix C.

Phase 6: Establishing partnerships with community health providers

The best problems to deal with are the ones you prevented in the first place. It seems simple, right? Obviously, it's not. However, the thought does convey the incredible importance of preventive efforts and the role they play. If you look at the research funding for many fields of medicine, a substantial amount is directed toward preventive screenings and promoting healthy lifestyles, which minimize the chance for costly ailments such as heart disease, stroke, cancer, and more.[3] In many ways, the SEAL Ambassador Program is built upon the ideology of prevention. When educators can leverage learning experiences to develop and strengthen self-esteem, self-efficacy, and life skills, they promote mental health and reduce the chance of a bad outcome. This benefits students, schools, and the greater community.

All that said, educators can only offer so much. It will take qualified providers outside of the school district to fill in the preventative gaps and offer treatment for students. This is where critical partnerships with the community need to be forged.

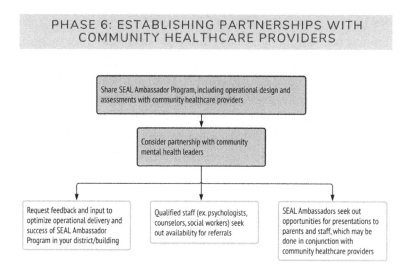

PHASE 6: ESTABLISHING PARTNERSHIPS WITH COMMUNITY HEALTHCARE PROVIDERS

Share SEAL Ambassador Program, including operational design and assessments with community healthcare providers

Consider partnership with community mental health leaders

Request feedback and input to optimize operational delivery and success of SEAL Ambassador Program in your district/building

Qualified staff (ex. psychologists, counselors, social workers) seek out availability for referrals

SEAL Ambassadors seek out opportunities for presentations to parents and staff, which may be done in conjunction with community healthcare providers

Developing community partnerships enhances care for students in need and their families. Often, families are at a loss regarding when to ask for professional help, let alone where to find these services. Well-connected schools can serve as a resource regarding care. And, in specific situations that are mutually agreed upon, referral pathways to various providers can be built and offered to the school community. It may seem simple, but these pathways and connections between schools and mental health experts are desperately needed, as an article in *The Journal of American Medicine Association - Pediatrics* reports that nearly half of children with mental health disorders **are not treated**.[4] This inadequacy could be due to several barriers to care, but it also may be due to stigma, lack of education, and not knowing where to turn. Partnerships between schools and local health providers are one way to improve this situation.

Additional resources

Before we turn the final page on this section of the book, I remind you that Chapter 9 comes with some additional resources. They have been referenced throughout the graphics and text, allowing me to clarify the available information.

Appendix A: This adjunct contains several pieces of information that SEAL Ambassador Teams (particularly Team 1.0) will find extremely useful to begin shifting from traditional teaching to leveraging teachable moments to include positive mental health determinants and life skills. More specifically, SEAL Ambassador Teams will find:

- Recommended strategies for educators regarding improvement of student self-esteem and self-efficacy

- List of vital skills recommended by leading corporations and organizations

- Five complete lesson plans that incorporate self-esteem, self-efficacy, and life skills that have been taught in the classroom setting multiple times

Appendix B: In this section, you will find thoughtfully designed evaluations of the SEAL Ambassador Program for students, counselors, and SEAL Ambassadors. As mentioned earlier, the self-efficacy and self-esteem portions of the student-specific evaluations have been validated and cited in many prior studies with high efficacy and predictive value. Should you need it, confirmation of the validity of the Rosenberg Self-Esteem scale and General Self-Efficacy scale can be found within Appendix B.

- Student evaluation collects quantitative data regarding self-esteem and self-efficacy utilizing previously validated measures and includes assessments regarding SEAL Ambassador-led classroom experience.

- Counselor/school psychologist/social worker evaluation collects quantitative data over time to determine the trend in caseload as well as the severity of cases (Tier

1-3). Additionally, mental health staff evaluations examine relationships between students in need and SEAL Ambassadors.

- SEAL Ambassador evaluation examines thoughtful questions that address lesson plan performance and staff impressions on a frequent basis, as well as a quantitative assessment regarding how the strategies are meeting goals over time.

Appendix C: The final adjunct to Chapter 9 offers a thoughtful list of additional mental health resources. These are meant to be *informative* and not a mechanism to certify educators or create the impression that they have the necessary skills to diagnose or treat mental health conditions. The *After the Mask* team does not advise teachers (or anyone in education) to perform any duties or functions outside their licensure or scope of training.

Chapter 9 References

1. Hollingham, R. (2019, July 19). *Apollo in 50 numbers: Time*. BBC News. https://www.bbc.com/future/article/20190718-apollo -in-50-numbers-time

2. Lavy, S., & Naama-Ghanayim, E. (2020). Why care about caring? Linking teachers' caring and sense of meaning at work with students' self-esteem, well-being, and school engagement. *Teaching and Teacher Education, 91*, 103046. https://doi.org/10.1016/j.tate.2020.103046

3. U.S. Department of Health and Human Services. (2020, January). *Prevention and public health fund*. HHS.Gov. https://www.hhs.gov/ open/prevention/index.html

4. Whitney, D. G., & Peterson, M. D. (2019). US national and state-level prevalence of mental health disorders and disparities of mental health care use in children. *JAMA Pediatrics, 173*(4), 389–391. https://doi. org/10.1001/jamapediatrics.2018.5399

10

Much ado about something...
Improved mental health for ALL

nd so, here we are. After nine chapters and a few field trips to the appendix, we've finally hit the point in the book where we smile softly, promise to text each other, and head our separate ways. Right? Maybe not. I have always struggled when inevitable goodbyes creep closer. How do you close things out? What's the right thing to say when you've really enjoyed chatting with someone yet understand that it will probably be quite a while before the universe allows you to cross paths again? Clearly, I still don't know. And perhaps this is why I have held onto the same four best friends for all of my life...I couldn't succumb to a devastatingly awkward goodbye. It's tough to say.

But all jokes aside, we are nearing the close of this book. And as the lead author, I want to make sure I did everything within my skill set to prepare you for the first minute after this book. You know—the exact moment where you finish reading and have to make a decision regarding whether you will change your classroom, grade level, department, or school district to address the overwhelming data you explored. What will be your role in improving the youth mental health crisis that Gen Z is wading through? Your response, of course, is personal, as is your decision to act. But before you begin weighing in on the pathway you might follow, allow me to toss a few more thoughts your way. Some of these ideas represent a continuation of a prior dialogue. Others I have held in reserve until Chapter 10.

The importance of conversation

First and foremost, this book presented a hefty amount of youth mental health data stemming from a wide bandwidth of respected agencies and leading research institutions. More than 150 citations helped shape your exposure to the depth and impact of mental health stressors upon school-aged children, along with some evidence-based strategies that should lead to change. It was my job to deliver that information to you. I would argue that all of it is important. It may have been time-consuming to sift through, but critically important.

All of the data and expert insight also had an alternate purpose...one that I would humbly suggest was just as vital as the information itself. We needed a conversation—an open and honest conversation that asked us to put daily life on hold and consider the dialogue before us. Why? The sad reality is that educators, myself included, have been hearing murmurs about the decline in student mental health for decades. Our counselors chat about mental health during professional development, and we aim to do something about it, but lesson plans, grading, and work emails consume us. We see posters over the school water fountain that draw attention to depression and anxiety, but they have been there for years and are now just a part of the traditional hallway decorations. And, occasionally, news headlines infiltrate our social media feed when there is a tragic student outcome, making us feel genuinely despondent, but only for as long as it takes to swipe past the story.

Sadly, moments like these are becoming so insidious and common in our daily lives that they have morphed into a type of background chatter, residing somewhere in the back of our brain. This is extremely dangerous. It sets up the potential for accidentally normalizing the decline of youth mental health as part of going to school. I don't think any of us want that, but we are all at risk for it. As such, this book intends to drag communities (educational and at large) out of their slumber, providing a platform to discuss the totality of the youth mental health crisis and how schools can be a vital part of the solution. So, although I was not standing before you, I made every effort for my writing to sound like a conversation in the hallway after class.

It is my sincere hope that you will now go and have an in-person conversation with a colleague, friend, or family member about this book. I believe the data and topic warrants one. There is also a hopeful side effect to that conversation. A decade in secondary schools has taught me that when teachers bounce conversation off of each other, truly amazing things take place, benefiting children in ways that typically don't make the news headlines or win awards but remain in those students' hearts for the rest of their lives. Your students are waiting. I suspect most of them will welcome the help. So, when the time is right, don't be afraid to have a conversation with them too.

The importance of first steps

Let's be honest, sometimes a call to action is not enough. Sometimes, there also needs to be a persistent force that nudges willing participants in the right direction. That's normal. So, let the various parts of this book help with that meaningful nudge. The pages within this book should serve as a familiar guide when you need any of the following: i) reliable data, ii) argumentation for action, iii) lesson plan considerations, and iv) a scaffold for how to leverage current academic content into teachable moments about self-esteem, self-efficacy, and life skills. All of this material is here to help you get started. It's my sincere hope that one gentle nudge forward leads to another until you reignite your passion for teaching. And, continue nudging until you find yourself consistently focused upon how to better the life of a child and willing to have that important conversation with colleagues that we discussed in the prior section.

What you, as an individual educator, need to combine with the resources that this book offers is a hefty dose of confidence. Please have faith in yourself. I know I do. I genuinely mean that. Although I don't have a graph or data set regarding your personal efficacy as an educator, I do believe in the skills of teachers. I have seen what they are capable of, even in the worst situations—not just in my own school district but also from the many others I consulted for all across the United States. And so, friends, when I combine 10 years of teacher observations with the evidence at hand, I am excited for teachers to get started.

Once "the nudge" gets rolling at your school, there is one critical operational guideline that I recommend you follow. Actions inspired by the SEAL Ambassador Program need to be **teacher-led**. Other staff are available to support, but teachers should take the reins and call upon their innate skill sets. It's the teachers that need to leverage curricular content in thoughtful and specific ways. They are well trained for this type of role and practice connecting concepts on a daily basis. As an educator, you know this is true. And if you're hesitant, think about the operations of the school:

- Teachers know their lessons better than anyone in the building.

- Teachers know the strengths and pitfalls of each class better than anyone else in the building.

- And most of all, teachers have some level of relationship with the students in their class that, on average, far exceeds any connection that an outside speaker, video, or presentation could offer.

Teachers possess every key component of knowledge and ability needed to implement this preventative strategy to positively impact student mental health. We need to let them do so. Because when given the latitude and support, it's only a small matter of time until frequent discussions regarding self-esteem, self-efficacy, and life skills are a regular occurrence in math, science, English, art, and music. Yep, regardless of subject matter, ALL teachers are trained for this calling.

However, if you're a teacher that is worried about the workload that might come with the SEAL Ambassador Program, I understand. Pretty much every educational initiative I ever volunteered for made my life more complex. This was mostly because the task at hand didn't play to my passion for teaching, and also because these new initiatives often added additional work. The more veteran you are as a staff member, the stronger you may align with the sentiment of my prior sentence. Please don't. Fight the urge. Allow me to reiterate, my friends in education, that you don't need to change a single unit or lesson's content or curriculum unless you want to. Save yourself some work, continue to follow the state standards and district expectations, but allow yourself permission to trim some areas so that you may insert discussions and teachable moments that promote the specific mental health determinants and skills that fall within your training and licensure: self-esteem, self-efficacy, and life skills. If anyone else tried to integrate these preventative moments into daily classroom life, they would seem awkward, forced, and lacking efficacy. You know it. And I know it, both as a former clinician and educator. No one takes better care of kids at school than teachers. The SEAL Ambassador Program is built on this guiding principle, and that is why it will succeed for the staff and schools that engage.

That being said, there will be some individuals outside the world of education who might challenge this claim. And for those that still question, or strongly doubt, how educators will connect academic lessons to positive mental health determinants, allow me to highlight something that is often overlooked: the art of teaching. Thoughtful creativity and just the right amount of finesse translates into an uncountable number of actions within the classroom. Educators and administrators are aware of this. And for that matter, so are most parents. One fan favorite amongst parents is how educators seem to magically help their children connect the dots between topics. It's not an easy process, but it's one of the most rewarding moments in the classroom. From first-year teachers all the way up to veteran staff, the ability to link concepts, identify relationships, and foster connections between school and the outside world is something educators do with a smile on their face. That moment of understanding is where most of our effort goes. And when one of our colleagues has an exceptionally good day with their artful teaching, it's all we hear about in the teacher's lounge for lunch. And that's how it should be.

Use your art of teaching. Get back to having fun with your lessons that go beyond mastery of content. Give yourself permission to show students how what they did in math class today promotes self-efficacy. Or, how about showing your students in the classroom that the skill they just practiced in their Spanish class is also used by software engineers at Google, architecture firms, and construction companies? Educators, it's your challenge and, in a way, your personal art project. So please, go and paint a metaphorical Rembrandt for your kids. Their mental health deserves a masterpiece, don't you think?

The importance of reigniting passion

Up until now, nearly 100% of this book focused on students. All the mental health data, expert insight, and evidence-based strategies are offered with the intent of helping students. I make no apologies for that decision, as improving the mental health of our students is the overarching mission of this book. Additionally, I am an educator, and we are used to students coming first. They are children, after all, and need to be protected while they learn. This is why educators naturally tend to student needs, emotions, and actions throughout the school day. We consistently make our students the most important priority in our lives for at least 40 hours a week. And why? Because it's just what teachers are born to do.

But there is a trap in that line of logic. It establishes a practice pattern where teachers become so habitually selfless that they neglect their own lives. It's often subtle at first. Perhaps some weekend grading deters you from a bike ride. Or maybe, you skip an opportunity to have some wine and watch an extra hour of Netflix with your partner because you need to start tomorrow early and set up a cool lab for your kids. That's how it begins. And then it grows. Teaching can consume you a little more as it starts to impact your necessary requirements of life. For example, what about the time you delayed an annual medical exam or dental evaluation because there was too much work to get done? Sound familiar? Until teachers set limits, the habit of putting others first can be an all-consuming and draining process. And this is assuming you are working within the framework of an average year, where a novel virus hasn't shut down life as we know it across the globe.

I mention all of this because there is a certain level of sacrifice educators are willing to donate to the children in their classroom. It's become an industry standard. Or, as my business friends might say, this level of sacrifice kind of "comes with the gig." All of us in education come to realize this reality at one time or another. And to be fair, there are some upsides to education, especially when it comes to the element of time.

- Generous amounts of holidays, along with a lengthy spring and winter break, are certainly appreciated

- Eight weeks of vacation in the summer is a rarity for many jobs

- No travel requirements for most

- Predictable schedule to allow for planning events

- And most of all, the smiles, hugs, and thank you notes from students YEARS after they left our classrooms that confirm we DID make a significant and lasting difference

I suspect that this last bullet point is the greatest motivator for educators across the globe to cut into their personal time to optimize their job. Students represent the driving force for why educators sacrifice our personal lives. And that's an important distinguishing factor to recognize. Teacher sacrifice is for the kids, not the other aspects of the job.

But what happens when the job itself becomes bigger than the kids? What happens when state assessments,

PTO initiatives, outside requests from the community, parent meetings, principal evaluations, and test prep (even in elementary school) become as important as your students' needs? Unfortunately, there is more to consider, courtesy of SARS-CoV-2. What happens when we are asked to teach from home, while watching our own kids, yet making sure we are still reaching parent and administrative expectations? And one more thought. Kindly tell me how you feel when your classroom becomes a political battleground regarding mask mandates, social distancing, and the safety of vaccines? You and I both know the answers to those questions. You become exhausted—for so many reasons. But, do you know what I believe is the most influential cause? The last 10 sentences didn't mention anything about forming relationships with students and positively impacting their lives for years to come. It was all background noise that encroached on our daily thoughts. And because of it, our favorite part of teaching was lost in the shuffle during the pandemic school year.

What I just described is a concise version of pandemic teaching. Educators know that I could have gone on for many more pages. For some, the newfound job requirements and reduction of student interaction pushed them out of education forever. It was too much. For other staff, this added adaptation nearly extinguished their flame and passion for the art of teaching. Various rules, guidelines, and community arguments put a damper on staff creativity and willingness to go the extra mile. In fact, it drove a lot of staff into bouts of anxiety and depression. I certainly don't mind admitting that I fell prey to a slump this year. Everything in my daily life of health advising quickly became about navigating a field of educational landmines and very little to do with students. I am willing to bet a lot of money that many of you felt the same at one time or another.

So, what now? What do educators do? No one wants to limp through the rest of their career, exhausted and consumed by the background noise of their job. I suspect some of you may worry that's exactly what lies ahead for many educators in the foreseeable future. And I certainly am in no position to tell you if you're right or wrong. However, I can share this. It was no coincidence that the evidence-based strategies found within this book play to the **strengths and passions** of teachers. We need to fuel the love for the classroom more than ever.

The SEAL Ambassador Program asks teachers to use all the skills, passion, and talent they possess to better a child's life. Go ahead and make that personal for you. Does that offer you a ray of hope? I certainly hope so. The SEAL Ambassador Program is built upon the exact same attributes that attracted you to being a teacher in the first place. And based on the press releases in 2020 regarding teacher job dissatisfaction, I think that's a welcome change that I see most educators getting behind.[1]

The SEAL Ambassador Program has more to offer. It is not just designed for the next academic year or two but rather to be sustainable for decades to come. SEAL Ambassadors have been provided enough data to launch this initiative, and that's critically important to student and staff buy-in at the start. Keep in mind that throughout this book, educators were deliberately introduced to reliable agencies and resources that track youth mental health data in real-time and can be followed by motivated schools *indefinitely*. The American Academy of Pediatrics, CDC, American Psychological Association, and American School Counselors Association will continue to offer information regarding trends, concerns, and improvements related to youth mental health. The Youth Risk Behavior Survey will continue to be administered every year. And even data from FAIR Health regarding insurance claims should remain accessible to the public for quite some time. As such, there will be a never-ending supply of credible evidence to support your decisions regarding the promotion of self-esteem, self-efficacy, and skill development in the classroom.

While no one should go rogue and abandon the curriculum and state standards, teachers should feel justified in making changes in their classrooms. Permit yourself to let the academic fluff go. We all know as educators to what depth we need to address topics. And we know how relevant and applicable they are for children. Allow me to pick on myself and provide an example. I'll be the first to admit that I never took the time to have kids in my anatomy class memorize every bone in the human skeleton. Why? Because as someone who went through medical school, I knew high school students didn't need that information yet. However, they do need to develop critical thinking skills. So, if we could learn some of the bone types and unique characteristics, then we could replace "death by worksheets" and rote memorization with discussions about sprains, fractures, dislocations, leukemia, and other bone disorders—which were far more exciting for students and opened up spontaneous conversations about pain tolerance, athletic ability, proper training, and how scary cancer must be. And you know what? I **never** had a parent attack me for those conversations, the ones where we connected relevant anatomy to emotion, curiosity, and the human body's limitations. And my principal wasn't upset either. But don't hang your hat on my stunningly average example of teaching. Trust your own judgment, along with the colleagues in your building that you respect. We can easily create time each week to delegate part of our precious class time to get back to the things you love about teaching. The kids *need* this, and frankly, so do you.

Millions of vaccines will be administered by the time you read this, and thousands of more hours of collaborative research will have been completed regarding SARS-CoV-2 variants. Science, combined with resilience and empathy, should continue to push us forward in terms of dealing with the fallout of COVID-19. But it will take time. And along those lines, it's important to understand that all of us will be operating on **different** timetables as we journey back to "normal." This pandemic has impacted all of us in different ways. That holds true for the students that enter our classrooms as well. *But all that aside, there will be life after the mask, and we need to prepare for it.*

Before you go... our personal aspirations for your journey

Although the *After the Mask* team believes in the necessity of data, evidence-based decisions, and performance-based analysis, we are also human and acknowledge the emotional component of what students and staff have endured for the last few decades, and especially the last few years. So, allow us to close this enormous conversation regarding youth mental health with our hopes and aspirations for your life after the mask.

Rachael Sorcher - future public health practitioner, aspiring global storyteller, travel enthusiast, lover of reality TV

By the end of this book, I hope you may also believe in the fundamental link between mental health, well-being, and education. This belief has fueled my educational career thus far and helped shape my contributions to *After the Mask*. As a Master of Public Health candidate, I believe recognizing this connection can help us best understand, support, and appreciate school-aged youth for their resilience and the obstacles they navigate—I say this as a student myself, which made writing this book even more special.

We all have people we look up to, or people we hope to "be," and these inspirational role models may change throughout our lives. For example, I can divide my life into distinct stages of wanting to be a Disney Channel Star, Simone Biles, and the President. However, the consistent role models in my life have always been my teachers—and as a graduate student, they continue to be. Looking back at my K-12 education, I don't know how my teachers managed to both teach and control our rambunctious energy, and motivate us to overcome our sleepiness. But the thing is, they ALWAYS did. My teachers consistently found ways to overcome the numerous daily obstacles present in the classroom. They never failed to teach us because they knew how to *connect* with us.

Speaking for myself, I felt especially heard by my teachers. Somehow, they could always sense when I was anxious about a test and knew exactly what to say to boost my confidence. Their support flowed both inside and outside of the classroom as my teachers were always the first people to congratulate me after dancing at a school-wide assembly. My story is just one out of millions of students in the world. But I guarantee that many of your students would share similar sentiments. So, on behalf of your past students, your current students, and your future students, thank you for not being afraid to jump hurdles in order to help us be happy on the daily, and reach our dreams in the long-term. Like *After the Mask* lays out, student mental health is one, albeit large, barrier that you will have to navigate as an educator. But fret not; you have been practicing the skills needed to tackle this challenge your entire career, and you have succeeded in doing so. Believe my story, and take my word for it! I feel so lucky to have been able to play a role in creating this book with the hope of returning a favor to the people who have given me the world—my teachers!

Jessica Sorcher - community health PhD student, health educator, adventure seeker, shameless celebrity gossip follower

Nothing is more rewarding as a human, public health graduate student, and future public health practitioner than translating research into practice, and making a measurable difference in communities. *After the Mask* strives to do just this. I hope you see the value in the presented strategies and are encouraged to take the first step towards impacting youth mental health, as it is a prominent public health issue we will continue to endure. We must start somewhere, and what better time to do so than right now?

While I may be well into my public health graduate education, I confidently know my K-12 teachers impacted the trajectory of my life. I despised geometry, but my math teacher taught me how to persevere through a semester-long struggle with geometric proofs. My business teacher taught my quiet and reserved 17-year-old self how to use my voice and share my ideas with the world. My health-science teacher ingrained in me the importance of empathy and helped to ignite my passion for public health. But, beyond all of this, it is the connections I made with former teachers that made an imprint in my mind and heart. Thank you for being the bright spots in students' lives, encouraging them to reach for the stars.

There were countless teachers that made a positive impact on my life, but there is one that stands out from the rest. I may be biased, but I also know that several former students would agree with me that this individual may have been the best high school educator in America. Beyond their witty sense of humor and engaging lessons was a person with the biggest heart who wanted nothing more than to see students happy and succeed in whatever life path they chose. Somehow, this teacher made the classroom my favorite place to be, where we laughed as much as we learned. While I may not be on the path to becoming a chemist or physician, I continue to act on the lessons I learned from this teacher's classes: always be kind, think before you speak and act, the world is your classroom, don't take yourself too seriously, and lastly, "stay out of jail!" Surprise! You may know who this teacher is, so keep reading to find out.

Christopher Jenson - former physician, educator, profoundly amateur triathlete, embarrassing father

I confess that I am a data driven guy. It's a product of my former life as an emergency medicine physician, where quick decisions were necessary, and every action should have evidence to support it. That mentality still carries over into my personal and professional life today and it helped shape *After the Mask*. As such, I wanted this book to live up to its title and truly serve as a guide regarding how to care for students and schools after the pandemic—a guide that gives you data driven information and definitive reasons for the implementations you launch in your classroom, department, school, and district.

I encourage you to have faith in your innate strengths and skills as an educator. Mountains of research demonstrate that your talents are exactly what students need right now, and furthermore, connecting your current lessons to positive self-esteem, self-efficacy, and life skills offers a chance to revitalize your love of teaching...after an exceedingly hard year. So, please take the evidence-based chance. Further yourself as a leader. Volunteer to be a SEAL Ambassador. See the purpose behind every action you take—even when you swear at the photocopier.

But above all else, I encourage you to create the kind of relationships that allow you to invest in your students and give them what they need for their future. *After the Mask* provides evidence regarding how teacher engagement positively impacts students from all demographics and backgrounds. As a data driven guy, I threw that information, along with much more, into the book for you to consider. What I can't provide, however, is any reliable data for how you FEEL when your students navigate the hardships of life and have the skills to succeed in all aspects of life.

Now is the time where I share something personal and important to me. My twin co-authors, Jessica and Rachael, were also my former students. They entered my classroom one day as two kind and diligent students, and transformed me with their questions and ideas. We chatted about inadequacies in education, how to deal with peer pressure, setting up non-profits (which they subsequently did), the skills needed to overcome adversity, and how acknowledging a crappy day with a hug can offer a lot of healing for someone in need.

Most of the diverse conversations we enjoyed somehow flowed out of my lesson plans. I found that interesting. Until one day, I realized something. Jess and Rach were teaching me. They had slowly and thoughtfully shown me that taking time to leverage your class content can open doors you never knew existed and provide students with a mindset that will carry them in the right direction, long after your final project. That lesson hit me in the heart, and it changed me forever. Because of Jess and Rach, I made it my mission to connect classroom content with real world concerns, ideas, and emotional stressors. And once I did it, I found further joy in teaching that I didn't know was possible.

I can't put into words what a thrill it was to write *After the Mask* with Jess and Rach, who are now well into adulthood and pursuing advanced degrees. They continue to be an inspiration to me, and more importantly, they have captured the hearts of my two daughters...who regard both of them as a much cooler version of their parents and 541,000 times as smart. The connection with these two former students is one I will always cherish. And, if you are a teacher, you completely understand.

Please give yourself permission to leverage content to make connections. Go change lives through your art of teaching and evidence-based strategies. Please enjoy seeing your efforts years later, manifesting in life accomplishments, which you promised your students long ago were possible. I doubt Jess and Rach remember much from what I taught them in terms of anatomy and chemistry. But, all three of us remember the silly conversations that came out of that content. Those casual moments somehow grew into strength, admiration, and a feeling of family. And that, my friends, may be the most powerful piece of data I can give you. Good luck!

Chapter 10 References

1. Singer, N. (2020, December 3). *Teaching in the pandemic: 'This is not sustainable'*. The New York Times. https://www.nytimes.com/2020/11/30/us/teachers-remote-learning-burnout.html

Want more information?

Please visit our website, www.afterthemask2020.com, for more content and updates regarding the After the Mask platform.

You can also contact our team via the website for consulting requests regarding in-person presentations, webinars, teacher trainings, and specific concerns for your district or school!

Appendix A

Examples of Macroscopic and Microscopic SEAL
Ambassador Opportunities

Appendix A contains several pieces of information that SEAL
Ambassador Teams (particularly Team 1.0) will find extremely
useful as they shift from traditional content-based instruction
to leveraging teachable moments. SEAL Ambassador opportunities should focus on the evidence-based mental health
determinants (self-esteem and self-efficacy) and specific life
skills that provide confidence in the midst of uncertainty. This
material is divided into three sections:

- SECTION 1 - Recommended strategies for educators
  regarding optimizing self-esteem and self-efficacy in
  students of all levels and demographics.

- SECTION 2 - Five complete lesson plans that are
  content-based and contain specific notations regarding
  the timing and scope of specific SEAL Ambassador
  teaching moments

- SECTION 3 - List of vital skills recommended by leading corporations and organizations.

SECTION 1 - Strategies for optimizing student self-esteem and self-efficacy

Review the suggestions below from three credible sources. Consider how to leverage current lessons and classroom experiences by embedding the strategies into parts of your lessons. Keep in mind, it's perfectly acceptable to adapt these strategies as needed to fit with the experience. Lastly, there are enough ways to address self-esteem and self-efficacy that SEAL Ambassador moments should not appear forced or unrelated to the classroom experience.

1. American Psychological Association: www.apa.org/ed/schools/primer/self-esteem

This website offers an evidence-based list of suggestions that correlate with positive mental health outcomes, entitled "What Can Teachers Do?" This list provides numerous examples of specific actions teachers can take to improve student self-esteem, such as pointing out concrete signs of progress, showcasing student accomplishments in class, and engaging students in conversation about their interests. This reference may serve as a guide for implementing daily practices in your classroom that support positive metrics of self-worth. Additionally, it is worth noting that licensed psychologists approve of these educational strategies.

2. The American Academy of Pediatrics: www.healthy children.org/English/ages-stages/gradeschool/Pages/Helping-Your-Child-Develop-A-Healthy-Sense-of-Self-Esteem.aspx

The American Academy of Pediatrics contributes to a website entitled "healthychildren.org." It contains a large number of resources that are recommended by pediatricians and benefit the physical and mental health of children. One section devoted to enhancing self-esteem and self-efficacy outlines characteristics students can adopt to develop a healthy sense of self. This specific resource highlights strategies that parents can utilize at home and practical high yield strategies for educators. The goal is to ensure that the efforts of trusted adults will positively influence the mental health determinants of a child. There are 11 points of emphasis, each of which falls within the scope of training and licensure of an educator. Examples applicable to students include: fostering a sense of trust, accepting mistakes and failures, and developing a sense of contribution.

3. The Education Hub: www.theeducationhub.org.nz/wp-content/uploads/2018/03/6-strategies-for-promoting-student-self-efficacy.pdf

The Education Hub is a research-driven organization that provides evidence-based solutions to challenges present in education. Founded in New Zealand by Dr. Nina Hood, Education Hub seeks to bridge the gap between educational research and teaching practice. Their group of experts has created a resource that defines self-efficacy, what students' self-efficacy beliefs are based on, and outlines six practical strategies teachers can utilize to promote student self-esteem on a daily basis. Some of these strategies include using peer modeling, administering self-assessments, and fostering daily problem-solving opportunities for students. There is in-depth information provided for each strategy, ensuring readers understand its purpose and importance.

SECTION 2 - Examples of Unit and Lesson Opportunities for SEAL Ambassador Teams

To provide additional assistance to SEAL Ambassador Teams, section two models HOW units (macro perspective) and individual lessons (micro perspective) could be adapted for teaching self-esteem, self-efficacy, and/or life skills. Of note, the SEAL Ambassador Program adaptations received high praise from students when provided with a post-experience evaluation.

SEAL AMBASSADOR STRATEGIES - EXAMPLE UNIT PLAN

Anatomy and Physiology - Unit 6 Cardiovascular Standards and District Expectations

1. Identify the critical structure and function of a normal human heart

2. Understand the determinants of cardiac output and how the following impact them: fitness, age, various disease processes

3. Explore the cardiac conduction system and apply to an EKG tracing

4. Analyze and interpret various heart rhythms, connecting them to changes in cardiac performance

5. Investigate current cardiac research and heart transplant

Example Calendar (Note: Abbreviated timeline to showcase various SEAL Ambassador opportunities)

Date	Concept to Explore	SEAL Opportunities	Homework
Mon.	Four chambers and valves of the human heart	Break students into groups. Each group has key information that leads to an understanding of WHY the human heart has specific design elements. *Self-efficacy*: discuss how students were able to integrate new content with current understanding (similar to separate divisions in a company working together) *Life skills*: public speaking, negotiating	Draw a human heart and the direction of blood flow
Tues.	Electrical conduction through the heart	Work with the physics circuit models and then predict what kind of interruptions or problems a physiological circuit might have *Self-efficacy*: students can see results of their model manipulation (measure ohms and amps) *Life skills*: using models to connect concepts and solve problems	Design a circuit diagram of the heart (speculative) and justify your design

Wed.	Cardiac output	In the gym, with teacher exercise volunteers, compare resting hearts rates, exercise heart rates, and 5 min recovery heart rates to determine relative scales of fitness *Self-esteem and life skills*: Display understanding and sensitivity when discussing someone else's personal performance. What considerations did you make before giving feedback?	Write a fictitious "medical report" to give to one of the subjects
Thurs.	Heart transplant	Group discussions and share out for the best process to prioritize and distribute hearts for transplant when there is a shortage *Self-esteem*: discuss the intrinsic value of helping those in need *Self-efficacy*: validate the strengths of each plan and how doctors also struggle with these decisions *Life skills*: strategies for difficult choices	None

SEAL AMBASSADOR STRATEGIES- EXAMPLE DAILY LESSON PLANS

1. Lesson #1 - Children's Oncology Book Project

Cells and Tissues represent a difficult unit for students. It involves working hard to understand structures you can't see, making the content seem distant and irrelevant. However, that changed when I had the idea to connect this content with cancer (which is abnormal cell growth) and the field of oncology. The classroom lit up! Students of all abilities came alive, asking more questions than you can imagine about the diagnosis, treatment, and realities of cancer. It became a free-flowing seminar on SEAL Ambassador Program concepts. This convinced me to replace the unit test with the development of a children's book, which would be given to a patient undergoing cancer treatment IF it was well written and supported with accurate science. This assignment represents one of my favorite examples of how course content has plenty of opportunities to tie in SEAL Ambassador moments!

Oncology Book Project - Children's Hospital

Project Goal
Collaborate with your small group team to produce a children's book for a patient at Children's Hospital that creatively explores the disease process, diagnosis, and treatment of pediatric cancer. The book will be illustrated by select upper-level students in the art department.

Project Expectations
The book you create will be given to a specific patient undergoing treatment at Children's Hospital. As such, your information

MUST be accurate and the book must be age-appropriate. Most importantly, your project needs to be extremely well designed because **what you write will impact a child.** *This is SO much more than a grade...this is for a kiddo in need.*

Required Elements for the Book
Your team will have a great deal of latitude and creativity in the design of your book. That being said, your book needs to be at a level that young children will understand. Make sure you include the following elements:

- *Explanation of the science behind cancer and how cancer develops*

- *Some reference to how cancer may make a child feel (ex: scared, anxious, sick)*

- *Discussion of how cancer is often diagnosed*

- *Exploration of what cancer treatment may involve and why it works*

- *Plotline that shows the main character with cancer improves*

Examples of Books
Your team will need to be creative. We are working with select art students and staff to illustrate the book. As such, you will need to pitch your idea early for review and approval. Possible ideas for a book include:

- *Traditional book paperback print* (preferred)*

- *Comic Book*

- *Online book that will be illustrated digitally*

- *Real-time animations with voice over (See health sketch channel - YouTube)*

How will I learn enough science content to write this book?
During this unit, we will cover a great deal of information about normal tissue growth and development and how it can (rarely) become cancer. Your activities, case studies, and teacher-led discussions will place an emphasis upon:

- *Types of tissues within the human body and their organization*

- *Normal cell cycle and tissue growth*

- *Abnormal tissue growth and development of cancer*

- *Fundamental concepts of cancer & types of cancer*

- *How we diagnose and assess cancer for severity*

- *Standard treatment of cancer (surgery, chemotherapy, radiation)*

- *Cutting edge treatment of cancer (immunotherapy, stem cell, arterial intervention)*

- *Stressors and social considerations of cancer patients*

*If you pay attention and work hard at your practice activities and hands-on experiences, you should gather MOST of what you need to write an effective book. That being said, **it is HIGHLY likely you will need to research outside what you learn in class to go the extra mile!***

2. Lesson #2 - Outbreak Game!

Just a few years before COVID-19, my final assessment for the immunology unit was to navigate an outbreak situation. It served as a wonderful performance-based assessment that also drew out SEAL Ambassador moments: i) having a defined role in the game by leveraging personal strengths to benefit the group (self-esteem), and ii) promoting organization, leadership, personal responsibility, and group dynamics—as all parties had to work together and rely on each other to solve the game before the timeline ended. **Pay close attention to assessment question #7.** I wrote it before 2020 and enjoyed looking back at their predictions in 2019.

Timber Town - Outbreak Case

Why am I doing this?
The following outbreak case will push your ability to problem solve and apply your knowledge of the immune system. Your case scenario is modeled after a real infectious disease outbreak! Get ready for the challenge of investigating the same illness and concerns that scientists and health care workers did in real-time.

What is the mission?
Your team will survey facts and use your knowledge of immunology and infectious disease to identify the outbreak agent, how it's spreading, and create a solution for the crisis. Your overall plan should follow the public health model (adapted from CDC) seen below.

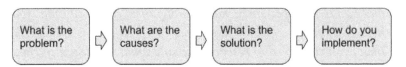

*To answer these questions, you should thoughtfully investigate **one box at a time**. Make sure you have evidence to back up any and all claims you make. You have the ability to investigate a great deal of information (see below). Take your time and do it right!*

How do I gather evidence to back up my claims?
Your team will have the opportunity to gather information in the following ways:

- *INTERVIEWS: You will have the opportunity to "speak" with three individuals from Timber Town each simulated day. You should prioritize the residents admitted to the hospital FIRST as you don't know the extent of their illness, and they could die by the next simulated day.*

- *TRACKING: Just like in Contagion, it's important to establish whom the sick individuals come into contact with and identify any overlap. Additionally, gaining insight as to where people like to spend most of their time can be helpful.*

- *MEDICAL TESTS: Your group will have the ability to order medical tests as you see fit. This includes labs (such as blood chemistries, blood counts, antibodies, cultures, etc.), medical imaging, and group-designed requests known as "Doctor's choice." Keep in mind, you have a budget, so you can't order every test on every resident.*

What are the important resources and actions for the game?
You will start the game on the pretend date of NOVEMBER 1st. That is day one!

- *Map that represents the town ("Timber Town") to view geographical relationships.*

- *Character pieces - representing important people in the town. The number assigned to each character correlates with their home on the map. They are optional to help you organize information.*

- *Information cards -*

  o *Interview cards—Request a meeting and information from major characters. You may interview up to three people a day.*

o *Health care cards—Request specific tests to be run on characters (ex: antibody tests, complete blood counts). You may run as many tests per day as you have money for.*

o *Tracking cards—Learn the route that characters travel each day and the locations in town they typically visit. You may only track up to three people a day.*

o *Press releases—Provided by the teacher regarding news in the town. Each day in the game, all groups will receive new information.*

o *Pathogen reference table—Lists all the possible pathogens the state health department is concerned might be the cause of this outbreak.*

How will you be evaluated - Questions to answer
Before you move on to the next problem-solving envelope, you must first answer the following questions:

1. *What organ system (or systems) does this outbreak seem to affect? Use patient information and evidence to support your claim.*

2. *You will need to determine if this outbreak is a virus or a bacteria. Take a moment to name three differences between bacteria and viruses.*

3. *What is your* **working case definition** *for the symptoms of this community outbreak?*

4. *Explain where and how the outbreak started in terms of location (bonus points for "index patient").*

5. *What is the trend for this outbreak over three days: i) fairly steady impact on the community? ii) increasing impact on the community? or iii) decreasing impact on the community? (NOTE: you must have scientific data to present!)*

6. *What is your ONE leading pathogen for the outbreak now? Justify with evidence!*

7. *How will you change the daily operations of the town to CONTAIN the outbreak at this time? How will you justify your interventions? What additional problems might this create for the people in this town? What is your argument that your plan is the LEAST restrictive option yet still safe?*

   o *What will you do to MEDICALLY treat the illness at this time? Are antibiotics and/or vaccines an option? Please justify your answer –and keep in mind, you have been allocated a specific budget. If you run out of money BEFORE you implement a successful plan, you receive NO points and lose the game. (NOTE: a list of costs will be provided to you so that you can budget!)*

   o *CDC help card – During the course of the entire game, you may request TWO phone calls for advice from a fictitious public health expert. Your team may ask one specific question per phone call. (NOTE: The CDC will NEVER offer you a comprehensive solution—your group needs to design that!)*

* *Smartphone timer – Will be used to keep track of time and symbolically represent days.*

* *Anatomy and Physiology notes – You are free to consult any part of your anatomy and physiology notes during the exercise.*

3. Lesson #3 - Checking Chest X-rays

After spending two class periods discussing chest x-rays and the pulmonary system, I offered the students a challenge— reading chest x-rays in teams. The goal is to analyze the radiographs and comment on seven specific points of interest. Admittedly, a tough assignment. But the assignment is a segue to a more important topic - the importance of value and decision making. To experience this, students determine which two points of interest they are best at assessing, advertise those skills to their peers, and then construct groups from that information. It is wise to have student "experts" in all areas. Some groups follow that recommendation, and others do not. In the end, I only offer extra credit for "correctly" reading the chest x-rays. We spend class time discussing how each team member has tremendous value and how groups maximized strengths and minimized weaknesses.

Checking Chest X-rays

Part 1
Please answer the following questions regarding density and radiology films:

1. *How does the x-ray beam transmit through a patient, and what captures the image?*

2. *Please explain why bone appears white, and air appears dark black? Why does the normal lung have "wispy cotton fibers" through it on x-ray...what are these representing?*

Part 2
Please use your alphabet pneumonic ("ABCDEF") to systematically investigate the following x-rays.

- *Comment on each part of the x-ray you have been taught for a grade.*

- *After each individual chest x-ray evaluation, take your best guess at a diagnosis for extra credit!*

1) Chest x-ray - Station One: (NOTE - there were multiple stations - abbreviated for the purposes of this book)
Please comment on the seven areas of interest discussed in class.

Part 3- Group Assessment (Content and SEAL Ambassador Program Questions)

1. *Was it difficult to be an expert in all areas of reading chest x-rays?*

2. *What was the value of collaborating together with other chest x-ray experts?*

3. *What was difficult about forming your group? Were their barriers, or did this go smoothly?*

4. *Based upon this exercise, why do you think doctors and nurses are often trained in specific subspecialties? How does this impact patient care that you or a family member might get?*

4. Lesson #4 - Student-Designed Cardiac Fitness Test

The cardiac stress test project remains one of my favorites! It connects a fun academic venue with SEAL Ambassador lessons with ease. In this lesson, students design and implement their own cardiac fitness test, but there is a catch. They have to create an informed consent document and schedule a time to sit down and talk to the teacher volunteers. This forces students to apply their science knowledge in a real-time environment by addressing questions and concerns from the volunteer staff. One might say that preparing for and carrying out this conversation is the most vital part of the lesson.

Cardiology Unit – Performance-based Assessment

Objective
Your team needs to work together and design a cardiac fitness test that allows you to record meaningful data related to cardiac fitness. Your test must be safe for all parties involved and appropriate for a high school environment. You CANNOT use the traditional treadmill test design we discussed in class.

What is the goal of a cardiac fitness test?
Your activity should measure cardiac fitness. This can be determined in many ways, but the main focuses of your test should look at the following:

1) *Baseline Data*

   - *Establish information about the participant regarding baseline diet, weekly exercise, and sleep habits that could affect cardiac demand throughout the week.*

   - *Determine baseline vital signs that you feel are important and analyze them against typical norms*

2) *Exercise Data*

   - *Establish how the designed activity will challenge the following body systems:*

      i) Cardiac

      ii) Pulmonary

      iii) Musculoskeletal

- *Record changes in all three systems as they change with exercise (Ex: respiratory rate, accessory muscle use for breathing, skin temperature, subjective muscle fatigue, etc.)*
- *Change in cardiovascular vital signs throughout exercise*
- *Identify extraneous variables that may affect exercise performance that given day/ week*

3)   Post Exercise Recovery

- *Change in vital signs*
- *Assessment of fatigue*
- *Time to return to baseline vital signs (significance of duration)*

What does our fitness test need to demonstrate?

- *Graded exercise plan that increases the level of resistance, cardiac output, and effort required to complete.*
- *Analysis and understanding of all pre- and post-exercise data. Relevance of data should relate to cardiac fitness and comment on the dynamic changes of all three body systems being studied. This does not come from your personal assessment but must be supported by knowledge from anatomy and physiology and research you have explored.*
- *Overall assessment of cardiac fitness that is supported through research your group has performed.*

Who can exercise for the fitness test?
Exercise subjects must meet at least one of the following criteria:

- *Teacher that volunteers for the study (with YOUR informed consent).*

- *You must set up a time and discuss your stress test with the staff member. They will evaluate your discussion with them (see grading rubric).*

Where can I gain information about fitness tests and stress tests?

It is your responsibility to engage in the assigned reading AND research how current stress tests are performed. I recommend you look up "Bruce protocol stress test" as a starting point.

Can we use a treadmill test?

No. We will discuss in class the Bruce Protocol treadmill test. Because this will be a model for us to analyze, you need to think of ANOTHER exercise plan for your participant. No treadmill tests will be allowed.

How do I know when a participant has completed our stress test?

Your project will need to be approved, and all exercise tests need to have the following considerations for your athletes:

- *Participant MUST stop if they feel anything above moderate fatigue*

- *Max time limit that is reasonable (should the participant NOT feel moderate fatigue)*

- *75% of the max heart rate (even if symptoms free) requires stopping as well*

- *At ANY MOMENT, the school nurse or Dr. Jenson may stop the test*

GRADING RUBRIC

CATEGORY	4	3	2	1
Stress test research/ background	Provides specific information and relevant facts from articles or textbook that explain all aspects of a stress test, how it assesses cardiac fitness, and explanation of how other organ systems change with exercise	Provides some information and facts that explain the most aspects design of a stress test, how it assesses cardiac fitness, and mostly explain how other organ systems change with exercise	Provides information and facts that explain some aspects of a stress test, how it assesses cardiac fitness, and mostly explain how other organ systems change with exercise. Incomplete explanations	Provides little specific information and facts that are not sufficient to explain how a stress test affects cardiac fitness and how other organ systems change with exercise
Stress test study design	Safe, with high likelihood majority of population able to perform with seemingly flawless transition through a graded level of exercise	Safe, and most of the time easy for general population to perform with minimal gaps as participant transitions through a graded level of exercise	Safe, but often difficult for general population to perform and/ or has some gaps that fail to demonstrate a smooth transition with graded level of exercise	Safe, but difficult for general population to perform and/ or does not demonstrate a smooth transition with graded level of exercise

	Relevant, well explained, and has strong correlation to baseline cardiac fitness. Answered all teacher volunteer questions. Put the teacher volunteer at ease. Teacher volunteer has confidence in your process.	Relevant, reasonably well explained with moderate correlation to baseline cardiac fitness. Answered all teacher volunteer questions. For the most part, put the teacher volunteer at ease. Teacher volunteer has confidence in your process.	Mostly relevant with moderate explanation and a decent correlation to cardiacfitness. Answered most of the teacher volunteer questions. Put the teacher volunteer at ease on some. Teacher volunteer has some concern about your process.	Lacking significant relevance, explanation, or correlation to cardiac fitness. You need to redesign the stress test, as your teacher volunteer will not be participating
Pre-exercise information (SEAL Ambassador Program moment)				
Data table for exercise	Measures selected to change are realistic to record and have direct correlation to cardiac fitness	Measures selected to record are realistic to record and have moderate correlation to cardiac fitness	Measures selected to change are mostly realistic to record and have some direct correlation to cardiac fitness	Measures selected to change are potentially difficult to record and have minimal correlation to cardiac fitness
Post-exercise information	Measures selected to change are realistic to record and have direct correlation to cardiac fitness	Measures selected to record are realistic to record and have moderate correlation to cardiac fitness	Measures selected to change are mostly realistic to record and have some direct correlation to cardiac fitness	Measures selected to change are potentially difficult to record and have minimal correlation to cardiac fitness

Analysis of data	*Data was collected numerous times. It was summarized, independently, in a way that clearly describes what was discovered.*	*Data was collected more than one time. It was summarized, independently, in a way that clearly describes what was discovered.*	*Data was collected at one point in time. Moderate assistance was needed to clearly summarize what was discovered.*	*Data was collected poorly and summary was not reflective of results*
Conclusion	*The data is clearly explained and trends and differences are clearly discussed. The conclusion created is well justified*	*The data is clearly explained and trends and differences are mostly discussed. The conclusion created is reasonably justified*	*The data is somewhat explained and trends and differences are somewhat discussed. The conclusion created is lacking justification*	*The data is poorly explained and/or trends and differences are discussed minimally. The conclusion is not well supported*

5. Lesson #5 - Neurology Stroke Assessment

In this lesson, students are tasked with two directives: i) design and prepare thoughtful questions that explore the changes to life encountered by a stroke patient and select neurologic tests for strength and sensation (from those discussed in class), assessing the patient's neurologic function, and ii) utilize these questions and exam results to suggest where our guest/volunteer underwent a stroke. As you might imagine, this requires a lot of soft skills, professionalism, empathy, and planning. Students are often proud of their efforts and how they handled a delicate situation. Please take note of the question assessments. The guest/volunteer was present for all ten potential questions. However, I only modeled one example here to be concise.

Stroke Investigation

Objective
Take the time to review your notes and activities regarding ischemic and hemorrhagic strokes. You will need to design 5-10 questions that you believe will help identify the area of the brain where a kind volunteer endured a stroke. You will also be allowed five exam tests. These tests must come from the list of skills you learned in class.

Questions Chosen
Each question has a feedback component. Make sure you complete the feedback, or you will not be able to use the question. All questions you recommend must be turned in to me one week before the scheduled volunteer.

1. *Example Student Question #1—Did you find that sometimes you could think of an action in your brain, but it wouldn't happen after your stroke? If so, how do you deal with that?*

2. *Student Reflection Questions*

    1. *What does this question offer me in terms of the stroke investigation?*

    2. *Does this question exhibit empathy? Please explain.*

    3. *Are there any ways this question could be misconstrued and hurt feelings?*

SECTION 3 - Recommended Life Skills for Adaptive Situations

Students add to their positive self-esteem and self-efficacy when they develop vital skills that apply to a wide range of career paths. This provides confidence in that students begin to feel prepared for any future or uncertain situations before them. As you might imagine, the acquired skills should be critical to most professions and situations and adaptable to an evolving workplace. Below are two additional resources beyond the skills list from Forbes in Chapter 8.

1. University of Colorado Boulder: www.colorado.edu/care er/2019/04/18/10-essential-skills-youll-need-career-success

Many universities understand the importance of developing soft skills or transferable skills to excel in any career after graduation. However, the Career Services at the University of Colorado Boulder commits to a specific portfolio of skills they believe their students need for career success, regardless of their field of study. The top three essential skills include communication, problem-solving, and teamwork. They note that students should focus on developing these skills both inside and outside of the classroom through research, study abroad, internships, and more.

2. Indeed.com: www.indeed.com/career-advice/resumes-cover-letters/skills-employers-look-for

Indeed.com is a career search engine that is utilized by approximately 610 million users in 20 countries. The website showcases a list of the top 11 skills employers look for in candidates. This list was generated by consistent and repetitive feedback from hiring managers in diverse career fields. The top three skills hiring managers look for in potential employees include communication, leadership, and teamwork. This resource outlines marketable skills that will help ensure students are competitive applicants for any job they pursue.

Appendix B

Student Evaluations: SEAL Ambassador Program

The purpose of the student pre-program, unit, and post-program evaluations are to assess the impact of the SEAL Ambassador Program over time from a student perspective. Each evaluation examines three distinct sections: general SEAL Ambassador Program impressions, self-efficacy, and self-esteem.

The self-efficacy questions originate from a validated instrument known as the General Self-Efficacy Scale. Along the same lines, the self-esteem questions come directly from another validated instrument known as the Rosenberg Self-Esteem Scale. The general SEAL Ambassador Program impression questions were created by the *After the Mask* team after peer review from counselors and school staff. You may decide to modify these general SEAL Ambassador Program questions to match specific concerns within your school or district.

NOTE: We strongly encourage using the same questions (both validated and general) throughout the entirety of the program so you can evaluate trends over time. The student evaluations also include several free-response questions that will provide the SEAL Ambassadors with narrative insight into students' experiences.

Pre-Evaluation: Use Questions 1 - 25
Unit Evaluation: Use Questions 1 - 25
Post-Evaluations: Use Questions 1 - 31

1. In general, I see how the things I am learning in this class are relevant to the "real world."

    a. *Strongly disagree, Disagree, Undecided, Agree, Strongly agree*

2. I feel confident in my ability to apply what I have learned in this class beyond academics (ex. work, extracurriculars, relationships etc.)

    a. *Strongly disagree, Disagree, Undecided, Agree, Strongly agree*

3. I feel like I could speak to my teacher about my life.

    a. *Strongly disagree, Disagree, Undecided, Agree, Strongly agree*

4. I feel like my teacher cares about supporting and empowering me to succeed in class.

    a. *Strongly disagree, Disagree, Undecided, Agree, Strongly agree*

5. I feel like my teacher cares about supporting and empowering me to succeed outside of school.

    a. *Strongly disagree, Disagree, Undecided, Agree, Strongly agree*

6. I can always manage to solve difficult problems if I try hard enough.

    a. *Not at all true, Hardly true, Moderately true, Exactly true*

7. If someone opposes me, I can find the means and ways to get what I want.

    a. *Not at all true, Hardly true, Moderately true, Exactly true*

8. It is easy for me to stick to my aims and accomplish my goals.

    a. *Not at all true, Hardly true, Moderately true, Exactly true*

9. I am confident that I could deal efficiently with unexpected events.

    a. *Not at all true, Hardly true, Moderately true, Exactly true*

10. Thanks to my resourcefulness, I know how to handle unforeseen situations.

    a. *Not at all true, Hardly true, Moderately true, Exactly true*

11. I can solve most problems If I invest the necessary effort.

    a. *Not at all true, Hardly true, Moderately true, Exactly true*

12. I can remain calm when facing difficulties because I can rely on my coping abilities.

    a. *Not at all true, Hardly true, Moderately true, Exactly true*

13. When I am confronted with a problem, I can usually find several solutions.

    a. *Not at all true, Hardly true, Moderately true, Exactly true*

14. If I am in trouble, I can usually think of a solution.

   a. *Not at all true, Hardly true, Moderately true, Exactly true*

15. I can usually handle whatever comes my way.

   a. *Not at all true, Hardly true, Moderately true, Exactly true*

16. I feel that I'm a person of worth, at least on an equal plane with others.

   a. *Strongly agree, Agree, Disagree, Strongly disagree*

17. I feel that I have a number of good qualities.

   a. *Strongly agree, Agree, Disagree, Strongly disagree*

18. All in all, I am inclined to feel that I am a failure.

   a. *Strongly agree, Agree, Disagree, Strongly disagree*

19. I am able to do things as well as most other people.

   a. *Strongly agree, Agree, Disagree, Strongly disagree*

20. I feel I do not have much to be proud of.

   a. *Strongly agree, Agree, Disagree, Strongly disagree*

21. I take a positive attitude towards myself.

   a. *Strongly agree, Agree, Disagree, Strongly disagree*

22. On the whole, I am satisfied with myself.

   a. *Strongly agree, Agree, Disagree, Strongly disagree*

23. I wish I could have more respect for myself.

   a. *Strongly agree, Agree, Disagree, Strongly disagree*

24. I certainly feel useless at times.

   a. *Strongly agree, Agree, Disagree, Strongly disagree*

25. At times I think I am no good at all.

a. *Strongly agree, Agree, Disagree, Strongly disagree*

26. How would you describe your SEAL Ambassador classroom environment?

    a. *Free response*

27. What differences did you notice between your SEAL Ambassador-led and non-SEAL Ambassador-led classes?

    a. *Free response*

28. How did your teacher being a SEAL Ambassador impact your class experience? Was this impact positive, negative, or neutral?

    a. *Free response*

29. What did you enjoy about class that you hope your teacher continues to implement in the future?

    a. *Free response*

30. What conversations have you had with your peers about your experience in a SEAL Ambassador-led classroom? Please explain.

    a. *Free response*

31. Would you like to continue or discontinue with the SEAL Ambassador Program? Please explain why.

    a. *Free response*

Student Evaluations: Scoring

Below, you will find information on how to score the pre, unit, and post-program evaluations.

Notes on scoring individual evaluations:
The following three sections are included in every pre, unit, and post evaluation: i) general SEAL Ambassador Program impressions, ii) self-efficacy, and iii) self-esteem. They should be scored and interpreted individually given their use of different survey instruments. As such, a total score should **NOT** be calculated for any evaluation (pre, unit, or post). Instead, you will have three separate scores for each section of the evaluation: one score for the General SEAL Ambassador Program questions, one score for the self-efficacy questions, and one score for the self-esteem questions. Note that a total score can only be calculated among the non-free response questions, so questions 26-31 on the post-program evaluation cannot be numerically scored.

Notes on scoring evaluations over time:
Please note that a total score should **NOT** be calculated for every evaluation completed in a given program duration (semester, school year, or another timeline). However, all unit evaluation scores can be compared over time. Additionally, the pre-program evaluation may act as a baseline to which you compare the post-evaluation scores.

Scoring Scales
General SEAL Ambassador Program Impressions
Questions 1 - 5

- Score questions 1 - 5 using the assigned values below.

    o Strongly disagree = 1

    o Disagree = 2

    o Undecided = 3

    o Agree = 4

    o Strongly agree = 5

- Add up items 1 - 5 to get a total score ranging from 5 - 25.
  - o A greater score indicates a more favorable feeling towards the statements.

Self-Efficacy
Questions 6 - 15 (General Self-Efficacy Scale)
Schwarzer, R., & Jerusalem, M. (1995). Generalized Self-Efficacy scale. In J. Weinman, S. Wright, & M. Johnston, Measures in health psychology: A user's portfolio. Causal and control beliefs (pp. 35-37). Windsor, UK: NFER-NELSON.

- Score questions 6 - 15 with the assigned values below.
  - o Not at all true = 1
  - o Hardly true = 2
  - o Moderately true = 3
  - o Exactly true = 4
- Total score is calculated by adding up all of the items.
  - o Total score ranges from 10 to 40 (a higher score indicates greater self-efficacy).

Self-Esteem
Questions 16 - 25 (Rosenberg Self-Esteem Scale)
Rosenberg, M. (1965). Society and the adolescent self-image. Princeton, NJ: Princeton University Press.

- Scores questions 16 - 25 with the assigned values below.
  - o For questions 16, 17, 19, 21 & 22
    - ▪ Strongly agree = 3
    - ▪ Agree = 2
    - ▪ Disagree = 1

- Strongly disagree = 0
  o For questions 18, 20, 23, 24, & 25
    - Strongly agree = 0
    - Agree = 1
    - Disagree = 2
    - Strongly disagree = 3
- Total score ranges from 0-30, with 30 indicating the greatest possible score (high self-esteem).

Teacher Evaluations: SEAL Ambassador Program

The purpose of the teacher evaluations is to inform and tailor discussion at SEAL Ambassador Team meetings and guide self-reflection among SEAL Ambassadors. These questions, stemming from the unit evaluations, will allow you to identify talking points on a periodic basis throughout the SEAL Ambassador Program experience. Additionally, the pre and post evaluations highlight strengths and weaknesses with classroom instruction before and after SEAL Ambassador Program implementation. Finally, we offer a validated job satisfaction survey instrument (TJSS-9) listed below. It is optional, but could be used in the pre and post evaluations as you see fit.

Pre-Evaluation: Use Questions 1 - 12,
Unit Evaluation: Use Questions 13 - 23
Post-Evaluation: Use Questions: 24 - 42
Teacher Job Satisfaction Survey (TJSS-9) 43 - 51

Pre-Evaluation

1. Please describe your current expectations for the SEAL Ambassador Program implementation in your classroom.

    a. Free response

2. What do you currently hope to gain on a personal level from being a SEAL Ambassador?

    a. Free response

3. How do you currently hope to transform your classroom through the SEAL Ambassador Program?

    a. Free response

4. How do you think students will receive the SEAL Ambassador content and respond to the program?

   a. *Free response*

5. How do you think the SEAL Ambassador Program implementation will impact students' overall classroom experience?

   a. *Free response*

6. What do you anticipate to be the largest barriers to implementation of SEAL Ambassador Program content? And how do you intend to address these barriers?

   a. *Free response*

7. Ultimately, what do you want to see occur as a result of SEAL Ambassador Program implementation in the short term? In the long term?

   a. *Free response*

8. What resources do you need to make the SEAL Ambassador Program content integration go smoothly? Who do you need to ask to help you with this?

   a. *Free response*

9. What class activities or lessons did you think will engage students the most?

   a. *Free response*

10. I see a benefit in leveraging course content to teach life skills and improve self-esteem and self-efficacy.

    a. *Strongly disagree, Disagree, Undecided, Agree, Strongly agree*

11. My school and/or district administration supports my autonomy in implementing the SEAL Ambassador Program in my classroom as I see fit.

    a. *Strongly disagree, Disagree, Undecided, Agree, Strongly agree*

12. Overall, I believe I connected well with my students.

    a. *Strongly disagree, Disagree, Undecided, Agree, Strongly agree*

Unit Evaluation

13. How receptive were your students to SEAL Ambassador Program content?

    a. *Free response*

14. How do you think the implementation of SEAL Ambassador Program content impacted students' overall classroom experience in this unit?

    a. *Free response*

15. What were the barriers to implementation of SEAL Ambassador Program content in this unit? How did you address these barriers?

    a. *Free response*

16. Did any of your students comment on the integration of SEAL Ambassador Program content into this unit? If so, describe the feedback and if it was positive, negative, or neutral.

    a. *Free response*

17. What class activities or lessons did you notice engaged students the most in this unit?

  a. *Free response*

18. I see a benefit in leveraging course content to teach life skills and improve self-esteem and self-efficacy.

  a. *Strongly disagree, Disagree, Undecided, Agree, Strongly agree*

19. My school and/or district administration support my autonomy in implementing the SEAL Ambassador Program in my classroom as I see fit.

  a. *Strongly disagree, Disagree, Undecided, Agree, Strongly agree*

20. My students were very engaged during this unit.

  a. *Strongly disagree, Disagree, Undecided, Agree, Strongly agree*

21. I integrated the SEAL Ambassador Program content well into this unit.

  a. *Strongly disagree, Disagree, Undecided, Agree, Strongly agree*

22. The enjoyment associated with my teaching has increased since implementing the SEAL Ambassador Program.

  a. *Strongly disagree, Disagree, Undecided, Agree, Strongly agree*

23. Overall, I believe I connected well with my students during this unit.

  a. *Strongly disagree, Disagree, Undecided, Agree, Strongly agree*

Post Evaluation

24. Did the SEAL Ambassador Program meet your expectations?

    a. *Free response*

25. What did you personally gain from being a SEAL Ambassador?

    a. *Free response*

26. How did you transform your classroom through the SEAL Ambassador Program?

    a. *Free response*

27. How did your students receive the SEAL Ambassador content and respond to the program?

    a. *Free response*

28. How did the SEAL Ambassador Program implementation impact students' and their overall classroom experience?

    a. *Free response*

29. What were the largest barriers to implementation of SEAL Ambassador Program content? And how do you address these barriers?

    a. *Free response*

30. Ultimately, what short term outcomes occurred as a result of SEAL Ambassador Program implementation? What do you believe the long-term outcomes will be?

    a. *Free response*

31. Did any of your students comment on the integration of SEAL Ambassador content during program

implementation? If so, describe the feedback and if it was positive, negative, or neutral.

    a. *Free response*

32. What resources do you need to make the SEAL Ambassador content integration go smoothly for SEAL Ambassador Program 2.0? Who do you need to ask to help you with this?

    a. *Free response*

33. What class activities or lessons did you notice engaged students the most throughout SEAL Ambassador Program implementation?

    a. *Free response*

34. Given what you know now, would you choose to continue with SEAL Ambassador Program updates/implementation in your future classes?

    a. *Free response*

35. In general, I think my students benefited from the implementation of the SEAL Ambassador Program.

    a. Strongly disagree, Disagree, Undecided, Agree, Strongly agree

    b. *Please elaborate.*

36. I see a benefit in leveraging course content to teach life skills and improve self-esteem and self-efficacy.

    a. *Strongly disagree, Disagree, Undecided, Agree, Strongly agree*

37. My school and/or district administrations supported my autonomy in implementing the SEAL Ambassador Program in my classroom as I saw fit.

   a. *Strongly disagree, Disagree, Undecided, Agree, Strongly agree*

38. My students were very engaged during all the units included in SEAL Ambassador Program implementation.

   a. *Strongly disagree, Disagree, Undecided, Agree, Strongly agree*

39. I integrated the SEAL Ambassador content well into all the units included in SEAL Ambassador Program implementation.

   a. *Strongly disagree, Disagree, Undecided, Agree, Strongly agree*

40. Overall, I believe I connected well with my students during SEAL Ambassador Program implementation.

   a. *Strongly disagree, Disagree, Undecided, Agree, Strongly agree*

41. As an educator, I felt empowered being a SEAL Ambassador at my school.

   a. *Strongly disagree, Disagree, Undecided, Agree, Strongly agree*

42. As an educator, I felt fulfilled being a SEAL Ambassador at my school.

   a. *Strongly disagree, Disagree, Undecided, Agree, Strongly agree*

The Teacher Job Satisfaction Scale (TJSS-9)

Pepe, A. (2011). Measuring teacher job satisfaction: A quantitative empirical tool. Paper presented at the 8th International Conference of European Research Network About Parents in Education, Milano, Italy.

43. The quality of your relations with co-workers.

    a. *Highly dissatisfied, Dissatisfied, Neutral, Satisfied, Highly satisfied*

44. The extent to which your co-workers encourage you and support you in your work.

    a. *Highly dissatisfied, Dissatisfied, Neutral, Satisfied, Highly satisfied*

45. Your overall satisfaction with your co-workers.

    a. *Highly dissatisfied, Dissatisfied, Neutral, Satisfied, Highly satisfied*

46. The extent to which students act in a self-disciplined manner.

    a. *Highly dissatisfied, Dissatisfied, Neutral, Satisfied, Highly satisfied*

47. Your satisfaction with the behavior of students in your school.

    a. *Highly dissatisfied, Dissatisfied, Neutral, Satisfied, Highly satisfied*

48. Your overall level of satisfaction with student discipline in your school.

    a. *Highly dissatisfied, Dissatisfied, Neutral, Satisfied, Highly satisfied*

49. The degree of interest shown by parents in the education of their children.

   a. *Highly dissatisfied, Dissatisfied, Neutral, Satisfied, Highly satisfied*

50. The extent to which parents are supportive of the school and its programs.

   a. *Highly dissatisfied, Dissatisfied, Neutral, Satisfied, Highly satisfied*

51. Your overall level of satisfaction with parents where your work.

   a. *Highly dissatisfied, Dissatisfied, Neutral, Satisfied, Highly satisfied*

Teacher Evaluations: Scoring

Unlike the student evaluations, a total score can be calculated for the pre, unit, and post teacher evaluations. Please look below for information on how to calculate a total score. Note that a total score can only be calculated among the non-free response questions. Additionally, this total score does **NOT** include the Teacher Job Satisfaction Survey (TJSS-9) as this measure should be scored and interpreted separately.

Scoring Scales:
SEAL Ambassador Program Impression Questions
Questions 10 -12, 19 - 23, & 35 - 42

- Score these questions using the assigned values below.
    - o Strongly disagree = 1
    - o Disagree = 2
    - o Undecided = 3
    - o Agree = 4
    - o Strongly agree = 5
- Add up the scores of the questions to get a total score ranging from 16 - 80.
    - o A greater score indicates a more favorable feeling towards the statements.

TJSS-9 Scoring
Questions 43 - 51

- Score questions 43 - 51 using the assigned values below.
    - o Highly dissatisfied = 1

o Dissatisfied = 2

o Neutral = 3

o Satisfied = 4

o Highly satisfied = 5

- Add up items 43 to 51 to get a total score ranging from 9 - 45.

    o A greater score indicates a more favorable feeling towards the statements (higher job satisfaction).

Counselor Evaluations: SEAL Ambassador Program

School counselors act as support staff for the SEAL Ambassadors. They also play a significant role in evaluating the impact of the program on students. The purpose of these questions is to monitor any change in mental health support needed among students of SEAL Ambassadors. The hope is that preventative efforts through the SEAL Ambassador Program will demonstrate a reduction in volume of Tier 1 support counselors need to offer and/or a reduction in the intensity of intervention required for complex cases.

NOTE: other mental health providers (ex: school psychologist) could also complete these evaluations.

Pre, Unit, and Post Evaluations

1. What was the weekly average of student cases you counseled since the last evaluation? (Total number cases seen since the last eval date divided by number of weeks)

   a. *Free response*

2. Since the last evaluation, how many SEAL Ambassador Program students did you work with regarding concerns or challenges connected to mental health?

   a. *Free response*

3. Since the last evaluation, how many SEAL Ambassador Program students that you saw required Tier 2 support?

   a. *Free response*

4. Since the last evaluation, how many SEAL Ambassador Program students that you saw required Tier 3 support?

   a. *Free response*

5. Consider all the SEAL Ambassador Program students that you saw since the last evaluation. How many of these students have a teacher they can turn to for help with stressors or concerns? (Please list as a fraction - ex: 8 out of 14 students would be 8/14)

   a. *Free response*

6. Please comment on any positive or negative trends regarding the impact of the SEAL Ambassador Program upon students since the last evaluation.

   a. *Free response*

Counselor Evaluations: Scoring

Evaluation questions 1-5 are numeric values, and therefore, can be graphed and tracked over time. This allows counselors to identify if there are any consistent trends associated with SEAL Ambassador Program implementation. Note there may not be any immediate change—this survey instrument targets more long-term outcomes.

Appendix B References

1. Schwarzer, R., & Jerusalem, M. (1995). Generalized Self-Efficacy scale. In J. Weinman, S. Wright, & M. Johnston, Measures in health psychology: A user's portfolio. Causal and control beliefs (pp. 35-37). Windsor, UK: NFER-NELSON.

2. Rosenberg, M. (1965). Society and the adolescent self-image. Princeton, NJ: Princeton University Press.

3. Pepe, A. (2011). Measuring teacher job satisfaction: A quantitative empirical tool. Paper presented at the 8th International Conference of European Research Network About Parents in Education, Milano, Italy.

Appendix C

Additional Resources

Important Disclaimer
Listed below are additional resources for you to review at your convenience. Please note, these resources are not associated with the SEAL Ambassador Program. We selected these unique institutions because we believe they align with the mission of *After the Mask*. These resources are for educational purposes only, as they exist to enhance your understanding of student mental health and associated topics.

There are many other insightful resources out there. However, we were selective in choosing those who do NOT advocate for cross-training educators or encourage teachers to go beyond their licensure to address student mental health.

The Mental Health Technology Transfer Center Network (MHTTC): www.mhttcnetwork.org/free-smh-course

MHTTC is a wonderful resource funded by the Substance Abuse and Mental Health Services Administration (SAMHSA) and strives to disseminate and implement evidence-based practice for mental health in various fields, including education. We want to draw particular attention to Classroom WISE (Well-being Information and Strategies for Educators), a self-guided online course, video library, resource collection, and website aimed at educator mental health literacy. Classroom WISE is launching, for free, in June 2021.

Classroom Mental Health: www.classroommentalhealth.org

This website was created by the University of Michigan Depression Center and presents a wide range of information for educators regarding mental health concerns among students, including depression, anxiety, and substance abuse. The website includes a section on how to best support students whom you believe are struggling or have approached you with their worries. Another section worth noting is "Classroom Climate," where various tactics are presented regarding reducing stigma surrounding mental health, stress reduction, and communication for sensitive topics in the classroom.

Child Mind Institute: www.childmind.org/audience/for-educators/

The Child Mind Institute has been referenced several times in this book and serves as a leader in advocating for children's mental health. Please browse the website for a deeper look into their reports, community programs and initiatives, as well as guides—all revolving around kids' mental health. We want to specifically draw your attention to their School and Community Webinar Program - Mental Health 101: Signs and Symptoms. This specific webinar provides insight into strategies to help identify those students who may need additional support.

The University of Nebraska Medical Center—Behavioral Health Education Center of Nebraska: www.unmc.edu/bhecn/education/online-training/teacher-training.html

The University of Nebraska Medical Center recognizes that educators play an important role in helping students improve their mental health. On this website, you will find 26 videos taken from a lecture by a licensed psychologist that provides in-depth information about various aspects of student mental health, including depression, anxiety, self-injury, and more.

The University of Maryland School of Medicine—Maryland Behavioral Health: www.mdbehavioralhealth.com/training

This website functions as an online training site for a variety of individuals, including educators, physicians, and mental health providers for supporting the behavioral health of youth and families. You might find value in a particular training titled "Mental Health to Support Student Learning: Training Modules for Educators and School-based Staff." This online training module is meant to be informative and aims to increase mental health proficiency among educators and other school-based staff.

Made in the USA
Coppell, TX
24 June 2021